The Important Things of Life

WOMEN IN THE WEST

Series Editors

Susan Armitage
Washington State University

Sarah J. Deutsch
Clark University

Vicki L. Ruiz
Claremont Graduate School

Elliott West
University of Arkansas

DEE GARCEAU

The Important Things of Life

Women, Work, and
Family in Sweetwater
County, Wyoming,
1880–1929

UNIVERSITY OF NEBRASKA PRESS
LINCOLN AND LONDON

All photographs courtesy
of Sweetwater County
Historical Museum,
Green River, Wyoming.
©1997 by the
University of Nebraska Press
All rights reserved
Manufactured in the United States
of America
⊗ The paper in this book meets
the minimum
requirements of American
National Standard for
Information Sciences—Permanence
of Paper for
Printed Library Materials,
ANSI Z39.48-1984.
Library of Congress Cataloging-
in-Publication Data
Garceau, Dee, 1955–
The important things of life :
women, work, and family in
Sweetwater County, Wyoming,
1880–1929 / Dee Garceau.
p. cm. — (Women in the West)
Includes bibliographical
references and index.
ISBN 0-8032-2163-0 (alk. paper)
1. Women pioneers — Wyoming —
Sweetwater County — Social
conditions. 2. Women pioneers —
Wyoming — Sweetwater County —
Social life and customs.
3. Frontier and pioneer life —
Wyoming — Sweetwater
County. 4. Sex role — Wyoming
— Sweetwater County —
History. 5. Family — Wyoming
— Sweetwater County —
History. 6. Sweetwater County
(Wyo.) — Social conditions.
7. Sweetwater County (Wyo.) —
Social life and customs.
I. Title. II. Series.
F767.S9G36 1997 97-9485
978.7′85 – dc21 CIP

ISBN 978-0-8032-4348-4
(alk. paper: paperback)

For Craig

Contents

List of Illustrations viii
Acknowledgments ix
Introduction 1
1. Sweetwater County: Desert Highway, Company Town, Cowboy West 15
2. Family Networks: A Web of Support 39
3. "I Got a Girl Here, Would You Like to Meet Her?": Courtship, Ethnicity, and Community 53
4. "My Wife Just Doesn't Like It Here and I'm Going to Let Her Go Back": Marriage and Patriarchal Authority in Transition 74
5. Group Partnership and Cowboy Myth: The Gendering of Ranch Work 89
6. Single Women Homesteaders and the Meanings of Independence: Places on the Map, Places in the Mind 112
7. From *Klenickso* to Main Street: Town Women's Work 129
8. "Grasping at the Shadow": The Paradox of Change 151
Appendix 161
Notes 165
Selected Bibliography 203
Index 209

Illustrations

PHOTOGRAPHS
Following page 114
High plains desert near Green River, Wyoming
Union Pacific Company Store
Eggs-Spinner-Gaensslen clan
Mine Safety wagon in Superior
Mr. and Mrs. Felix Taucher
Annie and Norris Austin, 1908
Stewart homestead
Margaretta Kemp, secretary to clerk of court, Rock Springs, 1921
Female clerks in Rock Springs Commercial Store, 1912

MAPS
Five-County Map of Wyoming, 1869,   14
The Lincoln Highway,   18
Wyoming Counties and County Seats since 1923,   35

Acknowledgments

I am grateful to the women of Sweetwater County who shared their life stories with me and other interviewers. Their humor, candor, and spirit gave life to this study. I am equally indebted to Dudley Gardner, who made available his vast archive of oral histories at Western Wyoming Community College in Rock Springs. From the oral history collections at the Wyoming State Archives and Historical Department in Cheyenne, Ann Burns and Nancy Cranford stand out as models of interviewing skill. Their good listening and astute questions drew forth stories that animated this study. I was fortunate, too, to hear some women's stories firsthand. My heartfelt thanks to go Jerrine Stewart Wire, Ann LeVar Powell, Mary Lou Anselmi Unguren, Pat Huntley LeFaivre, Louise Spinner Graf, and Elinore Gaensslen Schofield, for giving their time, honesty, and energy to my queries.

Others in Sweetwater County opened their homes and businesses to me, making it possible to complete this research. Special thanks go to Marcia and Mike Hensley of Farson, Wyoming; to Lois Brandner and Ruth Lauritzen of the Sweetwater County Historical Society; and to Mary Tebedo and Diane Butler of The New Studio in Rock Springs.

I am indebted to my colleagues as well, for their part in bringing this study to fruition. Elliot West and Karen Merrill offered invaluable criticisms that transformed the work from dissertation to book. Betsy Jameson, Susan Armitage, Sherry Smith, David Emmons, Ken Lockridge, and Mary Murphy gave key portions of the manuscript careful readings. Their observations, challenges, and encouragement further improved its quality. My dissertation committee, MariJo Buhle, Howard Chudacoff, and Bruce Rosenberg did yeoman's work, reading numerous early drafts. MariJo Buhle, in particular, supplied clarity and wide-ranging expertise at crucial points as the project took shape. William Farr and Kath McChesney-Lape, Tim Huebner and Mike LaRosa, colleagues at the

University of Montana and Rhodes College, respectively, also provided moral support and fine tuning.

Finally, no author survives without friendship. Antonia Baum Farrell, Sarah MacNamara, Cathleen Waters, Terri Sears, Carla McNellis, Bonnie Craig, Terry Peterson, Suzanne Stoeckmann, Woody Kipp, and John Harris sustained me throughout this long process. The same may be said of Craig Rayle, with whom all things were possible.

The Important Things of Life

Introduction

"Why does woman long for the ballot?" asked the editors of the *Big Piney Examiner* in 1915. Newspaper to ranchers in the Green River Valley of Sweetwater County, Wyoming, the *Examiner* opposed woman suffrage. With rhetorical flourish, the editors deemed the national suffrage campaign a misguided effort:
> When all is said and done, is not the selection of the butcher more important to the home, than the election of mayor; is not the employment of the dairyman a far more important event in the life of children than the appointment of a postmaster; is not the selection of books for the family library more important than voting books for the jail and courthouse? Why does woman lay aside the important things of life? Why leave the substance and grasp at the shadow?[1]

According to the *Examiner*, the "important things of life" for women were "the substance" of home and family, not "the shadow" of female equality, sentiments that echoed Victorian mores from the nineteenth century.[2] The *Examiner*'s editorial revealed the paradox of conservative gender consciousness in a setting where material adaptation to frontier conditions was gradually broadening women's roles. But the story behind such conservatism is not told in political speeches. Rather, it begins with subtler changes that characterized the informal spaces of work and family life, where so much of female activity took place.

On the late-nineteenth- and early-twentieth-century Sweetwater County frontier, survival required adjustments that expanded women's work roles and increased their domestic authority. At the same time, survival on this ranching and mining frontier heightened the value of group cooperation. On ranches, such cooperation was grounded in familiar, older traditions of separate gender spheres and patriarchal authority. In mining towns, such cooperation placed women squarely within reciprocal kin and ethnic networks, which restricted as well as supported them in their expanding roles. The combined needs for gen-

Introduction

der role flexibility and reliable systems of mutuality made for paradoxical changes in women's roles.

Women's role flexibility in Sweetwater County coincided with a liberalization of women's roles nationwide. By the 1920s, Victorian mores had given way to more individualistic, egalitarian models of gender. Relationships of mutual obligation on the frontier, however, implied subsuming personal ambition—women's in particular—to group needs. Sweetwater County thus brought into relief conflicts between individualism and community that characterized debate about woman's place nationwide. In this respect, the American West was like a laboratory of gender role change, where migration, relocation, and new settlement underscored processes of reconstructing social identity.

Sweetwater County lies in southwest Wyoming, bisected by the Green River, running north to south; and by the Union Pacific Railroad, running east to west. As early as the 1860s white settlement dotted these two transportation routes, but most emigrants merely passed through on their way to Oregon, California, or Washington. White outposts remained sparse until late in the century, when discovery of coal made the region a destination in its own right. From the close of the nineteenth century through the first three decades of the twentieth century, the population burgeoned. Arable land along the Green River drainage and liberalization of homestead law drew sheep and cattle ranchers to the region. Rich coal seams under the desert floor, industrial demand, and Union Pacific capital generated a mining boom that lasted through World War I.

Mining towns developed as urban industrial islands dominated by the Union Pacific Railroad and Coal Company. These company towns housed a working-class population of striking ethnic diversity. Rural communities, on the other hand, developed a decentralized agricultural economy consisting of widely scattered, privately owned, family ranches. These ranches were home to a largely native-born, middle-class population. In both settings, women shared the common milieu of domestic responsibility. In both, women made vital contributions to the family economy. In both, the frontier experience broadened women's work roles and subtly increased their household authority. And in both, the necessity for group cooperation mediated the liberalizing effects of such changes. But there the similarities end.

Indeed, it was the differences between rural and mining-town women that exposed these processes of change and mediation. For gender identity on the Sweetwater County frontier was also situational, embedded in class, ethnicity, and regional economy. Mining-town women's lives highlighted the importance of women's informal networks as forces of social cohesion. Such networks eased the transition from Europe to Wyoming, and helped to build ethnic community

Introduction

within the shifting and heterogeneous populations of company towns. In the coal-town economy, what was an extractive-industry frontier for men became a service-industry frontier for women. First-generation immigrant women kept house for miners without families, an economic role that doubled as the locus of social networks crucial to immigrant survival. Among the second generation, some women left housekeeping for retail and office work, positions that symbolized Americanization and New Womanhood. In short, within these ethnically diverse mining towns, the processes by which women shaped gender boundaries were also processes of acculturation. Moreover, because the challenges of survival on an industrial frontier heightened the value of informal kin and ethnic networks, the opportunities that called to women also sometimes posed choices between individual ambition and obligation to family or countrymen.

Rural women's lives brought into focus the confluence of western myth and constructions of woman's place. Despite gender-based divisions of labor on ranches, the rural economy increasingly required women to ignore such boundaries. By the second generation, ranch women frequently crossed over into men's work. But they framed such crossover as a temporary extension of familiar gender boundaries rather than a permanent set of new ones. At the same time, popular mythology about the cowboy defined a separate world of ranch work that reasserted distinctions between genders. Ranch women affirmed cowboy myth, with its idealized boundaries between masculine and feminine work. In these ways, ranch women mediated material changes in their role through a conservative value system that deflected challenge to the sexual order. The demands of survival in an agricultural economy heightened the value of family cooperation and stability, and thus perhaps, of familiar patterns of gender hierarchy.

Finally, during the second two decades of the twentieth century, single rural women found in homesteading both economic opportunity and a symbolic redefinition of gender. Some wrote about homesteading as a transformation of female identity, drawing on popular mythology about the West as a place of self-reinvention. Comparisons between rural women and coal-town women thus outline regionally distinctive processes of adaptation, mediation, and self-definition that shaped gender in the West. Taken together, they suggest a paradoxical process of change, in which some material and social adaptations held out the promise of individualism even as others bound women with the demands of community.

Women's narratives from Sweetwater County, 1880 to 1929, conveyed the exigencies of life on this ranching and mining frontier. They told of the sharp smell of big sage, of the massive and forlorn beauty of the high desert. They spoke of

Introduction

the black promise of coal, of the homestead claims that followed the courses of rivers, and the human effort that scored the land with mine tunnels and irrigation ditches, stopes and reservoirs. These were the visible yields of settlement. Against this background I have peeled away the demographic, economic, and social structure of Sweetwater County to expose informal systems of human exchange within which women played a central role. Here were unofficial institutions of mutual obligation and support, through which women shaped their own, their families', and each others' destinies. Kin and neighbor, elder and youth, citizen and greenhorn, all formed networks that sustained—and at times constrained—women's lives on the southwest Wyoming frontier.

Courtship, marriage, childrearing, and making a living, life processes central to women's experience, are like rivers and mines for the historian. They offer routes into the expression of gender identity, access to veins of meaning. Applying the methodology of community study to these life processes, one can explore changing constructions of gender, and map their connection to regional patterns of settlement and economic development. From census manuscripts, oral histories, written memoirs, city directories, local newspapers, and regional folklore, I reassembled women's work and family roles in two distinctive settings: coal-mining towns and ranching communities.

Constructions of gender in the West are complicated by ideological constructions of the West itself. "For more than a century," wrote Richard White, "the American West has been the most strongly *imagined* section of the United States."[3] Indeed, the West has become so identified with mythic themes of transformation that even historians are not immune. The idea of the West as a place where American society reconstituted itself on different terms remains compelling and underpins much of the scholarship on western women.

The first scholarly version of a mythic West was the Turner thesis, appearing in 1893 and influencing debate for decades after.[4] Frederick Jackson Turner proposed that the frontier experience had shaped American national character through a continuous process of renewal as white civilization advanced westward. Turner's frontier was a wellspring of innovation, individualism, and egalitarian values; it represented the successful evolution of democracy.[5] Critics would later note that Turner's theory of frontier history betrayed a late-Victorian, nationalistic bias. In this landscape, women appeared as scenery, rather than actors.[6]

Consequently, the first wave of feminist scholarship in western history tested the Turner thesis against women's experience. Proceeding from the concept of frontier as a catalyst of social and political change, these scholars asked whether

Introduction

the frontier was liberating for women. Focusing on westward expansion during the mid– and late nineteenth century, some argued that the frontier offered empowering economic opportunities to women and eroded hierarchical relations between the sexes.[7] Others concluded that the disruptions of migration undermined Victorian domesticity, causing women to lose important bases of autonomy and social power.[8]

These studies relied primarily on written narratives, which reflected the values of literate, white, middle-class Victorian society. In the wake of debate over the frontier as a democratic force for women, scholars began to question the scope of these studies and the relevance of Turner's paradigm. Noting Turner's assumption of Anglo-Saxon cultural superiority, historians now identified a plurality of cultures in the American West and recast westward expansion as a form of Anglo-European invasion and conquest.[9] Historians of women in the American West called for investigation of peoples and time periods beyond the boundaries of mid- to late-nineteenth-century Victorian society.

Multiculturalism became the new point of departure for investigation of western women's lives. "As in the East," wrote Sarah Deutsch, "race, class, and ethnicity as well as gender and region shaped the structure of life in the West."[10] Some scholars fear that multiculturalism will lead to intellectual fragmentation, that American history will suffer a loss of unifying themes.[11] But multicultural study does not imply a kind of relativism that stops short of conclusions. Rather, in the case of women's history, it implies an ecology of gender. That is, gender systems evolve through the regional adaptations of particular ethnic groups and classes and are further shaped by the interactions between different cultures.[12] In a review of western women's history, John Faragher wrote:

> Much of what is distinctive about the West, and America for that matter, is the mixed, the "miscegenated" nature of our culture. It is becoming ever clearer how important women were to the process of cultural change at the very heart of what the frontier was all about.[13]

Indeed, if frontiers were like laboratories where a plurality of interest groups met, then multicultural history can sort the ways that regional economy, class identity, and ethnic heritage mediated the evolution of gender roles. Revisionist western historians thus challenged Turner's nationalism, imperialism, and masculine focus. But his concept of frontier as a process of transformation endures.

Sweetwater County, Wyoming, provided a unique setting in which to further explore the significance of regional economy, ethnicity, and class in western women's lives. Between 1880 and 1910, rural homesteaders comprised 15.9 percent of the county population, railroad and mining town residents, 84.1 percent.

5

Introduction

Encompassing agriculture, mineral extraction, and small-scale service industries, Sweetwater County provided a microcosm for comparison between women in a ranching economy and women in a mining economy.

Ethnic distinctions echoed economic divisions within the county. Between 1880 and 1910, 66.1 percent of railroad and coal town dwellers were foreign born; 72.8 percent of rural residents were native born.[14] Among the foreign born who populated railroad and coal towns, over twenty nationalities were represented, including English, Welsh, Irish, Scottish, Canadian, French, Belgian, Dutch, German, Austrian, Hungarian, Tyrolean, Italian, Polish, Slovenian, Croatian, Serbian, Finnish, Danish, Swedish, Greek, Basque, Japanese, and Chinese.[15] In short, mining towns were characterized by pronounced ethnic diversity, ranching communities by a predominantly native-born population. Within this one county, then, one can compare the changing roles of women in ethnically diverse, industrial islands with those of women in culturally homogeneous, agricultural settlements.

To draw comparisons between native-born ranch women and immigrant coal-town women, I had to generalize from the diverse population of Sweetwater mining towns. It proved impossible to profile every one of the twenty-odd ethnic groups enumerated in these towns, for many appeared in proportions too small for quantitative analysis. Instead, I identified those immigrant groups that predominated numerically, and focused on them. They became representatives of foreign-born women in a mining economy.

Immigrants from the British Isles comprised 57.4 percent of the foreign-born population in 1880.[16] During the 1890s Scandinavian and German immigration increased, while immigration from Great Britain declined. By 1900 Britons comprised 32.2 percent of the foreign-born population, Scandinavians, 31.7 percent, and Germans, 11.8 percent.[17] After the turn of the century, the balance shifted, and Eastern Europeans became the fastest-growing, and then the largest immigrant group in Sweetwater County. The proportion of foreign-born residents from Eastern Europe jumped from 12.3 percent in 1900 to 29.9 percent in 1910. By 1910, Eastern Europeans outnumbered Britons, Germans, and Scandinavians.[18] Between 1910 and 1920, Wyoming saw the largest increase in Eastern Europeans ever, due to political and military unrest in the Balkans. In 1910, 825 Eastern Europeans were recorded in the Wyoming census. By 1920, the number of immigrants from Eastern Europe had more than tripled, to 2,671.[19] Accordingly, this study draws from the experience of those nationalities which formed the most significant proportions of the immigrant population during each time period. English, Scottish, and Irish women most represented Sweetwater County's early immigration; Swedish, Finnish, and German women rep-

Introduction

resented the second wave of European migration to southwest Wyoming; and southern Slav women represented the coal town population boom after the turn of the century.

Nuances of class status surfaced in clues from the census manuscripts and through expressions of social identity within personal narratives. The Federal census for Sweetwater County revealed the number of wage-earners per family, their occupations, whether they owned property, and the economic composition of their neighborhood. Oral history informants identified certain sections of town with class status. In Rock Springs, for example, the South Side housed the town's managerial classes and professionals; the North Side, miners and their families, small businessmen, and transient laborers.[20] In smaller company towns, such as Reliance, Superior, South Superior, Megeath, Lionkol, and Winton, working-class neighborhoods predominated throughout.[21] Finally, in the outlying rural areas, ranch women identified with an agrarian, middle-class tradition aimed at securing property ownership and self-employment.[22] Sweetwater County, then, also presented a microcosm for comparison between middle- and working-class women on a modernizing frontier.

What is meant by a modernizing frontier? Sweetwater County history from 1880 to 1929 marks a transitional period between the first generation of white settlement and the emergence of the modern West. Women who arrived in Rock Springs by train saw their daughters leave by automobile. If one generation gathered at corner saloons to trade news and gossip, the next flocked to movie houses for the latest celluloid thriller. During the late nineteenth and early twentieth century, the dominant culture nationwide shifted from Victorian to modern mores. Technological advances accelerated the pace of industrialization, and industrial growth intensified migration to urban areas. Completion of railway networks, invention of the automobile, and improvements in mail service connected areas that were isolated only a generation earlier. Agricultural and industrial development in southwest Wyoming became more fully integrated into the national economy. At the same time, popular media and mass-marketed retail goods linked people nationwide through a common consumer culture. So, too, gender roles were in flux. As more women entered public life through higher education, reform activity, and wage work, a "New Woman" challenged Victorian notions of True Womanhood. The First World War magnified these trends, boosting industrial production, catalyzing further migration to urban centers, and sharpening differences between generations.[23] It was precisely during this transitional era, from the 1880s through the 1920s, that white migration to Wyoming peaked.[24] In Sweetwater County, then, frontier women's roles took shape within the context of modernizing America.

Introduction

Sweetwater County thus framed the evolution of gender in the West within regional boundaries encompassing modern development. But this should not be mistaken for a comprehensive case study of the county. This work details neither the institutionalized politics nor the formal community organizations particular to each ranching community and mining town. Instead, this study focuses on women's informal activity—on the everyday business of making a living, of forming and sustaining relationships.

Exploration of women's informal activity sounded three conceptual notes relevant to this study. First, women's informal activity made visible heretofore unseen bridges between private and public life. Indeed, outside the parameters of Victorian gender ideology, strict separation between public and private worlds was neither an article of faith nor a common practice.[25] In Sweetwater County, for example, the construction of intimate partnership played a significant role in the life of the community. That is, courtship activated reciprocal obligations between single women and their community. In mining towns, single women held the power to reinforce ethnic cohesion through their choice of spouse. In ranching communities, a double moral standard held single women responsible for sexual control. In each case, single women answered to a community agenda that spoke to the demands of survival on a mining or ranching frontier. Thus courtship highlighted the interplay of private and public life, of individual and community needs. Relations between individual and community, in turn, informed constructions of gender in the West.

A second conceptual base for the investigation of women's informal activity is the historical significance of women's household relations and work. In a review essay on western women's history, Glenda Riley cautioned against devaluing women's household work as historically unimportant:

> If men's work becomes the normative standard against which we judge the worth of women's work, do we not demean domestic labor? To assume that women were only actors when they expanded, or fled from, the domestic realm is to impute powerlessness to women's world, power to men's.[26]

One way to avoid this pitfall is to ask how women's household work fit into the family and regional economy, and to explore how women's household relations linked household residents with the larger community. For women's household activity was not only economic, but relational as well. John Faragher urged historians to reconstruct the lives of women and men "from the inside out," by examining relations of reproduction and work within the family, and by analyzing the structures of domestic authority.[27] In Sweetwater County, households in ranching and mining communities alike veered away from the privatized

Introduction

nuclear family structure associated with modernizing middle-class culture. Rather, household life typically centered around a nuclear family plus kin or boarders. Relations between kin, and between host families and boarders, in turn, demonstrated that women's social responsibilities within households figured in patterns of social exchange that shaped the larger community. Additionally, changing structures of domestic authority revealed the significance of ethnicity in constructions of womanhood on the mining frontier.

Finally, a third consideration in the study of women's informal activity involves keen appreciation for the power of ideology in people's lives. Popular mythology about the West informed women's and men's behavior and shaped the stories they told about their westering experience. Robert Hine has argued that the West was "motivated by and continually selecting its own myths and legends." That is, Westerners themselves both absorbed and transformed the myths that informed "Western" identity.[28] By the turn of the century, dime novels, Wild West shows, and serialized popular fiction presented the American West as a land of cowboys and wide-open spaces—symbols of rugged individualism and the opportunity for self-reinvention, respectively.[29] Western lore also emphasized the themes of triumph over adversity, of resourcefulness and endurance.[30]

Sweetwater County's rural settlers wove popular ideas about the West into their daily lives. Ranch wives translated the pioneer myth of triumph over adversity into domestic terms, giving their home production of consumer goods larger meaning as emblems of family success, symbols of family survival. Ranchers projected cowboy myth onto their work routines in order to reinforce the idea—if not the practice—of gender-based divisions of labor. Study of women's informal activity, then, must consider how women drew from Western lore to give meaning and order to their daily work.

Single women homesteaders also responded to the possibilities inherent in Western myth. Those who wrote about homesteading constructed a vision of female independence based on property ownership. Though the reality was more complex, homesteading became a compelling metaphor for female egalitarianism. In this way, literary homesteaders created a Western version of New Womanhood. Women homesteaders thus demonstrated another way that Westerners internalized and transformed Western myth.

Gendered analysis of this process is crucial. As suggested by the example of single women homesteaders, women contributed to the creation of a mythic West in ways different from men. Indeed, as women reinterpreted Western myth, they rewrote the female roles within it. Study of women's informal activ-

Introduction

ity in Sweetwater County, then, must also recognize how women used Western lore to reshape gender ideology.

Finally, while literary homesteaders created a brave New Woman in the pages of popular magazines, their numbers were few in southwest Wyoming. Most ranch women in Sweetwater County held to more traditional notions of womanhood, even as their behavior diverged from it. That is, ranch wives drew on Victorian ideals of female devotion to family, to make sense of their encroachments into men's work. And so study of women's informal activity in Sweetwater County might also consider how traditional gender ideology flexed to accommodate transgression of boundaries.[31] Traditional gender ideology appeared in the lives of ranch women as a powerful reference point with which to mediate role change.

Questions about how gender systems take shape within informal work and family systems pose a methodological challenge. Few women in Sweetwater County memorialized their experience in writing. Those most likely to leave behind diaries or memoirs were literate, middle-class women. Demography, folklore, and oral histories expanded the range of archival sources on Sweetwater County women to include a more diverse sample. Demographic analysis of the Federal census manuscripts for Sweetwater County highlighted women's regional, generational, class, and ethnic differences. Content analysis of popular folksongs revealed contemporary gender role prescriptions and common emotional issues. Personal narratives, spoken as well as written, supplied the depth of individual experience. Local newspapers, business directories, and land records supplemented these sources, locating individual women in time and place.

Demographic analysis of the county census outlined the structure of women's lives. Household by household, street by street, patterns of family size, national origin, class status, and neighborhood composition unfolded. Census manuscripts made visible women's significant life decisions: their marital status, their age at marriage, the number of children they bore, the number of boarders they kept or servants they employed, and changes in their occupations. Subtler patterns could be discerned as well. Dates of immigration for each household member signaled years of separation or reunion with husbands, parents, or siblings. Children born in different states revealed a trail of family migration. Boarders who shared the same nationality as their host family suggested ethnic housing networks. And the presence of extended kin in households hinted at family systems of relocation and support. From a random sample of one hundred households for each census year from 1880 to 1910, such information yielded comparative profiles of coal-town women and their rural peers.[32]

Introduction

Folklore provided clues to popular values and attitudes, including those shared by people who could not or did not have time to write. For the purposes of this study, "folklore" refers to rural American oral traditions in song and story. Some historians are leery of folklore. As American West folklorist Bruce Rosenberg observed:

> Those who seek verifiable immutable "facts" in the swarm of events we term "history" have been suspicious of folklore. . . . Oral transmission is said to be particularly unreliable. People forget details, add others, change still more. And it is true that while oral traditions are seldom accurate in the positive sense sought by contemporary historians (although some traditions are quite accurate, particularly in those cultures where it is of the utmost religious significance to be so), they do often reflect psychological and cultural truths.[33]

Popular folksongs of the late nineteenth and early twentieth century expressed intense feelings—sexual passion, revenge, grief, anger—that were socially unacceptable in daily life.[34] Expression of such emotion was taboo in personal narratives as well. But folksongs dramatized taboo situations and feelings, allowing singers and listeners vicarious expression. Indeed, the popularity of certain songs suggests that they sketched out common emotional issues.

Of course, historians have no way of knowing which women sang which songs. Still, for this study, some inferences could be made. Rural women's narratives from Sweetwater County referred to box socials and dances at which fiddle tunes and folksongs were played. Folklorists and folksong anthologies indicated the region and time period in which songs were well known. Consequently, one can identify certain songs as part of Sweetwater County culture. These songs were analyzed for prescriptive content and emotional resonance in women's lives.

Personal narratives provided the most vivid impressions of women's lives. Autobiographies, memoirs, and oral histories added complexity and dimension to the faceless statistics of demography, the anonymous emotion of folklore. Oral histories, in particular, offset the literate, middle-class bias created by reliance on written materials alone. Like folklore, oral history has been criticized as an inexact tool. Critics note that the process of reminiscing can distort events, should informants become nostalgic, forgetful, or ingenuous. But proponents agree that the purpose of oral history is not to recreate events in perfect chronological detail. Rather, it is to reflect the meanings that the informant has attached to given periods of his or her life.[35] As such, oral history reveals how people make sense of their experience; the issues that most preoccupied them will surface, like hand-drawn maps for the attentive historian. This study drew from

Introduction

one hundred oral interviews with Sweetwater County residents who remembered back to the first three decades of the twentieth century.[36] In addition, several oral histories of Sweetwater County residents collected by the Wyoming Works Progress Administration (WPA) between 1936 and 1940 offered memories dating back to the 1890s. Both the WPA narratives and more recent interviews included native and foreign-born informants, from mining towns as well as ranches. For both constituencies, oral histories gave life to patterns discerned in the census, and individual expression to values conveyed in regional folklore.

The available written memoirs survived from ranching and homesteading women only. Ora and Lenora Wright's collected memoirs of Eden Valley settlers and the Sublette County Artists' Guild's collected memoirs of upper Green River Valley ranchers were principal sources.[37] Memoirs of rural life from other counties supplemented these sources, since ranching on the high plains in Carbon, Uinta, or Laramie Counties closely resembled that in Sweetwater County.[38]

Written memoirs occasionally present an interpretive challenge not unlike oral histories. Because memoirs often were written with publication in mind, they may reflect the author's construction of a public persona with a public agenda. In some cases, such an agenda may take over, to the point where fiction replaces memory. In a study of Montana pioneer memoirs, for example, Clyde Milner found that authors exaggerated the frequency and dangers of Indian contact, in order to meet reader demand for melodrama or white triumph in westering narratives. Comparing published memoirs with diaries kept at the time of migration, Milner argued that memoirs may not accurately replicate the facts, but their expression of shared values can be equally telling, for they do reveal processes of self-construction.[39] The challenge is to recognize the social meanings expressed in such constructions while weighing the "facts" against related sources. Not all written memoirs from Sweetwater County presented such a complex task. Some contained straightforward information about carrying mail, hauling water, or herding sheep. These narratives sketched in the texture of daily life. In short, oral histories and written memoirs from southwest Wyoming opened a window on women's everyday activities as well as on their shared values and their changing self-definition.

With one foot in the Old West and the other in early-twentieth-century urban industry, Sweetwater County history resists easy characterization. An aerial view of the county today still marks the physical boundaries that separated ranch women from coal town women. Mining towns appear as dense clusters of housing and businesses, islands in the midst of a vast yellow-gray desert. Miles of rolling hills, rock outcroppings, and buttes, remnants of an inland sea, stretch between Rock Springs and its distant cousin, the rural hamlet of Burnt

Introduction

Fork. In Burnt Fork, green quilt patches of irrigated field mark property lines, ranch to ranch, pasture to desert. To understand women's changing place in this geography, we must return to an earlier time. Sweetwater County, 1880 to 1929, tells a story of dynamic demographic and economic change that shaped gender relations on this modernizing frontier.

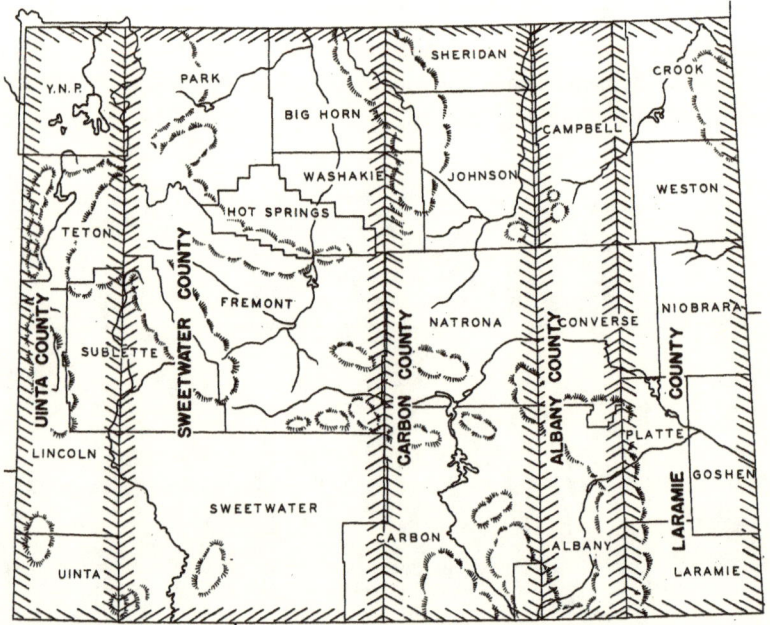

Five-county map of Wyoming, 1869. Reprinted from *History of Wyoming*, 2d ed., revised, by T. A. Larson, © 1965, 1978 by the University of Nebraska Press.

CHAPTER ONE

Sweetwater County: Desert Highway, Company Town, Cowboy West

In 1863 Overland Trail emigrant A. Howard Cutting passed through the region that is now Sweetwater County. Cutting spoke for many when he remarked on the strangeness of the landscape, the harshness of the climate, and the scarcity of natural resources:

June 8th . . . These rocks remind me of lumps of furnace stone magnified. . . . A miserable lonesome country here. No wonder the stage men charge for water, should think they would need to charge for being looked at. . . .

. . . The "Guard" for the first time, has to go two miles away from Camp to guard the stock [to the only place suitable for grazing] . . . and a cold job it will be as the nights in this miserable country are extremely cold.

June 9th . . . Green River is a very swift stream, about 150 yards wide and too high . . . to ford.

June 10th . . . Wood very scarce, have seen no timber with the exception of a few pine shrubs on the side of Mountains a long way off.[1]

Rocks like a furnace, freezing nights, dangerous river, sparse forage, and no wood—little wonder that westering migrants did not pause to settle this region for the better part of the nineteenth century. It is easy to imagine farm families squinting in the heat of what was then Dakota Territory and pointing their teams more determinedly toward the green valleys of Oregon.

Eventually the region would draw permanent settlement, but Cutting's observations foretold the difficulty of survival in this "miserable lonesome country." Miners and ranchers, venturing here some twenty to forty years later, would encounter profound physical and economic risks. They would have only their own resources upon which to fall back, for Sweetwater County's boom era ended before the New Deal—before federal programs guaranteed workman's compensation, old age pensions, workers' rights to collective bargaining, or subsidies to farmers. In short, Sweetwater County's pioneer settlers would have to create their own safety nets—their own ways of coping with industrial injury, death, unemployment, unpredictable weather, and loss of livestock.

Sweetwater County began as Carter County of the Dakota Territory in 1867. At that time, its boundaries extended north to Montana, south to Colorado, and west to Oregon. When Wyoming became a territory in 1869, the vast Carter County was renamed Sweetwater County. Between 1875 and 1886, Johnson, Fremont, and Carbon Counties were established in Wyoming, taking from Sweetwater County its northernmost, northeastern, and southeastern blocks, respectively. The establishment of Sublette County in 1922 pared off the north-central portion, and Sweetwater County assumed its present area of 10,249 square miles.[2]

What Cutting and other emigrants saw was high plains desert. The elevation averaged 6,600 feet above sea level; rainfall averaged less than eight inches per year. Only the Green River drainage, running through the western half of the county, broke the pattern of butte and plain. Tributaries of the Green evoked their character by name: Bitter Creek, Little Bitter Creek, Big Sandy River, Little Sandy River, Black's Fork, and Burnt Fork.[3] Where the Green River corridor widened into valleys, and along perennial creek bottoms, there was arable land. In the foothills of the Uinta Mountains, along the southwest border of the county, bluegrass, gramma grass, and wheat grass made good forage for livestock.[4]

But most of the county was an arid plateau where soils resisted cultivation, having too much salt and too few nutrients. Water was scarce, and vegetation ran to sage, greasewood, prickly pear, and alkali spike grass. On the high plains desert it could take thirty to forty acres just to sustain one cow.[5] Sparse forage, in turn, would shape ranchers' strategies of settlement. The challenge would be how to accumulate enough range to raise livestock. Still, while the land appeared spare, wealth lay hidden below ground. Once a vast inland sea, southwest Wyoming carried those secrets in its coal beds, where the detritus of life, over geologic time, had become fuel. Not until the coming of the railroad would this fuel become a commodity. For these reasons, Sweetwater County began as a highway, not a home, to white settlers. From the 1820s, when fur traders rendezvoused south of the county at Brown's Hole, through the 1870s, when the Union Pacific began to mine coal, thousands of whites traveled through, but few stayed.

During the 1700s Native Americans had migrated to the region from the Great Basin. By the early 1800s Shoshones and a few northern Utes inhabited the area that was to become Sweetwater County. Cheyennes, Crows, Arapahoes, and Oglala and Brule Sioux occasionally traveled through as well. Relations between Euro-Americans and Native Americans were peaceful during the early

1800s, when white contacts were few.[6] But in 1849 the California Gold Rush dramatically increased use of the Oregon Trail, which ran just north of present-day Sweetwater County from Laramie west to South Pass, then southwest to Fort Bridger. Emigrant traffic scattered buffalo herds, drove off game, and destroyed grass and timber. During the 1850s white emigration also brought fatal epidemics; cholera, smallpox, and measles decimated almost every tribe that came in contact with whites. Bands of Cheyennes, Arapahoes, and Sioux objected to these disruptions, and war broke out on the northern plains.[7]

In 1862 freighter Ben Holladay opened a new emigrant trail to the south to avoid warring tribes. Called the Overland Trail, this stage route ran east to west across the area that is now Sweetwater County.[8] Rock Springs, Bitter Creek Station, and the settlement called Green River took root as stage stations on this trail.

Skirmishes between federal troops and northern plains tribes continued throughout the 1860s, culminating in the Fort Laramie Treaty of 1868. This document relegated the Sioux to reservation lands in what is now the western half of South Dakota, the Cheyennes and Arapahoes to the Indian Territory in Oklahoma. That same year the Shoshones signed a treaty at Fort Bridger, removing them to a reservation at the edge of the Wind River Mountains, just north of present-day Sweetwater County.[9] Though the Cheyennes, Arapahoes, and Sioux would continue to fight, after 1868 these conflicts would be played out farther north in the Dakota, Montana, and Idaho Territories.[10]

The departure of the Shoshones, Cheyennes, Arapahoes, and Sioux coincided with the coming of the Union Pacific Railroad. In 1869 the transcontinental railroad was completed, connecting Omaha, Nebraska, to San Francisco, California. Union Pacific track followed the Overland Stage route across southwest Wyoming—present-day Sweetwater County. Surveyors chose this route because it had richer coal deposits than the old Oregon Trail through South Pass.[11] Coal fueled the trains and would soon become the Union Pacific Railroad's most lucrative resource. The Union Pacific, in turn, established a growing hold on the region, which would shape its history.

Tiny towns that had sprung up as stage stations now became railroad depots for the Union Pacific. Even at this early date, the Union Pacific flexed its power in southwest Wyoming. Settlers at Green River stage station, for example, anticipating the railroad's arrival in 1868, established a townsite on the east side of the river and named it Old Town. They assumed that the Union Pacific would build track, depot, housing, and offices in Old Town. Instead, the railroad bypassed Old Town and laid its own townsite on the west side of the river, naming it Green River City. Old Town could not survive without Union Pacific pa-

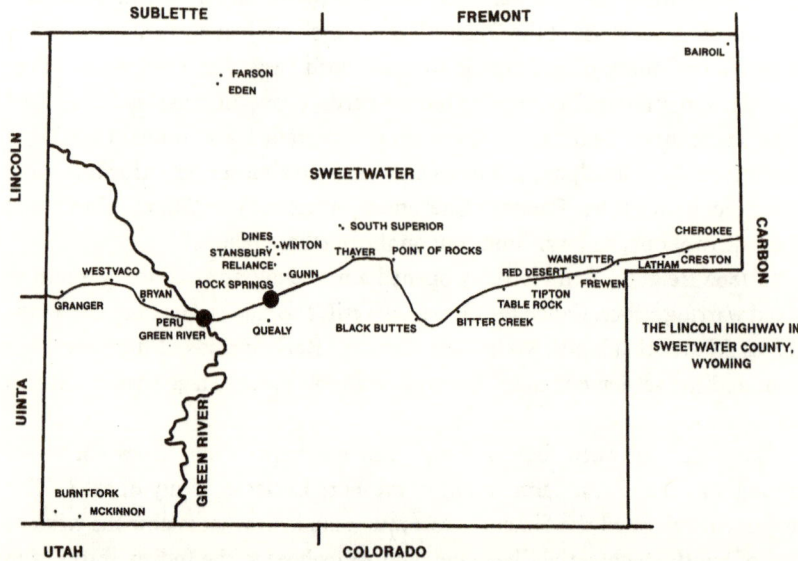

The Lincoln Highway paralleled the route blazed by the Union Pacific Railroad in 1869, which, in turn, had followed the Overland Trail. Reprinted from *Historical Images of Sweetwater County* by Dudley Gardner and Val Brinkerhoff, © 1993 by A. Dudley Gardner.

tronage, and within a year it folded. Residents moved across the river to Green River City in 1869 "and started anew on the railroad's terms."[12]

With the completion of the transcontinental railroad, emigrant traffic increased, though still, few stopped to settle in southwest Wyoming. Those who did clustered at the railroad depots of Green River City, Bryan Station, Rock Springs, Bitter Creek, and Point of Rocks. Green River City, the largest depot, boasted 101 inhabitants in 1869.[13] Early depot towns were makeshift at best. Wyoming historian Lola Homsher described Point of Rocks, circa 1868: "Lined along the main street, and extending to side avenues, were clapboard houses, tent abodes, and mortared shanties. Strings of lumber wagons heaped with cargoes pushed in and out near the freight depot."[14] These embryonic towns bloomed and faded, depending upon how much business the Union Pacific brought. From 1867 to 1868, Point of Rocks thrived as a freighting center since it linked the U.P. terminus with stages to South Pass City, Salt Lake City, and Oregon. But in late 1868, when the U.P. terminus was extended west to Bryan Station, Point of Rocks declined as Bryan became the new stage link to points north and west. Similarly, Bryan Station prospered until the U.P. extended farther west; then Bryan, too, dwindled almost to extinction.[15] With white outposts so transitory, those invested in the region's future looked for strategies to encourage permanent settlement.

In 1869 Wyoming became a territory. Surprising the nation, the new territorial legislature enfranchised women. Contemporaries reported that the woman suffrage bill in Wyoming was an advertising gambit, not the result of a female suffrage lobby. According to observer Edward M. Lee, legislators were eager for publicity that would attract settlers:

> The [woman suffrage] law was not adopted in obedience to public sentiment, but because territorial lawyers believed it would operate as a "first class advertisement," that their action . . . would be telegraphed throughout the civilized world, and public interest thereby aroused, resulting in increased immigration and large accretions of capital to their new and comparatively unknown territory. . . . The women themselves did not appear as petitioners.[16]

Wyoming historian T. A. Larson speculated that the woman suffrage bill was more publicity ploy than feminist triumph because so few women inhabited the territory at that time. In 1869 the sex ratio in Wyoming was six men to every one woman. An organized woman suffrage movement did not surface in Wyoming until 1890, when Wyoming gained statehood and the new state legislature addressed the territorial precedent of woman suffrage.[17]

Despite woman suffrage and a transcontinental railroad, southwest Wyoming failed to draw minions of settlers during the 1870s. The nationwide panic of 1873 had little effect on Wyoming, already in the economic doldrums. Larson summarized the situation in 1873 when he wrote,

> Few Wyoming people owned securities. Falling agricultural prices did little harm to Wyoming agriculture, since there were few farms and not many ranchers.
>
> . . . People simply were not coming to Wyoming except as sight-seers or tramps. The tramps rode the freight trains to California and back again.[18]

Still, Green River City and Rock Springs gained a toehold during the 1870s. Green River became the county seat in 1873, ensuring its permanency. And Rock Springs turned to coal mining.[19]

In 1868 two Scottish immigrants, Archibald and Duncan Blair, opened a coal seam near the Rock Springs stage station. Initially the Blair brothers had come to Rock Springs to run the stage, but they began mining coal in anticipation of the approaching railroad. They named their mines to mark the geological order of the coal seams. Number One Mine reached the No. 1 seam, Number Six Mine the No. 6 seam, and so forth.[20] Near their first mine, the Blair brothers erected a three-room clapboard building where they set up an office, living quarters, and store. This they called Blairtown.

By 1871 Blairtown coal claimed a steady customer in the Union Pacific Railroad. Scotch, Irish, and English immigrants, most of them from mining districts in Great Britain, staffed the Blairtown mines. Comforts were few in Blairtown; miners lived in dug-out homes burrowed into the steep banks of Bitter Creek. Meanwhile, a few miles east of Blairtown, two brothers called Wardell opened another coal mine, which they dubbed "Rock Spring."[21]

In 1874 both the Blair and Wardell brothers sold their interests to the Union Pacific Coal Company. Thereafter, the Union Pacific discouraged other coal companies from establishing mines in southwest Wyoming, by charging exorbitant freight rates and engaging in land fraud to lock up access to coal seams. The 1864 federal land grant to the Union Pacific for transcontinental railroad construction had given the corporation twenty square-mile sections of land for each linear mile of track. The railroad's holdings constituted the odd-numbered sections in a strip forty miles wide, twenty miles on each side of the track. Mineral rights came with the grant. Federal law prohibited the Union Pacific from buying even-numbered sections, not included in the grant, and limited land acquisition outside grant boundaries to 640 acres per corporation. But the U.P. found ways around such restrictions. To fill in gaps in coal-rich areas, the company used dummies, vagrants, and willing employees to file claims or buy land and then transfer title to the Union Pacific. In this way the U.P. acquired coal-rich even-numbered sections during the 1870s and 1880s, monopolizing access to coal seams in southwest Wyoming.[22]

While U.P. land claims consolidated power in the corporate world, construction of company towns consolidated power over labor. Company ownership of townsites, workers' housing, and mercantiles served the Union Pacific goal of establishing "absolute control of the town in case of trouble with employees."[23] The U.P. paid miners in scrip, forcing them to shop at the company store. The company store charged high prices, driving miners into debt and dependence on company largesse. Company housing supplanted company store practices in Union Pacific efforts to control labor. In 1875 Blairtown miners left their mud-ridden, dug-out shanties to rent two-, three-, and four-room, unpainted frame buildings owned by the Union Pacific. Such improvements in living quarters were double-edged, for miners who struck faced eviction. The threat of homelessness discouraged worker solidarity. To further discourage labor organization, the U.P. adopted a strategy of "divide and conquer," pitting rival ethnic groups against each other. During the late 1870s and early 1880s, if English,

Scottish, or Irish miners organized to protest wage cuts, the company fired them and hired Asian labor.[24]

In 1883 the Knights of Labor organized Rock Springs miners and railroad workers. But the Knights excluded Asian labor, claiming that their presence depressed wages. The Knights' hostility toward Asian workers foretold worsening conflict. The U.P. continued to undercut white miners with cheap Asian labor, until by 1885 Asians outnumbered white miners. In 1885, 150 whites and 330 Asians worked the coal mines in Rock Springs. The melting pot boiled over in 1885, when Welsh, Irish, Cornish, and Swedish miners rioted against the Asian miners. Mobs looted and burned Asian miners' homes, literally driving them out of town. Called the Rock Springs Massacre, the melee left 28 Asians dead and 15 wounded. Immediately following the massacre, most Chinese and Japanese left Sweetwater County in search of less hostile environs. Thereafter the Union Pacific began recruiting white, European workers.[25] But the U.P. strategy of "divide and conquer" persisted. Wyoming historian Dudley Gardner noted that the company made sure to hire from a variety of ethnic groups, "as a means of keeping down labor agitation."[26]

After the massacre, immigration from Asia and Great Britain declined, while immigration from Eastern European nations and the Scandinavian countries increased. The proportion of Eastern Europeans in Sweetwater County rose from 0.3 percent in 1880 to 7.2 percent in 1900. The proportion of Scandinavians rose from 5.3 percent in 1880 to 18.6 percent in 1900. And the proportion of British settlers in the county dropped from 27.4 percent in 1880 to 18.9 percent in 1900. With increased Scandinavian and Eastern European immigration, foreign-born began to outnumber native-born residents. By 1900 the county population stood at 58.6 percent foreign-born residents, 41.4 percent native-born.[27]

The Rock Springs Massacre was more than a demographic watershed. It exposed miners' grievances against the Union Pacific. Mining methods were primitive and dangerous: "The coal was pick-mined, shot with black powder, hauled by mules through the mine slope to the outside, loaded into wagons, and taken to the railroad track."[28] Rock Springs miners needed better exits and ventilation. They objected to child labor and to company store practices. In 1886 Rock Springs miners successfully lobbied the territorial legislature to prohibit boys under age fourteen and women from working in mines, to require coal mines to have at least two exits, to establish ventilation regulations, and to provide a territorial mine safety inspector. But the legislature voted down a bill that would have ended company store practices. This bill would have required the Union Pacific to pay miners' wages in U.S. currency rather than company scrip. It also would have prohibited withholding miners' wages to pay company store bills.

So company store practices continued, trapping miners in a cycle of debt. It was not until 1891 that the Wyoming legislature outlawed payment in scrip.[29] Cash wages paved the way for diversification of Rock Springs' consumer economy. During the 1890s independent businesses would take root, supported by miners and their families who avoided the company store.

Partial mechanization of coal mining between 1887 and 1892 doubled coal production. Cutting and drilling machines made extraction of the black rock more efficient. Union Pacific mines flourished. By 1893 the U.P. produced 63 percent of the state's total coal output. Though the panic of 1893 depressed fuel prices, during the late 1890s the coal market recovered.[30] By the turn of the century, coal mining dominated the county economy. Demographic patterns reflected this development, with more emigrants settling in mining/railroad towns than in rural areas. By 1900, 87.3 percent of adult women in Sweetwater County lived in town, while only 12.7 percent lived on homesteads or ranches.[31]

Green River City emerged as the freighting and supply center for ranchers moving through the Green River Valley. The U.P. railroad linked cattle and sheep drovers with eastern markets, attracting outfits from Texas who trailed herds north to Wyoming, then shipped them by train to Chicago. During the 1870s open-range practices prevailed. Cattle were turned loose in the fall to forage for themselves, and then cowboys gathered them up in the spring. In a 1938 interview with WPA historian Josephine Jons, rancher J. M. Huston described the early days of open-range herding in southwest Wyoming:

> The Green River Valley in those days was just one big ranch. We used the Green River and all of its tributaries north of the U.P. railroad for range. We used the west side of the river for summer range, and the desert and river in the winter time. There was very little feeding done then.
> . . . We would drift the cattle off the desert on to their summer range. Then late in the fall we would drift them back again.[32]

Wyoming cattlemen depended almost entirely upon free use of government land during this period. By 1877 assessors reported 11,377 cattle and 1,965 sheep in the county. But most of these herds belonged to nonresident owners who had established permanent ranch headquarters in the eastern part of the state, where the climate and terrain were less forbidding.[33]

The 1870s were an incubation period in Sweetwater County history. A ranching and mining economy began to take shape, but not in impressive, or even permanent proportions. The population, for example, grew by only 645 people between 1870 and 1880.[34] The Union Pacific Corporation controlled a nascent mining industry. Livestock grazed the open range, but ranching was not yet rooted by settlement in the county.

In contrast, the 1880s marked a decade of change. Between 1880 and 1890, Wyoming's population tripled, from 20,789 in 1880 to 62,555 in 1890. In Sweetwater County alone, the population doubled, from 2,561 in 1880 to almost 5,000 in 1890.[35] Cattle and sheepmen began to establish ranches in the county during the 1880s, in response to overgrazing on public lands. Competition for control of range became intense, and ranchers turned to land ownership, fencing out their rivals. The open-range era faded. "As time went on," said J. M. Huston, "the country became more settled up and everything changed. . . . There were others taking up ranches in different places, [and] they kept their cattle around their ranches, feeding them hay in winter."[36] Keeping cattle on a ranch required both pastureland and acreage to grow hay.

Ranchers found it difficult to acquire enough land to sustain a herd. The Homestead Act of 1862 made 160-acre claims available to U.S. citizens over age twenty-one who met a residency requirement of five years and built a habitable cabin. The catch, for ranchers, was that the law allowed only one claim per household head. But on the arid plains, 160 acres would not feed a herd. In 1877 the Desert Land Act allowed 640-acre claims on "desert land"—land that could not be cultivated without irrigation. In 1878 John Wesley Powell proposed to Congress that 2,560-acre claims be made available on arid lands west of the 100th meridian since ranching on the high desert required more acreage per head of livestock. But Congress rejected Powell's proposal. The 1877 law held to 640-acre desert claims, requiring three years' residency and irrigation of the claim to earn title.[37] Still, even 640 acres of desert forage could not sustain a herd of more than about twenty-five beeves.

So ranchers bent the rules to acquire more acreage. Some arranged for cowboys to file claims, then transfer title to their employer. Others filed dummy land claims in the names of nonresidents. Still others applied for 640 acres of "desert lands," which were actually streamside meadows. Finally—and slightly more legal—some persuaded relatives to file adjacent claims, creating a large family ranch. Most ranchers never earned title to fraudulent claims. Despite scores of land applications made during the 1880s, by 1890 only 10 percent of Wyoming public lands had been patented.[38] "Proving up" was perhaps less important to ranchers than the application process itself, which allowed them to use and fence the acreage in question.

Sweetwater County rancher Abner Luman's career reflected the nature of ranching in southwest Wyoming at the end of the century. Born in West Virginia in 1849, Luman migrated to Kansas with his parents, then further west on his own as a young man. From 1866 to 1876 he worked in staging and freighting from Utah to Montana. Next he herded cattle and sheep for several outfits in

Wyoming until 1880, when Luman established his own ranch in the upper Green River Valley.[39]

Though cattle ranching would capture the popular imagination, sheep ranching promised economic success. Luman found that sheep fared better than cattle on the sparse forage and extreme temperatures of the high desert. Moreover, the market for wool was strong during the 1880s. By 1884 the western Wyoming counties of Sweetwater, Uinta, and Fremont had become predominantly sheep-growing regions. The hard winter of 1886–87 secured this trend. Cattle herds suffered huge losses when the extreme cold killed healthy animals. For the next ten years following the winter of '86–'87, cattle ranching waned in Wyoming and sheep ranching expanded. By the late 1890s cattle herds on the Wyoming plains had been reduced by two thirds. Meanwhile, the number of sheep in Wyoming increased from 875,000 in 1885 to 3,366,000 in 1890.[40] By 1896 Abner Luman, like most Sweetwater County ranchers, had "largely extended his operations in sheep." Luman went on to become a livestock magnate, with ranches in Wyoming and Idaho and a sumptuous home in Salt Lake City.[41]

Though Luman's career reflected the spread of sheep ranching in southwest Wyoming, his wealth was atypical.[42] Between 1880 and 1900, 12.8 percent of Sweetwater County residents lived in rural areas. These settlers, by and large, lived on subsistence farms with herds of less than 100 cattle or sheep.[43] Some came in response to rumors of the profitable sheep industry. One WPA informant said, "According to rumor, one early operator [of a sheep ranch] . . . claimed a profit of 35 per cent for three years, while another in the Pole Creek region claimed a profit of 60 per cent in one year."[44]

Others came in response to Wyoming boosterism. In 1889 the Secretary of the Wyoming Territory printed *Resources of Wyoming*, a promotional booklet aimed at prospective settlers. Under "Sweetwater County," the booklet promised the following "Agricultural Advantages":

> It will not be many years before the extensive bottom lands lying along many streams in Sweetwater County are waving with golden grain; when its vegetables will be as celebrated as those of Colorado or Utah. We have the same soil and the same climate as our neighbors, and we only need water to raise good crops.[45]

One wonders how A. Howard Cutting might have amended such glowing terms. By 1897 local newspapers in Sweetwater County had picked up the same rhetoric, extolling the county's agricultural potential. "Sweetwater County has resources unequaled by any other county in the state of Wyoming," proclaimed one article in a special illustrated edition of the *Rock Springs Miner*, May 17, 1897. "Every acre of its hills and valleys," boasted the *Miner*, "is the very best sheep and cattle grazing land, native grasses and feed of all kinds growing in abundance."[46] Lured by the promise of grazing and irrigable lands, homesteaders from the British Isles, and from farming states in the Northeast and Midwest, began filing land claims in Sweetwater County.

Still, the pace of agricultural settlement did not meet boosters' expectations.[47] Indeed, the land was not as readily farmed as the boosters claimed. On many claims, creek levels were so irregular and soil so sandy that homemade irrigation ditches dried up, washed out, or clogged with silt. Migrants reading their *Resources of Wyoming* booklet may have overlooked the small print about irrigation and capital:

> Green River and its many tributaries offer an inexhaustible supply of water which only needs capital to divert it on to the lands. . . . Irrigation would have to be done on a very large scale and considerable capital be required to do this work.[48]

Sweetwater County soil and topography called for reservoirs, dams, and miles of canals to make arable land—projects beyond the scope of individual homesteaders.

The Carey Act of 1894 encouraged large-scale irrigation projects through donation by the federal government of up to one million acres of arid lands to each state willing to direct corporate reclamation and then settlement of such lands.[49] The first Carey Act irrigation project in Sweetwater County was organized in 1905, in Eden Valley on the Big Sandy River. The Eden Valley Irrigation Project comprised 56,323 acres of land segregated under the Carey Act. In 1907 Eden Land and Irrigation Company, the corporate investor responsible for constructing a large-scale irrigation system, began work on a main canal diverting water from Big Sandy Creek. By 1914 Eden Land and Irrigation had completed a reservoir and forty-five miles of canals. The company then sold water rights to settlers, who filed claims on project acreage.[50] Agricultural settlement in Sweetwater County picked up only after the Eden project married government lands to corporate capital, making irrigation viable on the sagebrush plains.

The first two decades of the twentieth century marked Sweetwater County's metamorphosis from sparsely settled ranching and mining frontier to booming region. Between 1898 and 1910 coal production in Wyoming doubled, from over three million tons to more than seven million tons. In Sweetwater County both the Union Pacific and rival companies opened new mines. In 1905, for example, the Superior Coal Company organized to prospect non–Union Pacific lands northeast of Rock Springs. Superior mines began production in 1906 and over the next ten years ranked second only to Rock Springs in coal tonnage.[51] The new town of Superior sprung up around the Superior mine sites. Meanwhile, the Union Pacific continued mineral exploration and opened the Reliance coal mines in 1910, seven miles north of Rock Springs. Within a year, the Union Pacific built on-site company housing, and the town of Reliance took root.[52] In 1916 the Union Pacific Coal Company bought out the Superior Coal Company.[53] With high-yield clusters of mines at Rock Springs, Superior, and Reliance, the Union Pacific again controlled coal mining in Sweetwater County.

But the Union Pacific failed to control the service industries that sprang up in mining towns. With pay in dollars rather than company scrip, miners patronized independent saloons, restaurants, laundries, bakeries, and mercantiles. Bertagnolli's Union Mercantile Store was typical of the independents. Henry Bertagnolli came to Wyoming in 1880 from Tyrolia, Italy. He worked in the Rock Springs coal mines until 1885, when the Chinese massacre disillusioned him. Leaving the mines, he began selling hay, grain, and feed, then expanded to include food and hardware. In 1893 Bertagnolli reorganized his retail business with three relatives and renamed it the Union Mercantile and Supply Company—a name chosen to honor union activity and to win customers away from the U.P. Company Store. Bertagnolli's Union Mercantile sold groceries, hardware, clothing, shoes, hay, grain, and feed. In 1905 the Union Mercantile opened a branch in Superior, and in 1907 another branch in neighboring Uinta County.[54]

Mining town women supported independent businesses. In charge of their household budgets, they found it more economical to buy dry goods, meats, and produce from noncompany stores. As Slovenian immigrant Helen Korich Krmpotich explained it,

> There was a Yugoslav family that had a store. You traded with the Yugoslav store . . . [because] well, the company store, they used to take your whole paycheck and you didn't have anything to pay anybody else with. Wasn't enough money.[55]

The "Yugoslav store" that Krmpotich referred to was the Rock Springs Commercial Store, run by the Suvik family in Superior. Mining town women, then, shared their husbands', sons', and brothers' distrust of the U.P. Company Store, and took their business to independent retailers.

Another reason independent businesses did well in Rock Springs, Green River, and Superior was that miners and their families had frequent interaction with the central community. In a study of late-nineteenth- and early-twentieth-century mining settlements, historian Earl Stinneford compared company towns in northern and southern Wyoming. Stinneford found that company towns in northern Wyoming rarely diversified, since they were built around isolated mines, far from principle cities. In contrast, southern Wyoming mines and their company towns were not isolated. Sweetwater County miners, for example, worked and lived close to central towns like Green River and Rock Springs. Consequently, these miners and their families experienced "more direct interaction with the community," and independent merchants found a ready market.[56]

Support for noncompany businesses also reflected pro-union sentiment among immigrant miners. In 1903 the United Mine Workers of America began organizing coal fields in northern Wyoming. Once this was accomplished, the UMWA turned to the coal mines of southwest Wyoming. By 1907 the union successfully organized locals in all Union Pacific mines throughout Sweetwater County.[57] On May 26, 1907, Rock Springs miners joined an industrywide strike. The Union Pacific Corporation threatened to fire and evict all participants, but this time worker solidarity extended to all ethnic groups, white and Asian alike. Without scab labor, company resistance crumbled. The strike secured an eight-hour day, a 20 percent wage increase, and use of checkmen chosen by the union.[58]

Mining disasters cemented miners' loyalty to the UMWA. On March 28, 1908, an explosion in nearby Hanna, Carbon County, killed fifty-eight men. Subsequent investigations proved the Union Pacific repeatedly negligent about safety underground. The union pressed for compensation, and won $800 for each widow of the Hanna explosion. Later that year the union struck again, this time against a wage reduction. This strike went statewide, involving over seven thousand miners. With safety standards inadequate and wage rates under siege, miners found what little protection they had in the UMWA.[59]

In the wake of union victories, labor activism entered electoral politics. In 1908 the Wyoming Socialist Party held its statewide convention in Rock Springs. Pledging support for state insurance, old age pensions, and miners' choice of state mine inspectors, the party found voters among Sweetwater County miners and their families. In 1910 the Rock Springs branch of the Wyoming Socialist Party ran candidates for mayor and city council, as well as for the state legislature and the governorship. Though Socialist candidates did not win, they made a strong showing. In the mining towns of Quealy and Superior, for example, 25 percent voted the Socialist ticket.[60] In 1911 Socialist leader Ida Crouch Hazlett spoke to enthusiastic crowds in Rock Springs. Thereafter, the party sponsored a lecture series at the Grand Opera House.[61] But enthusiasm for socialism waned in Sweetwater County after 1912, when a four-party race split the vote and fragmented the party. Still, while the Socialist Party lost support, the UMWA remained popular.[62] More importantly, both organizations spoke to miners' concerns about safety and insurance against injury.

European immigration peaked in Sweetwater County from the early 1900s through the early 1920s. The proportion of foreign-born residents in Sweetwater County rose from 58.6 percent in 1900 to 62.7 percent in 1910.[63] Of these, 29.9 percent came from the Eastern European countries of Czechoslovakia, Poland, Austria, Hungary, Romania, Croatia, Slovenia, Dalmatia, Bosnia, and Serbia. Another 25.3 percent came from Germany; 25 percent came from the Scandinavian countries of Finland, Norway, Sweden, and Denmark; and 17.2 percent came from Great Britain.[64] Between 1912 and 1920, military, political, and economic upheaval in the Balkans spurred emigration from Italy, Greece, and Eastern Europe. Between 1910 and 1920, Eastern European immigration to Wyoming rose from 825 to 2,671.[65] Relief from war, then, and the promise of jobs drew an ethnically diverse population to Sweetwater coal towns during the early twentieth century.

The majority of men in these ethnic groups found jobs with the Union Pacific Railroad and Coal Company. According to Gordon Hendrickson's study of immigration and assimilation in Wyoming, "As . . . new immigrants entered the state, the earlier, more experienced U.P. employees moved into positions of greater responsibility." By the early 1900s, for example, experienced Britons and Scandinavians became supervisors and foremen, while new immigrants—Slavs, Italians, and Greeks—entered the mines or railroad yards as unskilled laborers. In turn, members of these groups moved up through the ranks as they gained seniority and experience.[66]

Permanent ethnic neighborhoods rarely developed in twentieth-century Sweetwater coal towns. Upon arrival in a mining town like Reliance, Superior, or Rock Springs, miners and their families usually accepted whatever company housing was available. In his study of Wyoming company towns, Earl Stinneford observed that

> local saloon owners occasionally aided the new arrivals in locating housing as close as possible to others with the same ethnic background, but the effectiveness of these activities was, of course, circumscribed by the availability of housing . . . New immigrants frequently found housing wherever possible regardless of the ethnic flavor of the neighborhood.[67]

The result was that small, ethnic neighborhoods formed, changed, dissolved, and re-formed, as new arrivals settled in vacant housing, some families moved to bigger quarters, and others moved to nearby company towns. Rock Springs resident Mary Lou Anselmi Unguren observed that occasionally several families of the same nationality would cluster together on blocks where there was a mix of private and company housing. If an immigrant family successfully negotiated with the U.P. for a change of address, or accumulated enough savings to rent privately owned housing, they would move adjacent to another family of the same nationality if such housing were available. Mrs. Unguren's Slovenian mother, for example, grew up in a small "cluster" of her own nationality on Number One Hill. Similarly, her Tyrolean father lived in a small cluster of his nationality on "M" Street. "However," Mrs. Unguren wrote, "other nationalities lived close by—even across the street. . . . These 'clusters' would comprise only a small part of the neighborhood."[68] In short, the well-defined ethnic neighborhoods that characterized immigrant settlement in larger cities, such as "Little Italy" in Boston, or "Finn Town" in Butte, Montana, never emerged in urban Sweetwater County. There, mining and railroad towns remained ethnically heterogeneous, with mixed neighborhoods, their populations mobile.[69] This would have significant repercussions on the informal worlds of work and family life inhabited by women. The lack of residential ethnic cohesion would heighten the urgency of creating ethnic community through other means. Ethnically jumbled neighborhoods also would heighten the value of kinship ties as a source of support.

The hazards of coal mining compounded the unpredictability of life in Union Pacific company towns. If settlement patterns in company towns were somewhat chaotic, the work underground was no more predictable. Despite the union push during the 1880s to improve safety standards, and despite strikes for compensation in the wake of disaster, mining remained extremely dangerous. Rock Springs resident Henry Kovach remembered his father's stories of mine accidents during the first two decades of the twentieth century:

Walls would break through or . . . there would be cave-ins . . . and one of those would break through . . .

I can remember him talking many times . . . "It was a dangerous day today . . . in the mines.[70]

Cave-ins, coal-dust explosions, gas explosions, burns, sprains, back injuries, and falls were commonplace.[71] Then, too, a miner could drown in a sump, get scalded by steam, hit by a runaway ore car, or break his neck in a hoist frame. Moreover, "new accidents were constantly happening, the likes of which were never before heard of."[72] Indeed, though mechanization introduced during the early twentieth century made some tasks less arduous, it created new dangers. Some men lost fingers and limbs caught in machinery; others overestimated their endurance and dropped from heat exhaustion and dehydration. Asphyxiation, caused by accumulations of methane gas, endangered still others. Between 1900 and 1910 alone, 448 men died in coal mining accidents in Wyoming. Between 1900 and 1940, 1,748 men were killed in coal mine explosions in the intermountain West.[73] Finally, whether a miner used a pickaxe or an electric undercutter to dig into a seam, coal dust was the result. "Black lung," or "miner's consumption"—a variety of progressive pulmonary diseases—continued to plague coal miners well into the twentieth century.[74] The dangers of coal mining would take their toll on families, further underscoring the need for reliable systems of mutual aid among kin and ethnic groups.

If transience, chaotic settlement patterns, and hazardous work plagued coal town dwellers, rural communities faced a different set of challenges. Agricultural prices in Wyoming increased nearly 50 percent between 1900 and 1910.[75] This, along with changes in homestead law, lured homesteaders to the intermountain West. In 1909 the Mondell Revisory Act enlarged public land claims to 320 acres in semi-arid regions, bringing dry farmers to southwest Wyoming. In 1912 Congress reduced the homestead residency requirement from five to three years, seven months per year.[76]

But even as bull markets and generous land law drew homesteaders to the region, serious obstacles confronted them. Overgrazing, drought, and a hard winter in 1911–12 destroyed herds. In 1913 sheep growers lost the protective tariff on wool. And the creation of national forest preserves limited grazing on public lands. In response, ranchers scrambled to consolidate as much land as possible, by enlisting relatives to file claims, taking over unproven claims, and buying up deeded claims.[77] Land transfers in the upper Green River Valley (part of Sweetwater County until 1922) illustrate the trend toward consolidation of land. Over a fifteen year period, for example, rancher Jim Mickelson of Big Piney purchased homesteads at the head of South Cottonwood Creek, until he had accumulated a sizable range. A 1938 WPA history of ranches in Sublette County listed twelve claims acquired by Mickelson between 1895 and 1915:

> James Mickelson of Big Piney now owns the following homesteads at the head of South Cottonwood: Jack Blackman, Joe Fredell (1897), Noah Booker (1910), Jess Stull (1913), Johnny Nelson (1900), Winifred Nichols (1895), Charles Fredell (1898), Jim Crowe, Ray Small, Jack Curtis, August Testi, and Frank Bray [no dates].[78]

In 1916, grazing homesteads of 640 acres became available, making it somewhat easier for ranchers to secure range on semi-arid lands.[79]

World War I boosted the livestock industry in Wyoming. Demand for wool, mutton, and beef raised sheep and cattle prices. The federal government contracted with Wyoming livestock growers to supply the Allies. Likewise, World War I fueled the coal industry. Beginning in 1914, demand for coal surged. Federal contracts spurred Rock Springs mines to produce ten thousand tons of coal per day by 1917. The war boom intensified settlement; the county population swelled from 8,455 in 1910 to 13,640 in 1920.[80] Between 1917 and 1918, coal production in the United States increased by almost one million tons. The Union

Pacific opened new mines at Winton, Dines, and Lionkol, in the vicinity of Rock Springs.[81] As coal and livestock production increased, freighting boomed. Employment rose in Sweetwater County, and so did wages. Miner's wages jumped from $3.52 per day in 1916 to $5.42 per day in 1917. Railroad engineers, by 1918, earned $8.50 per day. Women's wages rose as well. In 1918 female stenographers' wages soared from $1.50 to as much as $5.80 per day.[82] Nationwide, more women entered the labor force outside the home, in some cases replacing men in industry. In Sweetwater County, the Union Pacific hired women to work as ticket agents and on section gangs.[83]

Communities mobilized to produce "victory gardens," to conserve staples on "Wheatless Mondays" and "Meatless Tuesdays," and to send care packages to servicemen. In Sweetwater County, women's organizations led the civilian volunteer effort. Rural and urban women's groups prepared bandages for overseas hospitals, collected books and knitted items for servicemen, and raised money for the Red Cross. Men from all ethnic groups enlisted in the armed forces, despite which some German families endured prejudice meant for the Kaiser.[84]

In Sweetwater coal towns, the service industries expanded to meet the needs of a growing population. New hotels went up; retail stores and food vendors opened shops; doctors, lawyers, accountants, and insurance agents established offices.[85] Commercial growth opened new job opportunities to women. Clerking jobs opened in retail stores, secretarial work in business and municipal offices. Restaurants hired female cooks and waitresses, and hotels, maids. Commercial laundries and bakeries hired women for day labor. Increasingly, Sweetwater County women entered the paid workforce outside the home, mirroring the national trend.[86]

At the close of the war, agricultural prices dropped, but homesteading increased. Flush from wartime prosperity, ranchers filed claims, bringing land entries to a peak from 1919 to 1921. Between 1915 and 1917, an average of 4,181 claims per year had been filed. In 1919, 7,083 claims were filed. And in 1921, the number of claims filed rose to 10,051. By 1923, the number of homestead claims filed had dropped back down to 2,914, and it never again rose above that figure.[87]

Notably, most of the claims filed during the peak years 1919–21 were taken up by ranching families wanting additional land—not by newcomers. Indeed, the rural population in Wyoming increased by only 5,829 between 1919 and 1929. According to Wyoming historian T. A. Larson, "People who were already on the land in 1919 sooner or later came into possession of most of the newly homesteaded land."[88] As before the war, ranchers, in their efforts to secure adequate grazing range, turned to relatives, and occasionally to employees or friends, to file claims and then transfer title to the rancher. Single and widowed women would take advantage of the demand for land, developing claims for sale to ranchers.[89]

With the war boom over, the Wyoming economy slumped. Agriculture and mining suffered setbacks during the 1920s, which presaged the Great Depression. Between 1918 and 1925, wool prices fell from eighty to twenty-five cents a pound; sheep prices from eighteen to six dollars a head; and lamb prices from eight to three dollars. Demand for coal dropped as well. The Union Pacific cut back production, and miners found their hours reduced. Some lost their jobs altogether.[90] As a result, the UMWA abandoned the no-strike pledge agreed to during the war. In 1919 UMWA President John L. Lewis called for a walkout to protest unemployment and wage cuts. After five weeks out, striking miners won a 14 percent pay increase, offsetting their decreased hours.

But the recession continued, and advances in mining technology further reduced the need for manpower. By 1920 the Union Pacific had laid off one third of its miners. For those who remained on the job, work was sporadic—only two to three days per week. Statewide, Wyoming coal production dropped by 3.4 million tons between 1920 and 1922. In 1922 the UMWA called another coal strike in Wyoming. This one lasted five months but gained little, and miners returned to work at 1920 wage rates.[91] With hours cut back and wages held low, a miner's paycheck would not support a family. Women's household work would become crucial to family survival during the postwar recession.[92]

Between 1923 and 1927, 1,872 more Wyoming coal miners lost their jobs.[93] Demoralized, in 1927 miners accepted a $1.28 wage cut without protest. Still, the UMWA influenced the state legislature during these lean years. In 1925 Wyoming lawmakers passed twelve statutes to improve safety in the state's coal mines. Provisions included mandatory sprinkler systems to reduce the accumulation of flammable coal dust; improved ventilation; and a "Coal Mine Catastrophe Insurance Plan," which allocated state monies to compensate the families of mining accident victims. Additionally, new safety standards limited the number of charges exploded per day, and required use of lamps that measured the amount of explosive gases present. Following this legislation, explosions and underground fires decreased.[94] It had taken over fifty years, since mining began in Sweetwater County, to secure adequate safety standards below ground.

Above ground, miners over the years had formed a variety of lodges and mutual aid societies, designed in part to ease the stresses of coal town life. Men's fraternal organizations offered health and life insurance plans. First-generation immigrant men founded ethnic fraternal lodges to meet this need. In Rock Springs alone, Irish workers formed a chapter of the Fenian Brotherhood; Scots formed a Caledonian Club; Germans, a Turnverein; Greeks, the Greek-American Progressive Association; Italians, the Andrea Hoffer Society and the Alphonso Lammamora Society; Croatians, the St. Joseph Society; and Slavs, the Slovenska Narodna Podporna Jednota.[95] Members of mutual aid societies paid dues, which accumulated against the day a member became ill, injured, or died. Member's families would be helped with funeral arrangements, compensation, and even volunteers to handle the disabled or deceased man's household chores.[96]

Second-generation men often joined American fraternal lodges, such as the Eagles, Elks, Masons, and Moose, all of which drew members from Green River and Rock Springs. By the 1920s, Germans, Britons, and Italians had assimilated into these organizations. The German Turnverein Society of Rock Springs, for example, folded during the first decade of the twentieth century as acculturated Germans joined American fraternal lodges.[97]

Women's associational groups, like men's, doubled as service and social organizations. Members of ethnic women's organizations shared skills, supplies, food, and support whenever major social events, like weddings and funerals, required group effort. And like their male peers, first-generation immigrant women usually joined ethnic associations, such as the St. Mary's Society, formed by Slovenian women in Rock Springs.[98] Second-generation immigrant women, like their male peers, were more apt to join "American" organizations, such as the Women's Club of Rock Springs, a branch of the nationwide General Federation of Women's Clubs. The Women's Club of Rock Springs focused on community service, organizing well-baby clinics in mining towns during the 1920s.[99] In short, men's and women's mutual aid societies absorbed some of the stresses of coal town life, particularly among first-generation immigrants anxious to pool resources with those of their own kind.

Though mutual aid societies provided social support and occasional financial aid, daily living conditions in mining towns remained harsh well into the 1920s. Housing, for example, remained primitive, even by contemporary standards. While middle-class homes in other parts of the country acquired plumbing and electricity during the 1920s, company housing in Sweetwater County was stuck in the nineteenth century.[100] One Italian miner bluntly called the Union Pacific houses in Rock Springs "shacks."[101] Wood-coal stoves provided heat and cooking surfaces. Kerosene or gas lamps provided light. Water for domestic use was hauled by railroad from Green River and Point of Rocks, and sold to company tenants for twenty-five cents a barrel. Home laundering took place in "shanties"—small, unheated shacks behind company houses. Women dipped buckets into their barrel water, heated the buckets over their stoves, and carried the buckets to the washtub in the shanty.[102]

Similarly, although modern appliances came into widespread use in middle-class electrified homes during the 1920s, few Sweetwater County women used vacuum cleaners, toasters, electric grills, coffee percolators, or washing machines. And while commercial food products and local markets encouraged consumerism, many working-class households still produced as much food as they could, well into the 1920s. Residents of Rock Springs and Green River remembered their mothers keeping a pig or chickens, or tending a vegetable garden in tiny company housing yards, and making their own sausage and canned goods.[103] Rural women, too, lived at the subsistence level well into the 1920s.[104] Nonetheless, for many European war refugees, even a Wyoming frontier in postwar recession looked more promising than their war-ravaged economies. European immigration rose after World War I, then tapered off during the mid- and late twenties. In 1924 Congress restricted immigration with the National Origins Act. This law set immigration quotas at 2 percent of the European ethnic composition of the United States, according to the 1890 census, at which time relatively few Southern and Eastern Europeans had arrived.[105] As immigration slowed after 1924, so did the pace of settlement.

From the 1880s through 1920s, Sweetwater County had been a region in transition. Ranching and mining brought permanent settlement; company towns and family ranches took root on the high plains. Open-range herding gave way to fenced herding, intensifying the competition for land ownership. Rich coal seams, technological advance, and demand for fuel culminated in the World War I coal boom. World War I also inflated the livestock industry. The war boom, in turn, accelerated commercial growth in railroad and coal towns, expanding the service industries. Finally, the postwar recession revealed the vulnerability of both mining and ranching to market fluctuations in the national economy.

The pattern of immigration, economic growth, and recession that characterized Sweetwater County history from the 1880s through the 1920s held serious challenges for those who came to stay. Coal town settlement patterns remained chaotic throughout Sweetwater County's frontier era, as company housing prevented formation of stable ethnic neighborhoods. Coal mining remained extremely dangerous, with new technology multiplying the kinds of injury miners risked. Ranchers, for their part, struggled with severe weather, harsh terrain, expensive irrigation, and competition for land. And so while thousands did, eventually, make Cutting's "miserable lonesome country" home, they faced decisive obstacles to their survival.

Given the themes of European immigration and dangerous industrial work, what made Sweetwater County different from industrial cities in the East? The

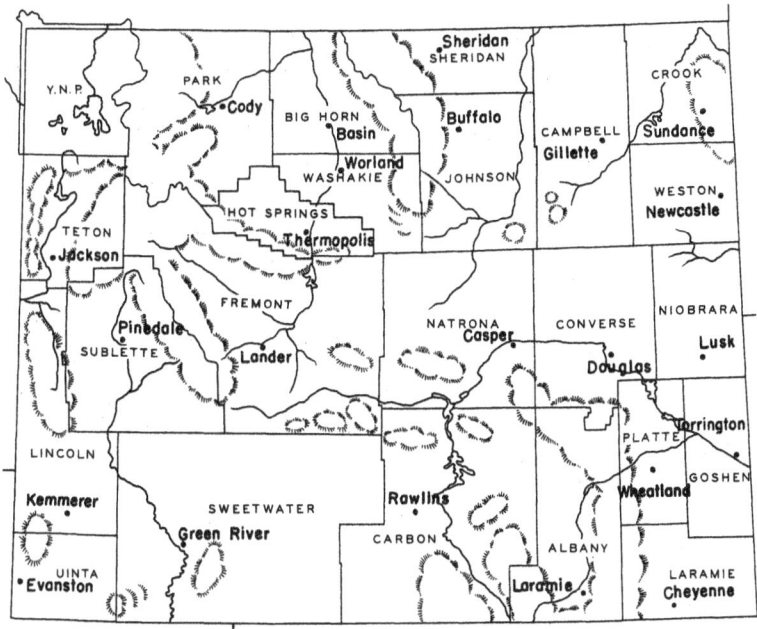

Wyoming counties and county seats since 1923. Reprinted from *History of Wyoming*, 2d ed., revised, by T. A. Larson, © 1965, 1978 by the University of Nebraska Press.

answer lies in the county's status as a frontier. From the 1880s through the 1920s, both urban and rural Sweetwater County answered to demographic, economic, and cultural definitions of frontier. That is, Sweetwater County embodied characteristics typical of regions labeled frontier, both by contemporaries and subsequently by historians.

Between 1890 and 1914 the United States Census Bureau designated a county "frontier" if the population density fell between two and six people per square mile. After 1914 the Census Bureau fixed the criterion for "frontier" at a population density of no more than two people per square mile.[106] During the late nineteenth and early twentieth centuries, rural Sweetwater County fit the census profile of a frontier region. Ranches and homesteads, widely scattered, fit the definition of frontier as a place of sparse population. Furthermore, Turner's 1893 definition of frontier as the "outer wave of settlement" for Anglo-American civilization implied subsistence conditions in which settlers were isolated, and the work of survival, labor intensive.[107] These characteristics, too, certainly described ranching communities in Sweetwater County from the 1880s through the 1920s.

In addition, Sweetwater County cattle ranches approached mythic notions of frontier as the land of the cowboy. Indeed, throughout this era, popular fiction, radio, and a fledgling film industry were defining the American frontier in terms of adventuresome cowboy life on the high plains.[108] Such imagery was not lost upon those who ranched in southwest Wyoming. Emblematic notions of western life would filter into the perceptions, and even the work routines, of Sweetwater County ranchers.[109] In short, rural Sweetwater County answered to contemporary popular images of frontier, with its sparse population, subsistence family economies, and cattle herds. As such, rural Sweetwater County veered close to the symbolic West in the American mind—even as open-range herding gave way to fenced ranches; even as discrete homesteads gave way to corporate irrigation projects.

But contemporary images of frontier, such as lone homesteads or cowboys on horseback, bore little resemblance to Sweetwater coal towns, where dense population and industrial development characterized settlement. In the case of these industrial islands, how does one distinguish between frontier and established city? Ethnohistorian Jack Forbes proposed a universal definition of frontier as a place of contact between different cultures, "an instance of dynamic interaction between human beings [which] involves such processes as acculturation, assimilation, miscegenation, race prejudice, conquest, imperialism, and colonialism."[110] This definition suggests that a developing community remains a frontier as long as new ethnic or racial groups are arriving and interacting with the existing population. Indeed, Forbes underlined immigration as characteristic of frontier areas. That is, a frontier occurs where "a portion of a people (as opposed to the entire group) migrate to a new area, evolve into a 'minority group' and subsequently have relations with the native born population and perhaps with other minority groups."[111] Forbes could have been describing Sweetwater coal towns, where immigration shaped the character of settlement for four decades.

Another useful definition for industrial frontier settlement comes from Carlos Schwantes's essay on the "wageworker's frontier" in the American West. Schwantes observed that the rapid expansion of wage work in the United States and Canada was contemporaneous with intensive exploitation and settlement of the western third of the continent. Both occurred during the seventy-year interval bracketed by the California Gold Rush and World War I. According to Schwantes, the wageworker's frontier occurred wherever the extractive industries, such as mining or logging, drew a large pool of unskilled or semiskilled laborers, dependent upon others for wages. Mining, logging, and crop harvests provided seasonal work, and so much of the labor force was transient, ready to move on when the job ended. "As late as the eve of World War I," wrote Schwantes, "it was common to find . . . miners living in Montana one month and Nevada or Arizona the next."[112] Because they were transients, many of these laborers did not marry, settle in town, and raise families. Hence, the population on a wageworker's frontier can be identified by a large proportion of single men. The sex ratio on the wageworker's frontier usually hovered around 60 percent men, 40 percent women.[113] Schwantes, too, could be describing Sweetwater coal towns. Work in the mines was seasonal, "on" in the cold months, "off" in the summer.[114] And for three decades at the turn of the century, men outnumbered women. In 1880, for example, Sweetwater County was 62.5 percent male, 37.5 percent female. In 1900 the sex ratio hovered at 60.7 percent male, 39.3 percent female; and in 1910, 67.7 percent male, 32.3 percent female.[115]

Like Forbes, Schwantes underscored the significance of ethnic diversity, noting that the wageworker's frontier was also identifiable by a higher percentage of foreign-born residents than other regions in the United States—including the coastal Northeast, which experienced immigration booms during the same period. Again, Schwantes could be describing Sweetwater coal towns, where, after 1900, foreign-born outnumbered native-born inhabitants.

Schwantes also noted that the appearance of a large pool of wage labor traditionally has been associated with the passing of the frontier and the beginning of urbanization. However, when that wage-labor pool was western, migratory, ethnically diverse, and predominantly male, it indicated an extractive industries frontier. Schwantes observed that settlements on the wageworker's frontier resembled factory towns in the East, "except they were frontier-urban and, more important, located in the West. This meant that residents of these industrial islands lived in close proximity both in time and place to attitudes and ways of life rooted in the classic American West of symbol and myth."[116] Once again, Schwantes could be describing Sweetwater County, where some miners homesteaded during the slack season, a "western" option unavailable to workers in eastern cities.[117]

But if Schwantes identified a recognizable economic and social configuration that he called the wageworker's frontier, he described only its masculine half. Sweetwater coal towns emerge plainly as extractive industry frontiers, characterized by seasonal wage labor, a skewed sex ratio, and a mobile, heterogeneous population. But they emerge incomplete without the female population. Investigation of mining town women will bring into focus the blurred background of Schwantes's wageworker's frontier, the gendered dynamics of Forbes's ethnic meeting ground. Though outnumbered in Sweetwater coal towns, women were by no means insignificant. Their lives revealed subtle patterns of informal acculturation and uninstitutionalized networking, which built community in the interstices of coal town society.

CHAPTER TWO

Family Networks: A Web of Support

Bertha Savo Husa Witka remembered crossing the ocean at age seven, with her parents, from Pori, Finland, to the United States in 1903. "At that time in Finland," she said, "the idea was . . . America . . . was the land of gold. Everybody had the idea that it was a very rich country."[1] Like Bertha Witka's family, migrants from Northern, Southern, and Eastern Europe came to Wyoming in search of jobs, income, and security. But often these goals proved elusive, or fickle at best. In Sweetwater County coal towns, accidents, disease, and unemployment dogged even the most optimistic of settlers. In 1923 Bertha married Eino Husa, and the couple settled in Rock Springs. Barely three years later, Eino Husa was dead, felled by a mining accident. Bertha was, at age twenty-nine, a widow.[2] Add to such loss the stresses of adjustment to a foreign culture, and immigration to Wyoming posed considerable risks.

Still, many survived to build a life in the coal towns of southwest Wyoming, and their stories are revealing. Central to these stories are the kin ties, which formed a skein of support through relocation, misfortune, and loss. Equally significant in these stories are the high rate of injury in mining towns, fluctuations in the mining industry, and the resulting impermanence of settlement. In the chaos and flux of coal town life, kin ties formed an infrastructure of support, less visible, perhaps, than mutual aid societies or fraternal lodges, but no less vital.

The importance of kin networks to immigrant survival is widely recognized, both by western and women's historians. Studies of both the industrial East and the frontier West have established the importance of kin ties in sustaining immigrant households through the vicissitudes of poverty, injury, and dislocation.[3] European immigrants in Sweetwater County were no different from, say, the Irish in Butte, the Italians in northern California, or the Slavs in Pennsylvania, in that they depended on kinship networks for crucial economic and social support.[4]

But Sweetwater County differed from other destinations in two respects.

First, the local economy and demographics were such that ethnic neighborhoods did not develop during the heyday of European immigration, which lasted from the turn of the century through the early 1920s. Without the security of residential ethnic enclaves, kin ties took on added importance, particularly for the first generation. Second, the lack of job opportunities for children and the value placed on their education, as well as the youthfulness of the immigrant population, shaped first-generation kin networks around adult sibling ties. By the second and third generations, kin networks expanded to include intergenerational reciprocity.

Men usually immigrated first, coming to Rock Springs, Superior, and other coal towns to find work. Some planned to work for a year or two, then return to the old country with their savings. Others planned to stay and send for their kin. But those who planned to return to Europe found it difficult to build savings on a miner's wages. Often they, too, decided to stay, and urged brothers and sisters, wives and children, to join them in the United States. The promise of jobs and the promise of reuniting fragmented families drew many a relative to follow their kin to Sweetwater County.

During the late nineteenth and early twentieth century, Sweetwater County drew immigrants from agricultural regions in Yugoslavia, Finland, Germany, and Italy.[5] While detailed investigation of rural, working-class family life in each of these countries is beyond the scope of this study, a few consistent impressions emerged from immigrant women's descriptions of Old World life. One was that rural peasant families expected every able member, even small children, to contribute labor and/or income to the household. Another was that older children routinely left home to ease economic pressure on the household. In short, reciprocal obligation between family members seems to have been a common rural tradition in late-nineteenth-century Europe.[6] So, too, was the practice of going far afield to support the family. Finn and Southern Slav immigrants to Sweetwater County had telling memories of these customs.

Anna Waananen was born in 1890 in rural Finland. Her father died when she was four years old, increasing the burden of support on her mother and siblings. "We had a little piece of land," Anna recalled,

> and mother tried to work that land with some vegetables, potatoes, . . . a couple of cows. She milked the cows and made her own butter, and we have food anyhow.
>
> . . . The biggest children have to go to work, make money. . . . The oldest ones leave.[7]

Even younger children who left home to attend school supported themselves, so as not to burden the family. At age eight, Anna began attending school in town, eleven miles distant. During this time, she lived away from home. "I started my own life," she said. "I worked for my room and board and went to school."[8] At age twelve, Anna finished school and left her home town permanently, in search of work. From ages twelve through nineteen, she worked as a servant for a wealthy Russian family living in Finland. Periodically she sent money home to her mother and younger siblings. Thus Anna Waananen learned the ethic of mutual support among family members during her youth and childhood in rural Finland.

Similarly, Slovenian immigrant Mary Jesersek grew up on a farm where all family members, including children, took responsibility for household support. When Mary was seven years old, her family fell upon hard times. "So I went from my home to work at this family, at another farm," she recalled. "I worked there for seven years . . . to help my family and myself."[9] In remembering her rural European upbringing, Mary Jesersek, like Anna Waananen, stressed the family tradition of reciprocal obligation. When the Waananen and Jesersek families struggled economically, sons and daughters left home as soon as possible to support themselves, and to send money back to kin left behind. Brothers, sisters, parents, and children thus shared responsibility for survival.

In the new country, the tradition of mutual obligation among family members proved invaluable. But it changed form. Family networks in the old country spanned several generations, from small children to parents and grandparents. In the new country, first-generation immigrant family networks revolved around adult sibling ties. Several factors in Sweetwater County changed the shape of European family networks. Unlike the old country, the mining economy of southwest Wyoming held few wage-earning opportunities for children. At the same time, the demands of assimilation increased the value of education for immigrant children. Children, then, lost significance as wage-earners in the family economy. In addition, coal mining was too arduous and dangerous an occupation to attract many men over the age of forty. Consequently, few elder European kin immigrated to Sweetwater County.

Coal towns held few opportunities for children as wage workers. As early as 1886 Rock Springs miners successfully lobbied the territorial legislature to prohibit children under age fourteen from working in the mines. By 1907 United Mine Workers had organized the coal industry in Rock Springs, Superior, and Reliance; and the UMWA maintained the ban on child labor.[10] The mining industry, then, would not hire children. Neither were there factories that would employ children on assembly lines or for piece work. Between 1880 and 1910, under "Occupation," Sweetwater County census manuscripts listed most children under age fourteen—including those in working-class, immigrant families—as "at home" or "at school." A few children, ages twelve to fifteen, worked as domestic servants.[11] But without an aristocracy or even a sizable middle class, there was little demand for servants after 1900. Instead of earning wages, working-class children in Sweetwater County coal towns went to school. Indeed, the availability of public education and the need to learn American language and customs encouraged immigrant families to send their children to school rather than out to work.[12] Statewide census figures for Wyoming in 1910 showed fewer than 1 percent of children ages ten to fifteen gainfully employed.[13] In the new country of southwest Wyoming coal towns, most European children became dependents rather than providers.

Elder kin also figured less significantly in immigrant family networks, for the simple reason that few elder kin immigrated. Most immigrants to Sweetwater County were under thirty years old. Mary Jesersek arrived in Rock Springs at age seventeen. Anna Waananen came to the United States at age nineteen.[14] Between 1880 and 1910, the average age of men and women in Sweetwater County was 23.2 years.[15] Census manuscript pages detailing settlement in Rock Springs and other mining towns in 1900 and 1910 showed scores of single immigrant men in their late teens and twenties, and single immigrant women likewise in their youth. Numerous, too, were immigrant families composed of parents, children, and siblings-in-law, in which adults in the household ranged in age from eighteen to forty-nine, with most in their twenties and thirties.[16] This is not surprising, for coal mining underground was young men's work.[17] Perhaps, too, older European family members had too many responsibilities and too few resources to risk pulling up stakes. Whatever their reasons, Europeans in their fifties, sixties, and older rarely migrated to Sweetwater County. Between 1880 and 1910 only 7.4 percent of foreign-born adults were over fifty years old.[18]

With few elder family members immigrating, and few wage-earning opportunities for children, extended-family networks in Sweetwater County revolved around adult sibling ties. Among first-generation immigrants, adult sibling ties buoyed newcomers through relocation and assimilation. Adult brothers and sisters linked each other to jobs, housing, and emotional support.

Anna Rizzi Magnagna was one of a trail of siblings who crossed the ocean from Europe to Rock Springs. Born sometime between 1875 and 1885 in the Italian Tyrol, Anna Rizzi grew up with five brothers and sisters. Her brother Eugene was the first to leave for America, sometime after 1895. In 1898, Eugene wrote the family from Rock Springs, Wyoming. Would Anna come and keep house for him? Perhaps he had tired of boarding-house life. For her part, Anna was unmarried, and, her parents judged, old enough to run a household for her brother. Anna agreed to go. On May 19, 1898, she arrived in Rock Springs and began keeping house for Eugene. She met his friends, including a Louis Magnagna, whom she married in 1899. Anna and Louis Magnagna remained in Rock Springs, where Louis held a partnership in Magnagna Brothers Sheep Company. Over the next ten years, Anna and her brother Eugene persuaded three more siblings to join them in southwest Wyoming. Sisters Dorothy and Marguerite immigrated to Rock Springs, married local men, and stayed. Brother John Rizzi also immigrated to Rock Springs, then settled in Kemmerer, Wyoming.[19]

Like the Rizzi brothers and sisters, adult siblings formed an informal support system, sustaining each other through the upheaval of moving to a foreign country. By asking sisters to keep house, unmarried brothers got free domestic service and re-created at least a part of the family life they left behind. Unmarried sisters, in turn, could begin life in the new country with economic support and filial companionship. Moreover, without benefit of parents or chaperones, unmarried women could, by living with a brother, enjoy a legitimate place in the community. Rarely did young, single, immigrant women set up housekeeping alone without being suspected of prostitution.[20] In short, adult immigrant siblings were like base camps for their newcomer brothers and sisters.

Equally common were adult siblings who immigrated together. Frank Metelko, a young, married Austrian, began hearing stories about Rock Springs from friends and acquaintances during the early 1900s. Frank's unmarried sister, Ursala, also paid close attention to these stories. As Frank told his daughter-in-law, Margaret, many years later: "It wasn't that people from there [Austria] just decided, 'We're coming to Rock Springs.' Either some of their relatives or some of their friends came to Rock Springs and then they would hear how well it was, [that] things were working out."[21] Some time between 1900 and 1910, Frank Metelko, his wife, and his sister Ursala decided to find out for themselves what kind of future Rock Springs held. At this time, Mrs. Metelko had recently given birth to her third baby. The other two children, Louie and Dorothy, were still young. Frank was reluctant to leave his wife, new baby, and the other two youngsters behind. Nor did Mrs. Metelko relish the idea of traveling alone with three small children at some unknown later date. So they chose to immigrate together. Ursala shared their ambition, and went with them. Crossing the ocean took three weeks, "and there were no facilities for washing or whatever on the boat. . . . Mrs. Metelko took care of the littlest baby, Mr. Metelko took care of Louie, and Ursala took care of Dorothy. So they had three people to take care of three children, . . . and that's the way they came across."[22] Ursala Metelko lived with her brother and sister-in-law in Rock Springs until her marriage to a Mr. Heppener. The Heppeners settled in Rock Springs, in the same neighborhood as the Metelkos, and the two families maintained social ties.[23]

Adult sibling relationships thus paved the way for young, single, European women to immigrate to Sweetwater County. Single women could travel in safety with in-laws and kin. Upon arrival, they could live and work in the households of their siblings until ready to marry and start their own household. Sweetwater County census figures confirm that a significant number of single, immigrant women chose this route to America. During the thirty-year period from 1880 to 1910, 12 percent of unmarried, foreign-born women lived in the households of their relatives.[24] As immigration increased during the early twentieth century, so too did the proportion of unmarried, foreign-born women living with relatives. By 1910, 33 percent of single, immigrant women lived in a relative's household.[25] Buoyed by adult sibling networks, single immigrant women gained a foothold in the new country.

Kin ties were one way that European immigrants built a community of support in a chaotic environment. Mining towns in Sweetwater County were, on the surface, melting pots, for ethnic neighborhoods never developed. In a landmark study of immigrants in the United States from 1830 to 1930, John Bodnar argued against the concept of insulated ethnic ghettoes as a given in urban life. Rejecting both cultural and structural determinism, Bodnar presented immigrants as active agents in history, individuals who mediated between ethnic tradition, economic reality, and political opportunity in order to meet "the central requirement in their lives: to secure the welfare and well-being of their familial or household base."[26] In some cases this included settlement in residential ethnic enclaves, but the formation of white, ethnic "urban villages" was by no means a foregone conclusion. Certainly, in Sweetwater coal towns, conditions discouraged residential ethnic cohesion.

Old photographs of Rock Springs neighborhoods show rows of narrow, clapboard homes abutting unpaved streets.[27] Had you walked these streets in 1910, you might have heard Italian spoken in one house, Austrian-German in the next, Slovenian in the next, and Finnish at the corner.[28] Two out of every three residents you met would have been first-generation immigrants from Europe. One of every three would have been a woman.[29] Finally, if you asked one of the men how long he planned to stay in town, he might have gestured toward the mines and replied, "As long as there is work."

Indeed, the possibilities for settling permanently in town were slim. Transience was the common denominator in this diverse population. Rock Springs, Reliance, Superior, Megeath, Winton, and Dines were single-industry towns, where coal mining dominated the economy. Every summer the coal market flagged, and hundreds of miners were laid off or found their hours cut back. In addition, the Union Pacific laid off miners each time a coal seam ran out.[30] Some left Wyoming for timber harvests in Oregon and Washington. Others looked for work in Nevada, Arizona, Utah, and Colorado. Even during the "on" season, mining accidents and injuries might send miners and their families packing.[31] In short, it was common for miners to move often, whether fleeing hazards or following shifts in the job market for semiskilled and unskilled labor.[32] The resulting transience of the population worked against development of ethnic neighborhoods.

Coal towns in Sweetwater County discouraged formation of ethnic enclaves in one other significant way as well. Rock Springs, Reliance, Superior, South Superior, Winton, Megeath, and Dines all were company towns, owned by the Union Pacific. The Union Pacific built and rented four-room houses to workers with families, as well as operating large bunkhouses for single men. Indeed, the Union Pacific so thoroughly controlled the housing market that "people moving into Sweetwater County mining towns after the turn of the century had little choice but to live in company housing."[33] By 1905, for example, only 4 percent of Sweetwater County residents owned their own homes. By 1915, only 8 percent did.[34] Thus, when newcomers arrived from Europe, they settled wherever a vacancy was available in company housing, regardless of what nationality lived next door. Saloon owners worked in cooperation with women who rented rooms, sending newcomers to board with families of the same nationality whenever possible. But their efforts inevitably were limited by the availability of housing.[35] And so Sweetwater coal towns became home to a mixed immigrant population without ethnic neighborhoods.

Pronounced ethnic diversity within neighborhoods and the transience of these neighborhoods made for an unpredictable social milieu. As immigration historian John Bodnar observed, when working-class ethnic neighborhoods did form in industrial cities, they could be "secure and friendly places," where neighbors visited on the street or gathered at each other's flats for communal work and socializing.[36] But in Sweetwater coal towns, where no "urban villages" developed, no such security existed. The ethnic diversity of these neighborhoods intensified the value of kinship ties. Extended kin could provide support where ethnic community did not exist residentially.

Memories of adult sibling networks were especially poignant in coal towns, where industrial accidents tore at the fabric of family life. Oral histories from early-twentieth-century Sweetwater County hold countless stories of relatives stepping in when kin were felled by personal tragedy. Sibling networks acted as safety nets in a sometimes hostile environment. Helen Korich Krmpotich's account of her parents' experience demonstrates how siblings activated kinship ties to cope with disaster. In 1906 the Korichs, a young Serbian couple, immigrated to Chicago with Helen, then a baby, and her five-year-old sister. Ten years later they wound up in the coal town of Superior, Wyoming. Getting there was a story of calamity, economic insecurity, and false starts.

In Chicago in 1906, Mr. Korich worked in the steel mills; Mrs. Korich ran the household. But the steel mills were dangerous, and before long, injury sidelined Mr. Korich. As Helen described it, her father "got burned, all his scalp, in Chicago in the mills. He didn't like that work after that because he was six months in the hospital. So then he heard—my Aunt Pearl lived in Pueblo, Colorado—that she wanted us to move there. . . . And so that's what we did."[37] As soon as Mr. Korich was able, the family moved to Colorado, where Pearl helped them to resettle. In Colorado they moved between mining towns, wherever there was work.[38]

But the mines in Colorado were no safer than the steel mills in Chicago. By 1912 the Korichs had settled in Hastings, Colorado, where gas collected like a time bomb in the shafts. Mr. Korich escaped the 1912 Hastings explosion, which killed 350 miners, but it convinced him to move on. That year he left the family to investigate mining jobs in Superior, Wyoming. Conditions seemed relatively safer there, and eventually he sent for his wife and daughters.[39] From Chicago to Pueblo to Hastings to Superior: in search of work that would not kill or maim, the Korichs had moved four times in six years. Mr. Korich's sister, Pearl, had been the crucial link in the first leg of that journey, from steel work in Chicago to mining in Colorado. Like siblings who drew their kin across the ocean, Pearl had served as base camp, offering her brother an alternative to the dreaded mills, a route toward recovery from disaster.

Adult siblings also stepped in to raise the children of kin struck by catastrophe. World War I found the Korich family living in Megeath, a war boomtown prospering on coal. But the great flu epidemic of 1918–19 killed 750 people in Wyoming, among them Mrs. Korich. At first, Helen, age twelve, quit school to run the household and tend her four brothers and sisters. Then Mr. Korich stayed home with the children while Helen worked at a boarding house, waiting on tables, washing dishes, peeling potatoes, "and whatever there was to help the cook."[40] But this became a tenuous arrangement, as Mr. Korich's health deteriorated. In 1920, he died of cancer. Helen, age fourteen, could not both watch the younger children and hold her job: "I had to stay home because my brother was only four years old and we didn't have babysitters like they have today. . . . So my uncle came from Toronto and took over the five of us and he raised us."[41] Mr. Korich's brother moved to Rock Springs and took over care of his orphaned nieces and nephews. Helen lived with her uncle and siblings until 1924, when she married.[42] Once again, another branch of the Korichs' adult sibling network stepped in when family survival was threatened. In an environment characterized by occupational hazard, economic instability, and frequent mobility, kinship networks like the Korich's supported families through transition and misfortune.

Sibling networks were common to the first generation of native-born emigrants to coal towns as well. Jean Hodge's family was typical. Born in Boone, Iowa, in 1876, Jean moved with her parents to Rock Springs in 1886. Mrs. Hodge had a sister there, Alice Paterson Kierle, who helped them resettle. Mr. Hodge found work in the coal mines. The following year, when Jean was eleven, Mr. Hodge was injured in a mine explosion.

> It was only after the miners were rescued that they [Mrs. Hodge and the children] learned the full particulars. After the first explosion, the buried miners were climbing up trying to work their way through to the top, when they saw a second explosion coming. Every miner knew that the thing to do in an explosion was to get down low, for the gas always floated to the top. They all sprang back except Dave Thomas, who lost his head and kept on climbing. Frank Hodge sprang up to rescue him, and both were caught in the gas—Hodge only down to his chest; the gas entered his lungs and injured them to such an extent that he was never able to do much work after that.[43]

In 1888, barely a year after Mr. Hodge's accident, Mrs. Hodge died. Jean, at age twelve, was the oldest of four children. Jean's father, disabled since the accident, could not provide for them. At this point, Mrs. Hodge's sister, Alice Kierle, stepped in. Alice brought the children to her household and raised them as her own. From 1888 to 1897 Jean lived with her aunt and worked in the Kierle family business, the Commercial Hotel in Rock Springs. By all accounts, Alice Kierle was generous to her sister's children. As Jean Hodge told a WPA interviewer in 1935, the Kierles had raised her and her sisters and brother with "the love and care that the best of parents bestow upon their children." Jean remembered "happy times" with her aunt.[44] In 1897, at age twenty-one, Jean Hodge married William Thompson and left her aunt's care.

Emigrants from the Midwest, the Hodge family had turned to Mrs. Hodge's sister for help relocating and for economic and emotional support in the wake of injury and death. Again, adult sibling ties formed the heart of first-generation coal town family networks. In an environment characterized by dangerous industrial work, adult brothers and sisters could sometimes mitigate the risks and losses in each other's lives.

In rural areas, however, first-generation settlers emigrated in complex, extended-family networks. Homesteaders often emigrated in multi-household groups of several generations. Multigenerational, multi-household groups could be advantageous for several reasons. First, in the relative isolation of rural homesteads, extended kin supplied extra hands for labor-intensive tasks. Second, several households could share the costs of travel, tools, and equipment. And finally, extended kin could combine land claims in order to accumulate sufficient range for livestock.

Extended-family migration was a common pattern among native-born agricultural settlers in the West. In a review essay on western women's history, Elizabeth Jameson used this point to debunk the "reluctant pioneer" stereotype. Though some Anglo women certainly grieved the family they left behind, "for many women, such concerns did not apply, because they brought their families with them."[45] Citing two studies of overland emigration, which encompass the mid– and late nineteenth century, Jameson observed that nearly half of all emigrant families traveled in extended-family groups.[46]

The demographic record in Sweetwater County suggests that this pattern continued with twentieth-century migration to rural western frontiers. Most emigrants to rural Sweetwater County were native born, coming from the Midwest or the eastern seaboard. Between 1880 and 1910, 67.2 percent of rural women were native born.[47] Notably, the average age among rural adults hovered at 32.7 years, significantly older than the countywide average age of 23.2.[48] The figures suggest, then, that elder members of native-born family groups were emigrating to rural Sweetwater County along with their youthful kin. Perhaps they did so, while their foreign-born peers did not, because their work would still be needed on the family farm; one's capacity to handle the physical stresses of mining was not at issue. Or perhaps relocation within one's own country was less daunting than relocation to a new country. Whatever the reasons, native-born emigrants to rural Sweetwater County arrived in multigenerational family groups of middle-aged and elder parents as well as young adults and their children.

The Wright family of Eden Valley illustrate this pattern. Ruth Ellen Day Wright and her husband, John Wright, farmed a spread in Princeton, Kansas, during the early 1900s. A vigorous couple in their mid-fifties, the Wrights had four children living at home, ranging in age from ten to twenty-one.[49] Their oldest son, Frank, and his wife, Carrie, had recently set up housekeeping in Indiana. As the youngest boy, Ora, remembered: "Father was desirous of making a change. He wanted to settle where his four sons could grow and develop with a new country. Having read the glowing advertisements and colorful brochures depicting the [irrigation] projects in Idaho and Wyoming, he and his friend Mr. Surtes decided to look things over."[50] In November 1907 John Wright and his friend Surtes boarded a train for Twin Falls, Idaho. During a stop in Rock Springs, they met a fast-talking land developer, ironically named Mr. Lemon. Lemon was promoting Eden Valley, a corporate irrigation project north of Rock Springs, with homestead sites and water rights for sale.[51]

Lemon showed Wright and Surtes a winter photograph of one of the project's large storage reservoirs, with the caption "Reservoir No. 2; Capacity Over 100,000 Acre Feet." It was actually a flat, snow-covered field. Wright and Surtes were leery, but the developer persuaded them to stay the night in Rock Springs and see the project the following day. The next day, Lemon avoided the dubious "Reservoir No. 2" and instead showed Wright an actual reservoir and canal under construction, fed by the Big Sandy River. John Wright was impressed. He made a down payment to the Eden Land and Irrigation Company and returned to Kansas to tell his family.[52]

Over the next year and a half, two households of Wrights prepared to move to Eden Valley. John, Ruth Ellen, and their children would build on one claim; their married son Frank and his wife Carrie would take an adjacent claim. Together, the two households rented an "emigrant car," an entire boxcar to transport their furniture, livestock, and food supplies.[53] In the spring of 1909 the two households arrived by train in Rock Springs and traveled by mule team forty miles to Eden Valley.

By 1910 both households were well established. Ruth Ellen and John had raised successful oat and potato crops the first year. Their adult sons, Walter, age twenty-four, and William, age twenty, worked the claim with them. Their twenty-two-year-old daughter, Lizzie Mae, boarded out as a schoolteacher during the week, returning to the ranch on weekends. On the adjacent claim, their married son Frank and his wife Carrie established residency. Carrie earned income as a store clerk in the town of Eden; Frank experimented with different methods of irrigation. All-day tasks, such as butchering and dressing hogs, brought the two households together.[54]

Emigrating in a multigenerational, extended-family group, the Wright parents and adult children shared travel expenses, helped each other with ranch work, and together claimed a sizable plot of land. Not only was this a practical way to relocate, it also reflected the emotional importance that the Wrights placed on family ties. Ora Wright wrote that once his parents (from Kansas) and his brother and sister-in-law (from Indiana) had relocated together to Eden Valley, "a great feeling of contentment was there; . . . the family could all be together again."[55] For the Wrights, extended-family networks were multigenerational sources of support.

By the second generation, urban as well as rural family networks became more complex.[56] First-generation urban families matured and branched, as children born to immigrants and emigrants grew up and established their own households. When second-generation offspring settled in the same town as their parents, multigenerational family networks grew.

Caroline Spinner and Charles Eggs began a family business network that eventually spanned three generations in Green River, Wyoming. Caroline Spinner, born in 1848 in Baden, Germany, traveled to the United States with her brother Carl in 1871. Age twenty-three, Caroline settled in St. Louis, Missouri, "where her family had many friends."[57] Her brother Carl moved farther west to Green River, Wyoming, where another brother, George, had established a butcher shop.

Back in St. Louis, Caroline met an ambitious young shoe merchant from Germany, Charles Eggs. In 1874 Caroline and Charles married. Within a year, they had their first child, Eleanor. By 1881 the Eggses had two more daughters, but Caroline had paid with her health. So, in 1882, she traveled to Green River to rest and recuperate at her brother's home.[58]

Caroline returned from Green River with stories of her brothers' business successes: Carl had set up a brewery; George's butcher shop prospered. At Caroline's suggestion, the Eggses moved to Green River in 1886. Brothers Carl and George helped them relocate. In Green River, the Eggses bought the Big Horn Hotel, which they managed together. As hotel proprietors, Charles and Caroline Eggs "became well and favorably known."[59]

By 1890 Charles Eggs felt ready to branch out and he opened the first shoe store in Green River. Caroline continued to manage the hotel. Daughter Eleanor, now age fifteen, helped her mother at the hotel. In 1891, at age sixteen, Eleanor Eggs started her own business, a ladies' millinery and ready-to-wear store in Green River. Backed by her parents' capital, Eleanor developed a successful retail outlet.[60]

A decade passed, with Charles handling the shoe business, Caroline running the hotel, and daughter Eleanor building the millinery and clothing trade. In 1901 Eleanor, now age twenty-six, met Emil Gaensslen, a German-American emigrant from Chicago. Emil had come to Green River to work with his brother at the Sweetwater Brewing Company as office manager, accountant, and stockholder. In 1907 Eleanor Eggs and Emil Gaensslen married and settled in Green

River. Over the next nine years, they had five children. Eleanor continued to manage her retail business.[61] In 1917 Charles and Caroline Eggs sold the Big Horn Hotel and retired to a new home on the north side of town. In 1921 Charles Eggs died. About this time, Eleanor and Emil Gaensslen expanded their interests to include real estate. During the 1920s, Eleanor and Emil built "at least a score of modern bungalows."[62]

Family business ties loosened among the third generation. Despite setbacks in the brewing enterprise, the third generation nonetheless reaped the benefits of their forbears' carefully built prosperity. Elinore Gaensslen Schofield, daughter of Eleanor Eggs Gaensslen, explained that she and her two brothers came of age during Prohibition, which forced the Sweetwater Brewing Company out of business. Elinore added that while the family shoe and millinery shops thrived during the 1920s, neither she nor her siblings "wanted to be storekeepers." Instead, Elinore Schofield's generation went to college. "We were encouraged to get a good education," she recalled, "and then fend for ourselves."[63] Similarly, third generation cousin Louise Spinner Graf enjoyed parental support, financial and emotional, for a college education. But unlike her independent cousins, Louise Spinner Graf drew upon family business contacts after finishing her degree. She returned to Green River and took a job at the State Bank of Green River, where her uncle, Hugo Gaensslen, sat on the Board of Directors.[64] Thus the third generation found such networks flexible. They functioned as sources of financial support, but required no fixed loyalty to family enterprise.

In the Spinner-Eggs-Gaensslen clan, then, family ties were business ties. Networks between siblings, parents, and children could be traced through the progress of the Big Horn Hotel, Eggs's shoe store, Eggs's (later Gaensslen's) Millinery, Spinner's Butcher Shop, Sweetwater Brewing Company, Gaensslen real estate office, and the State Bank of Green River. Spinner-Eggs-Gaensslen business ties demonstrated the expansion of family networks over the second generation, and the flexibility of these networks for the third generation. First-generation networks had formed around adult sibling ties: Caroline's brothers, Carl and George Spinner, had provided the Eggs with a link from St. Louis to Green River. Second-generation networks expanded to include multigenerational as well as sibling ties: Emil Gaensslen relied on his brother for his first job in Green River; Eleanor Eggs relied on her parents for support starting a retail business. Finally, the third generation capitalized on family prosperity, attending college yet still drawing upon kin networks, as Louise Spinner Graf did, for job opportunities.

Extended-family networks thus functioned like a web of support that buoyed settlers in Sweetwater County. Relatives acted as base camps on the trail of relocation and as safety nets in a hazardous and chaotic environment. Rural European tradition had rooted parents, children, and grandchildren in networks of mutual obligation. In Sweetwater County, the ethic of family reciprocity continued, but took new form. With few opportunities for child wage work and few older Europeans immigrating, extended-family networks among first-generation urban settlers formed around adult sibling ties. Adult sibling networks paved the way for young, single European women to immigrate. They could travel in relative safety with kin. Upon arrival, adult brothers or sisters provided housing, social contacts, and economic support. Unmarried women functioned symbiotically with their adult siblings, contributing domestic service, childcare, or income to their households.

Of course, European immigrants to Wyoming coal towns were not unique in their dependence on kinship support. Neither were single-industry towns, the hazards of mining, unstable employment, or a transient workforce unique to Sweetwater County. What distinguished these coal towns from like environments elsewhere in the country was the combination of pronounced ethnic diversity and the lack of ethnic neighborhoods. For ethnic groups in Union Pacific coal towns the lack of residential cohesion intensified the challenges of survival and thus compounded the value of kinship ties.

In rural Sweetwater County, first-generation family networks were multigenerational. Often several households of kin, including older family members, filed homestead claims together. Like the adult sibling networks of urban immigrants, rural family networks also pooled economic resources, contributed labor to each other's households, lived in proximity, and supported each other emotionally. By the second generation, multigenerational ties characterized urban as well as rural family networks. Among middle-class settlers like the Spinner-Eggs-Gaensslen clan, family ties became business ties, the ethic of mutual obligation expressed through shared enterprise, capital investment, and partial hiring practices.

Extended-family support did not stop at relocation, rescue from misfortune, and economic help. Family networks figured in a variety of situations, including courtship. Indeed, courtship practices in urban Sweetwater County revealed single immigrant women's roles in the formation of kin ties that built ethnic community. In rural Sweetwater County, courtship patterns suggested single women's centrality in the expression of community values. And in both settings, single women's responsibility to community shaped courtship in distinctive ways.

CHAPTER THREE

"I Got a Girl Here, Would You Like to Meet Her?": Courtship, Ethnicity, and Community

If one's kin formed the most immediate community of support, one's everyday associates—coworkers, housemates, employers—formed a world of potential support. There were no guarantees; such support would have to be built. Courtship, like migration, underscored informal but crucial processes of community-building. Through marriage, new relations broadened the circle of kinship support. And through the process of choosing a marriage partner that was courtship, single women also defined their relationship to the larger community of neighbors and associates, acquaintances and friends. But the web of community could also become a snare, a source of judgment and even exclusion. Indeed, in Sweetwater County, single women's responsibility to community constrained them from exploring the social and sexual freedoms of New Womanhood. Moreover, courtship, like settlement, revealed processes of community-building in regionally specific patterns.

Studies of courtship in the West have addressed neither the immigrant experience nor the early twentieth century.[1] With its European population and later period of settlement, Sweetwater County opens new ground to investigations of courtship in the American West. In studies of eastern and midwestern patterns of courtship from the turn of the century through the 1920s, historians have traced the emergence of modern behaviors like unchaperoned dating and sexual expressiveness.[2] As Victorian ideology faded and a separate youth culture took shape, courting youth increasingly rejected family authority in favor of a peer-controlled system of social and sexual mores.[3] In eastern cities in particular, commercialized amusements steadily drew youth beyond the ken of family and

---

This chapter originally appeared in Susan Armitage and Elizabeth Jameson, eds., *Writing the Range* (Norman: University of Oklahoma Press, 1997). Copyright 1997 by the University of Oklahoma Press.

neighborhood supervision.⁴ With these discoveries, historians have placed modern courtship hand-in-hand with New Womanhood; the modern single woman experimented with new social and sexual freedoms.

If local newspapers are to be believed, modern courtship came to Sweetwater County as early as 1907. A series of articles in the *Green River Star* in 1907 and 1908 introduced the idea of courtship as a time of experimentation for single women. Notably, these were outside voices, syndicated columnists from eastern urban newspapers, not local writers. Still, the editors of the *Star* ran these articles, and thus acquainted readers with the "New Woman," a single, independent female who accumulated a certain amount of cosmopolitan experience before settling down.

The virtues of worldliness and independence for single women first appeared in an article titled "Short Skirts Are All Right" in February 1907. The author began by championing the shorter skirt as a practical garment, worn by the most desirable women. The most desirable women, in turn, were those hardy souls who led the most independent lives: "Today, when he marries, man seeks a companion for the hard tramp over the hills and dales of life. . . . Let him turn his attention . . . to the girl who has probably paid for her gown with her own hard-earned money, the girl with the short skirt."⁵ This "companion" for the "tramp over the hills and dales of life" was, with her short skirt and earning power, a New Woman. Gone was the assumption of economic dependence on parents or beaux.⁶ The visual symbol of such independence was that of female athleticism, tramping over hills and dales in unencumbered clothing.⁷ "Short Skirts" thus implied that a period of self-reliance would better prepare the single woman for modern marriage.

Reinforcing the theme of female independence, other articles touted the value of delayed marriage and unchaperoned courtship. In April 1907 the *Star* ran a story headlined "Few Early Marriages Now" and subtitled "Men and Women Await Arrival of Years of Discretion."⁸ The author approved the rising age at marriage and predicted that it was "quite within the range of possibility that 41 will be regarded in the future as the equivalent of the present 21."⁹ The author next pointed to the rising age at marriage as evidence of women's intention to learn from experience how to distinguish trustworthy from unworthy men: "Women . . . fear that they may be deceived and . . . enter into a partnership with one who will turn out to be undesirable. . . . [They want] experience enough to enable them to judge character with fair accuracy."¹⁰ "Judging character with fair accuracy" was a virtue that came with worldly experience, according to the *Green River Star*.

In 1908 the *Star* ran an apocryphal story called "The Duping of Polly." In this tale, Polly, a single woman traveling alone, is wooed by the charismatic captain of the ship she has boarded. Halfway through the voyage, Polly makes the startling discovery that the ardent "Captain Brundage" is a married man. First she is mortified. Then she decides to exact revenge for his duplicity. But more importantly, she learns to be a better judge of character. Cleverly, she forces Brundage to confess, collects $250 from him as hush money, and uses it as dowry for her subsequent marriage to an honest man.[11] Polly emerges as an intelligent, self-reliant heroine. She learns from experience the difference between honorable and unscrupulous men. Moreover, in this story, worldly experience does not ruin the single woman; it matures her. A tainted courtship is not a disaster; it simply teaches a woman better judgment.

Indeed, articles about courtship in the *Star* were relatively sanguine about the trend toward unsupervised courtship. In December 1907 the *Star* ran a column, "American Lovemaking Has Stirred Up Things in Cuba," which linked Victorian customs of chaperonage with backwardness, and modern courtship behavior with the progress of civilization. Using hyperbole, the author opened with a series of rhetorical questions: "Think of taking your fiancée to the opera without a chaperone! Can you imagine anything worse? . . . Can the human imagination comprehend anything so daring as an automobile ride without a chaperone?"[12] The author explained that Cuban society still maintained customs of chaperonage which, in the United States, had faded in the light of modernity. "These questions of propriety have been settled in America," asserted the author, "and the chaperone has lost her job."[13] The author related these changes to "the progressive schools built by American enterprise and capital," and concluded that "younger people . . . think they [modern American courtship customs] are an improvement over the customs of the past."[14] Thus, "American Lovemaking" implied that modern behaviors such as unchaperoned courtship were an expression of civilized progress.

Local newspapers thus introduced Sweetwater County readers to popular images of New Womanhood and modern courtship. Articles like "Short Skirts," "Few Early Marriages," "The Duping of Polly," and "American Lovemaking" encouraged single women toward economic independence and unsupervised courtship. In subsequent years, syndicated columns occasionally reiterated this theme, affirming a period of self-support or social experimentation for women before marriage.[15]

Still, such articles were few and far between. Most of the time, the *Green River Star* and *Rock Springs Rocket* addressed women through more traditional venues—articles about cooking, sewing, cleaning, childrearing, decorating, and entertaining. If articles promoting New Womanhood appeared infrequently, and only in syndicated columns from eastern newspapers, to what degree did such images reflect actual courtship behavior on the southwest Wyoming frontier? Did the working-class immigrant women who settled mining towns try living on their own before marriage, New Woman style, in order to develop worldly wisdom? Did they venture into unsupervised dating? Did single women in ranching communities follow the dictates of a separate peer culture? Did they experiment with freer sexual expression?

Oral histories and memoirs from women in Sweetwater County, 1900–1925, suggest that courtship on this mining and ranching frontier did not fit the modern model. Instead, the regional economy and demographics of southwest Wyoming shaped women's courtship behavior in distinctive ways. The ethnic diversity, mobility, and economic instability of mining towns encouraged close supervision of courting couples among first-generation immigrants. In contrast, the relative stability and homogeneity of ranching settlements preserved a Victorian sexual standard while paradoxically allowing young women and men considerable freedom.

In neither case did a modern peer culture hold sway. Rather, courtship expressed community standards, which, in Sweetwater County, still were set by the larger, multigenerational, adult community. That is, courtship was not simply about romance, choosing a husband, or degrees of supervision and sexual activity. It was also an expression of shared values that were seen as important to survival on the southwest Wyoming frontier. In mining towns, courtship reflected the high value placed on kin and ethnic ties in a chaotic environment where ethnic community did not exist residentially. In rural areas, courtship underscored the secure sense of community and shared Victorian mores, which took the place of chaperones as a social control on courting couples. In each case, courtship highlighted single women's role in building community or maintaining community standards.

At first glance, the demographic record resembles the pattern of modern courtship. Women were marrying later, presumably to explore a few years of independence first. In Sweetwater County, second-generation women married later than their mothers: in 1880, the average woman married for the first time at age twenty. By 1900, she waited until age 21.9; and by 1910, she did not marry until age 22.4.[16] This was not due to any rejection of marriage as an institution. County marriage rates remained high between 1880 and 1910: 94.4 percent of women married by the time they reached their early thirties.[17] And so, at first glance, the rising age at marriage suggests that Wyoming frontier women *did* adopt the behaviors of New Womanhood, seeking a period of independent experience before settling down.

But the resemblance was superficial. On closer examination, delayed marriage had a very different meaning for southwest Wyoming women. Mining towns offer a case in point. First, unlike the Pollys of newspaper fiction, few single women in mining towns lived on their own outside a family setting. Second, the most common reason for delayed marriages lay in the mining economy, not in women's pursuit of independent social experimentation. Single immigrant women often delayed marriage while their fiancés struggled for job security in a fluctuating labor market.

Dorothy Pivik's father came from Yugoslavia to Wyoming shortly after the turn of the century. He drifted between mining camps as they hired and fired, from Rock Springs to Kemmerer, to Reliance, and back to Rock Springs. At the time he left Yugoslavia, Mr. Pivik had been engaged to a young woman in his village. He had planned to send for her as soon as he found a steady job. But with seasonal layoffs and closures of depleted mines, economic security was difficult to grasp. Four years passed before he sent for his fiancée, and they finally married in Rock Springs.[18] Like Dorothy Pivik's mother, many foreign-born women postponed marriage while their fiancés struggled for secure footing in an unstable, migratory labor market. Delayed marriage thus reflected the economic contingencies faced by working-class couples in company towns.

If pursuit of cosmopolitan adventure had been the focus of delayed marriages, residency patterns would have shown single women living on their own. Indeed, popular images of the New Woman depicted her escape from family authority to her own apartment. A "latchkey gal," she came and went as she pleased.[19] In the western vernacular, such a woman would have been "baching."

In Sweetwater County, "baching"—living alone or with single peers—was widely accepted for single men, but not for single women. Slovenian immigrant Dorothy Pivik provided a description of "baching" in Rock Springs during the early 1900s: "They had, let's say, a two-room shack or so, and the bachelor would live in the shack in back of the house. . . . [They] would just have a heating stove and a small room for a bed . . . just a plain little hut like. So they were living in the shack and eating in the house."[20] "Baching" was a common form of boarding out, in which the lodger rented a shack adjacent to the home where he bought his meals. In another variation, lodgers bunked together in rooming houses run by the Union Pacific, without meals or housekeeping. These boarders bought meals at restaurants and took their laundry to washerwomen.[21] Between 1880 and 1910 three quarters of all single men in Sweetwater County roomed at a hotel or company dorm, or boarded with a family unrelated to them. Only a fraction lived with their parents or relatives.[22]

The reverse was true for single women. They neither rented a "shack" alone nor lived with single peers. In 1880 only one in one hundred households sampled consisted of single women sharing a dwelling. In 1900 the percentage was the same. In 1910 none of the households sampled consisted of single women sharing a dwelling.[23] In short, single women did not "bach" on the Sweetwater County frontier.

During the early 1900s, working-class women's wages would not support living alone. Between 1903 and 1908, for example, miner's wages hovered between $55 and $68 per month. During the same period, women's wages averaged about half that. A boarding house waitress, cook's helper, or maid earned anywhere from $10 to $15 per month; a department store sales clerk, about $20 per month.[24] Even single women with more earning power did not "bach." Teachers and white-collar workers, for example, lived with parents, relatives, or boarded with a family.[25] Income, then, was not the only factor behind the single woman's reluctance to "bach." Sharing a household with parents or extended kin, or boarding with a host family provided single women with important social supports.

Living in a family setting was the most common residential pattern for single women. Between 1880 and 1910 slightly more than half of all unmarried women lived with their parents. Those who lived away from parents chose alternative family settings, such as domestic service, living with relatives, or boarding with a family of the same nationality.[26] Among immigrant single women, for example, 64 percent shared another family's household as servant, relative, or boarder during this period. The remainder lived with their parents.[27] Among native-born single women, 69.4 percent lived with their parents, and 30.5 percent shared another family's household as servant, relative, or boarder.[28]

For those women without parents, the shape of alternative family settings changed over time. Live-in domestic service gradually gave way to boarding with a family of the same nationality, or boarding with relatives. In 1880, 27.7 percent of single women lived with a private family as domestic servants.[29] By 1900, immigration swelled the ranks of working-class neighborhoods, and the demand for help in boarding houses far outpaced the demand for domestic service in middle-class homes. The Union Pacific hired married couples or widowed women to run their boarding houses. These boarding house keepers, in turn, hired single women to help with housekeeping.[30] Increasingly, single, foreign-born women who arrived without kin lodged at such boarding houses, where they worked as cooks, waitresses, maids, or laundresses, under supervision of the family who ran the lodge.

Annie Kujala was typical. Twenty-one years old and single, Annie immigrated to Rock Springs from Finland in 1900. She settled at a Union Pacific boarding house run by a Finnish couple in their early fifties, Emil and Mary Makka. About twenty Finnish miners roomed at Makka's, and Mary Makka needed help with the cooking and cleaning. Annie waited on tables and did dishes in exchange for room, meals, and a small wage.[31] Annie Kujala had found a household that, in some ways, replicated the home she had left, for the Makkas were the same age and nationality as her own parents. Like Annie Kujala, by 1900, 24.3 percent of single immigrant women boarded out, often with families of the same nationality, with couples of a parental age.[32]

Living with relatives was the other popular alternative for single women without parents, particularly after the turn of the century when immigration boomed. We have seen how adult sibling networks situated unmarried women with adult brothers and sisters in the new country. By 1910, 18.2 percent of young unmarried women lived with relatives.[33] All told, between 1880 and 1910, 63.6 percent of all unmarried women lived with parents or relatives. The rest, whether private maid in 1880 or rooming-house helper in 1910, boarded with families as hired help. Clearly, the modern "latchkey gal" was only a literary idea in Sweetwater County.

Courtship highlighted the role of household, kin, and ethnic ties in single women's lives. Unmarried women were bound by a social webbing that both supported and frustrated them. Family—blood relatives—constituted the most immediate and powerful network. Single women without kin created alternative networks based on household and ethnic ties. Family, household, and ethnic ties, in turn, made courtship a community event.

Single men and women comprised over half the population in Sweetwater County. Between 1880 and 1910, 53.7 percent of county residents over age fifteen were unmarried men and women.[34] After 1910, the exodus of young Europeans to America continued, some escaping political and military conflict; others, overpopulation and a landless future.[35] Even more striking, by 1910, single men outnumbered single women by five to one.[36] The possibilities for cross-cultural romance were many.

Ethnic diversity certainly influenced courtship in mining towns, but not as a force for blending. Given the chaotic mix of nationalities in Union Pacific neighborhoods, immigrants struggled to form ethnic community ties despite their scattered residences. Ethnic lodges and mutual aid societies, for example, emerged in Sweetwater coal towns as much in response to the need for social networks as to cushion the expenses of death and disability. But equally significant were immigrants' *informal* efforts to build ethnic community in the midst of heterogeneous neighborhoods. Indeed, it was their informal efforts to strengthen ethnic ties that shaped courtship on the mining frontier.

The example of Southern Slavs is instructive, for Eastern Europeans comprised the fastest growing ethnic population in Sweetwater County during the early twentieth century. From 1900 to 1910 the proportion of Eastern Europeans in the county more than doubled, from 12.3 percent to 29.9 percent.[37] Between 1910 and 1920 Eastern European immigration to Wyoming tripled, from 825 in 1910 to 2,671 in 1920.[38] Moreover, between 1910 and 1930 Southern Slavs comprised the largest group of Eastern Europeans in Wyoming. During this period, 2,842 Southern Slavs migrated to Wyoming, as compared to 1,148 Poles, 1,040 Czechs, and 961 Hungarians.[39] The term "Southern Slav" refers to those ethnic groups once encompassed by Yugoslavia—Slovenes, Croatians, Dalmatians, and Serbs.[40] The example of Southern Slavs, then, represents a significant portion of the first-generation immigrant experience in early-twentieth-century Sweetwater coal towns.

The most visible example of Southern Slavs' efforts to create an ethnic social space was construction of the Slovenski Dom in Rock Springs in 1914. Funded jointly by Croatian and Slovenian fraternal lodges, the Slovenski Dom was a social hall built to serve Southern Slavs from Rock Springs, Superior, Reliance, and other mining towns. Slovenski Dom means "Slovenian Home," and the hall became a gathering place for men's and women's groups, family and ethnic celebrations.[41] Less visible, but equally significant, was John Mrak's saloon on K Street in Rock Springs. Mrak's saloon functioned as a social space for Southern Slavs in a way that local neighborhoods could not. Men and women stopped in to exchange news and gossip. Weddings and funerals were held upstairs. Women gathered there to set up feasts for holidays. Miners socialized downstairs. Mrak's saloon also served as a clearinghouse where Rock Springs Southern Slavs could find countrymen to help them negotiate jobs or housing.[42] In many ways, then, John Mrak's saloon functioned like an ethnic neighborhood, as a social space where Southern Slavs counted on hearing their language spoken, seeing familiar faces, and sharing cultural tradition with others of similar background.

Outside the parameters of Mrak's saloon or the Slovenski Dom, Southern Slavs nurtured informal social ties with others of their own ethnic group whenever possible.[43] Nowhere was this more evident than in matters of courtship. Indeed, Southern Slav women courted within a close-knit web of familial and ethnic social networks. Relatives, acquaintances, co-workers, and employers assumed responsibility as matchmakers. Single women without kin sometimes formed quasi-parental relationships with their boarding house keepers and sought advice from them on matters of the heart. Parents chaperoned dates and dances and approved or rejected potential husbands. The degree to which

Southern Slavs brought family and ethnic ties to bear on courtship suggests that despite the lack of residential cohesion—or perhaps in response to it—their impulse to create ethnic community was strong.

The best-known matchmaker among Southern Slavs in Rock Springs was John Mrak, proprietor of the K Street saloon. Not only did Mrak foster job and housing liaisons, he also helped single men and women find marriage partners. As Dorothy Pivik described it: "Let's say if a woman came here, he [Mrak] would find a man [for her] and they'd marry, or vice versa. . . . It's like he mated them. He always found a partner for one or the other."[44] John Mrak was not the only one alert to possible matches. Older Southern Slav men and women seized casual, through not subtle, opportunities to suggest matches to their young, single acquaintances, co-workers, or employees. Dorothy Pivik described her husband's first marriage in Rock Springs as a match initiated by an older acquaintance: "The way he [Mr. Pivik] met her [his first wife] is through my uncle. My uncle worked for the Rock Springs Commercial store and he delivered groceries in Quealy, and he told my husband—of course, at the time he was just a young boy—he said, 'I have a girl picked out for you, and she works for my wife,' she was her maid. . . . So, he [Dorothy's uncle] brought him [Dorothy's husband, as a young man] in on the horse and buggy, and he met her and he said they were married soon after."[45] Similarly, Mary Jesersek was introduced to her future husband by one of her employers, an older woman of the same ethnic group whom she helped with housework: "There was a friend of Suvicks . . . the lady had a baby and she needed somebody to work for her, so I went to work in her home; and my [future] husband was working in the butcher shop and he'd deliver meat, and this lady says, 'I got a girl here, would you like to meet her?'"[46] Mary and the butcher began their courtship that day and married within the year. John Mrak, Dorothy Pivik, and Mary Jesersek's stories suggest that matchmaking was an accepted practice among Southern Slav immigrants. These matches were informal; a matchmaker introduced a young man and woman, then left the outcome to them.

Indeed, single women were free to refuse proposals. Before meeting the butcher, Mary Jesersek had refused to marry a man with whom she had been matched. The story behind her decision is revealing, for it also demonstrates how single women without kin sometimes found support by boarding with a family of the same nationality.

Mary Jesersek grew up in a Slovenian village at the turn of the century. When she was seventeen, one of her neighbors immigrated to Wyoming. Evidently this neighbor suggested Mary as a potential wife to one of his Slovenian friends in Rock Springs, for Mary received a written proposal in the mail from the young hopeful. She agreed to marry the Rock Springs suitor, on the recommendation of her former neighbor. So the Slovenian miner booked and paid for her passage to America. But when Mary arrived in Rock Springs and met her fiancé, she found, to her dismay, that she did not like him: "The first day I was here I stayed with the family of that fella that I came for . . . and he was boarding down at Number Four [mine]. Then the next day, there was a dance, Labor Day? And we went to the dance. . . . I don't know, that fella just didn't appeal to me."[47] At the dance, another Slovenian, Mrs. Luzan, noticed Mary's unease and questioned her about her plans. "She [Mrs. Luzan] says to me, 'You like that fella? Do you want to marry him?'"[48] When Mary explained her reluctance, Mrs. Luzan helped her to find work, a way out of the ill-advised marriage. Rather than marrying her long-distance "match," Mary took a job as housekeeper at a small boarding house run by a Slovenian couple, the Suvicks. She felt adamant about repaying her erstwhile fiancé for the cost of her travel: "I don't remember him saying that he wanted money for the ticket, but I thought, I don't want to be obligated to nobody. . . . I work until I pay my ticket; it was $105."[49] Having discharged that obligation, Mary remained with the Suvicks, where she had both a job and a home. They encouraged Mary to take more time to choose a spouse. By the time she married the butcher, Mary had lived with the Suvicks for two years, and she remembered them fondly: "They were really nice people."[50] Her story suggests that Southern Slav women without kin sometimes found a supportive "home" boarding with families of the same nationality.

Mary Jesersek's story also illustrates the informality of matchmaking. Clearly, the only commitment Mary felt toward her hapless fiancé was monetary; she reimbursed him for travel. Other than paying that debt, the arrangement carried no obligation.

On the other hand, parents sometimes forbade marriage to a partner independently chosen. Single women who ignored well-meaning matchmakers also risked their parents' disapproval. Such was the case with Dorothy Pivik. Pivik grew up in Rock Springs during the second and third decades of the twentieth century. Independent of matchmakers, she fell in love with a young man whom she met in high school. But Dorothy's parents disapproved of the match because the young man in question was not a Southern Slav. "Our folks always felt that we should marry the same nationality," she said. "Now this boy that I met, he was English and we were very much in love, but it didn't work out. . . . My parents were against it. And I listened to them."[51] Dorothy complied with her parents' judgment and ended the relationship. Though she felt some regrets later, at the time, she recalled, "We did listen to our parents; we had to listen to them."[52] In Dorothy Pivik's case, the family charge to marry within their nationality foreclosed the option of choosing her own spouse. The obligation to build ethnic community through endogamous marriage prevented Dorothy Pivik from exercising the freedoms of New Womanhood, such as independent courtship and choice of spouse.

Religion figured in this equation, for religion was inseparable from ethnic identity among Slovenes, Croats, and Serbs. Croatian immigrant Ann LeVar Powell remembered her parents' directive to marry a man of the same faith. "The unspoken rule," she said, "was 'Do marry a Catholic.'"[53] Mary Lou Anselmi Unguren confirmed that Southern Slav parents supervised courtship, and that Catholic Croats and Catholic Slovenes urged their daughters to marry within the faith, if not within the same nationality. Mrs. Unguren's mother, Louise Schuster, immigrated to Rock Springs from Slovenia with her parents before World War I. When Louise fell in love with Rudy Anselmi, an Italian, her parents initially frowned upon the match. But the fact that Anselmi was Catholic, and that Slovenians who worked with Rudy said he "had a good reputation," moved Louise Schuster's parents to approve the marriage.[54] Family authority carried weight in Southern Slav courtships, then, for women like Dorothy Pivik, Ann LeVar Powell, and Louise Schuster needed their parents' approval to continue a relationship. One had to pick a spouse whom one's parents would accept. The obligation to extend kinship networks through marriage within the faith or within one's ethnic group thwarted individualistic choice of spouse.

Not surprisingly, Southern Slav parents kept a close watch on whom their daughters saw. Louise Luzan Leskovec's story typified that of many single, Southern Slav women whose parents supervised courtship. Louise Luzan grew to womanhood in Rock Springs during the second and third decades of the twentieth century. During this time, John Mrak's saloon held dances several times per year. As Louise recalled, "I always went to dances with my mother and father. They wouldn't let us go alone."[55] The Luzans were not unique in this respect. Dances at Mrak's saloon took traditional working-class form. That is, they were intergenerational events attended by entire families. Usually they were sponsored by a local club or mutual benefit society, or in the case of wedding parties, by the families of the bride and groom. At these dances young women and men socialized in the constant presence of parents, relatives, and acquaintances.[56]

In her study of working-class women's recreation in eastern cities during the same period, Kathy Peiss found a gradual movement among ethnic youth away from traditional working-class dances and into commercialized dance halls. In these large dance palaces, far from the eyes of parents, relatives, or neighbors, couples enjoyed anonymity.⁵⁷ Commercialized recreation came to Sweetwater coal towns in the form of the Rialto Amusement Company. By 1914 Rialto had opened two theaters in Rock Springs, featuring movies, visiting musicals, drama, and vaudeville acts. Rialto did not, however, open any dance halls. As late as 1921, Rock Springs, Superior, Reliance, Megeath, and Green River had no commercialized dance palaces, like those found in the metropolitan East, which catered to a separate youth culture.⁵⁸ And so ethnic youth in southwest Wyoming coal towns continued to attend traditional working-class dances. There, under the watchful eyes of chaperones, young women and men found circumspect ways to court. Marion Buchan, a single Yugoslavian miner, arrived in Rock Springs in 1910. He described a custom in which if a boy danced the last dance with a girl, it meant he liked her especially.⁵⁹ This custom seems a far cry from courtship at the unsupervised, commercial dance halls of large cities, where working-class couples were openly sexually expressive.⁶⁰

Dances were not the only form of courtship subject to adult supervision. In an exchange with interviewers Ann Burns and Nancy Cranford, Louise Leskovec described dating in 1918, when her courtship with Matt Leskovec began:

LL: One year, he [Matt Leskovec] went to a convention with Mr. Plemel and he sent me a card. When he got back, he called me up for a date, and my mother said that, yes, I could go.

I: You did have to ask your mother?

LL: Oh yes. She never let me go on dates by myself.

I: Now, who went with you?

LL: My mother and dad. (Laughter) We went to the show.

I: You all four went to the show?

LL: Yes.⁶¹

Similarly, Helen Korich Krmpotich courted with her future husband when he came to visit her father. "My Dad wouldn't let us go out on dates," she said.⁶² Dorothy Pivik, Louise Leskovec, and Helen Krmpotich's accounts of their courtships and engagements in early-twentieth-century Rock Springs suggest that Southern Slav parents played a strong role in their daughters' choice of spouse. Chaperoned dating and dances, as well as granting permission to marry, gave parents considerable influence over daughters' marriage plans.

The purpose of such influence was to encourage daughters to marry a man of the same nationality. And judging from the demographic record, these efforts were successful. The 1910 census sample from Sweetwater County yielded 96 foreign-born women who immigrated while single, then married after settling in the United States. Of these, 25 were Eastern Europeans, all of whom married a man of the same nationality.⁶³

Census data from a national sample of the same period indicates that first-generation Eastern European women almost always married within their own ethnic group. In a study of immigrant marriage patterns using a national sample drawn from the 1910 census, Deanna Pagnini and S. Philip Morgan found that "new immigrants" from Southern and Eastern Europe usually married their own kind. Only 6 percent of Eastern Europeans and 2 percent of Italians in this sample outmarried. In contrast, exogamy (marriage outside one's ethnic group) was more common among "old immigrant" groups such as the British, Irish, Germans, and Scandinavians. Fifty-eight percent of British immigrants outmarried, as did 36 percent of Germans, and 18 percent of Scandinavians.[64]

Sweetwater County echoed the national pattern in that the majority of "new immigrants" married a man of the same nationality. Among the 96 foreign-born women who immigrated while single, then married after settling in Sweetwater County, 75, or 78.1 percent married within their own ethnic group. Among the 21 remaining who outmarried, all were matches between "old immigrants," for example, between a British-American and a German-American; or between Americans and "old immigrants," for example, a native-born American and a British-American.[65]

The difference between Pagnini's national sample and the Sweetwater County sample lies in interpretation. Pagnini and Morgan hypothesized that endogamy among "new immigrants" was due primarily to residential and occupational segregation, and secondarily to xenophobia on the part of "old immigrants" toward those whose language, customs, and appearance differed more dramatically from Anglo culture. In Sweetwater coal towns, however, there was neither occupational nor residential segregation. Working-class neighborhoods were ethnically mixed; so, too, was labor in the mines. Moreover, among "new immigrants" who came over as children, language barriers disappeared by the time they reached courting age because, by then, American schooling had made them fluent in English.[66] Instead, the evidence from Sweetwater coal towns suggests that endogamy reflected efforts to build and maintain ethnic community in an environment characterized by transient, ethnically diverse neighborhoods.

The Southern Slav example suggests several ways that courtship expressed community values. First, kin ties formed a crucial community of support in an environment characterized by occupational hazard, economic instability, and lack of residential ethnic enclaves. In this context, choosing a husband of the same nationality not only offered the comforts of shared religion, it also reinforced the likelihood of kinship support.[67] Married daughters or siblings often moved far from home as a consequence of their husbands' search for work.[68] If a woman married and moved away to another county or state, she would be beyond the immediate reach of her own kin networks. And if she married a man of another nationality, she might not be accepted by his kin.[69] Then, who could be sure that she or her children would have the support they needed in the event of illness, death, or economic disaster? Given the importance of extended kin ties to immigrant survival, Southern Slav parents encouraged their daughters to build kin and ethnic support through marriage within their own nationality.

The example of the Southern Slavs, then, suggests several ways that the demography and economics of early-twentieth-century Wyoming coal towns shaped courtship. The hazards of mining-town life underscored the value of kinship ties, hence marriage within one's own ethnic group. At the same time, heterogeneous, changing neighborhoods offered a smorgasbord of cross-cultural possibilities for romance. And so Southern Slav parents and elders steered young women toward their own kind by supervising courtship, suggesting matches, and approving or vetoing engagements. The extent to which familial and ethnic ties played a role in courtship was testament to Slovenian and Croatian efforts to build ethnic community—a form of social cohesion whose value was intensified by their lack of residential cohesion. Thus while single, immigrant, New Women in large cities rejected family and local authority, Southern Slav women in Sweetwater coal towns courted within an informal web of family and ethnic networks.

In contrast, women and men in rural Sweetwater County courted with far less supervision. Long distances between homesteads discouraged family control of courtship. Because of distance, visits between ranchers took the form of infrequent but extended stays. At the least, visitors stayed overnight; more often, they stayed two or three days.[70] During such visits, and during travel between ranches, couples often spent time together unchaperoned. But distance was not the only factor that relaxed rules of courtship. Ranching communities in Sweetwater County were relatively stable and culturally homogeneous. Hence, parents felt less need to monitor their daughters' social lives.

Rancher Mae Mickelson's account of Elsie Ann Johnson's wooing provides a telling glimpse of rural courtship. Born in Wyoming, Elsie Johnson grew up on a ranch in north Sweetwater County during the 1890s and early 1900s. In 1912 she married Jesse Chase, a neighboring rancher. As Mae Mickelson described it:

> Elsie and Jesse knew each other as children. Their families were always friendly.
>
> When she [Elsie] and Jesse started dating, [they went] . . . to a dance at Lot Haley's on Cottonwood above Big Piney. . . . Everyone in the country came and mixed with everyone. The dance lasted all night, which was

usual in those days. When daylight came, everyone started wending their way homeward.

. . . Helen Sargent was a young schoolteacher in the Basin, living at Bonderants, the first time Jesse came to take Elsie for a horseback ride. She said Claire Bonderant stood and watched them ride off and that he was heartbroken! He was in love with Elsie too.

. . . Ira Dodge, Justice of the Peace, married Jesse and Elsie in Big Piney on the 22nd of March, 1912. The snow was very deep. They had driven a sleigh from Cottonwood.[71]

This account of courtship suggests that young women and men in rural Sweetwater County were trusted with unchaperoned time together. Couples like Elsie and Jesse were free to go horseback riding, and to travel long distances unaccompanied by parents, relatives, or peers. In short, Elsie Ann Johnson enjoyed a less supervised courtship than did her Southern Slav peers in coal towns.[72]

Mickelson's narrative also alludes to the sense of community stability and homogeneity that contributed to more relaxed rules of courtship in rural areas. "Elsie and Jesse knew each other as children," Mrs. Mickelson wrote. "Their families were always friendly." With less turnover in the rural population, those who stayed developed long-term relationships with neighbors and shared a sense of rootedness. Parents like the Johnsons felt comfortable about their daughter spending time with Jesse Chase, a man they had known since his childhood. "Everyone in the country came and mixed with everyone" at the dance, continued Mrs. Mickelson, suggesting that no major cultural differences divided ranch folk in her area. Indeed, nearly three quarters of rural dwellers in Sweetwater County between 1880 and 1910 were native born, and most of these native-born ranchers hailed from the Midwest.[73] Among the 27 percent of foreign-born rural settlers, most came from the English-speaking countries of Great Britain.[74] The relative homogeneity of ranch culture seems to have made parents and daughters alike more trusting of social situations involving single men and women.

Other narratives from rural Wyoming reinforce this impression. Helen Coburn, single homesteader in Worland from 1905 to 1908, felt safe attending local dances on her own because those present shared her cultural background. Born in Iowa, Helen had moved to Wyoming to homestead with her friend Mary Culbertson. Before leaving Iowa, Helen had promised her father not to attend any ranch dances because the people might be "crude."[75] But she soon found that other homesteaders in her community "were all people from the Middle West, like myself, and were from families of good background."[76] So Helen attended ranch dances and wrote to her father that she "was not breaking her promise, but just taking it back, as he didn't know the true conditions of the West."[77] Similarly, Eden Valley homesteader Mrs. Nathan Hodson remembered most of the settlers in her area, from 1909 through the 1920s, as being from "Kansas, Missouri, Wisconsin, Iowa, Kentucky, and Illinois. . . . All were friends and interested in each other's welfare."[78] Helen Coburn, Mrs. Nathan Hodson, and Mae Mickelson's narratives suggest that rural ranching populations in Sweetwater County were stable and culturally homogeneous relative to the mobile and ethnically diverse populations of mining towns. Secure among native-born peers from similar backgrounds, familiar with homesteaders throughout their locale, rural folk were less guarded in their attitude toward courtship.

Despite the trust accorded unchaperoned couples, single ranch women were physically and socially vulnerable when they spent time alone with men. If sexual activity occurred, they risked unwed pregnancy and disgrace. Folksongs common to early-twentieth-century ranching communities warned single women to avoid premarital sex. In ballads about cowboy/ranch-girl romances, premarital sex led to abandonment and unwed motherhood. In scenarios involving unchaperoned courtship, cowboys appeared as charming playboys, single women as their willing victims.

"The Wild Rippling Water" is a popular western folksong based on a British ballad rewritten to fit ranch life. It tells the story of a "fair maid" who goes "a rambling" alone with a cowboy,

> Just down by the river,
> just down by the spring,
> to see the wild water
> and hear the nightingale sing.[79]

In this song, the "wild, rippling water," a metaphor for sexuality, proves too compelling to resist, and the fair maid winds up pregnant. She asks the cowboy if he will marry her. He declines and rides away. The last verse holds the moral of the story:

> Come all you young ladies, take warning from me
> Never place your affections in a cowboy so free
> He'll go away and leave you as mine left me
> Leave you rocking the cradle, singing "Bye, oh baby"
> Leave you rocking the cradle, singing "Bye, oh baby."[80]

Like "The Wild, Rippling Water," the popular western song "Bucking Broncho" recognized the power of sexual desire and warned single women of its consequences. The narrator of "Bucking Broncho" is a young woman in love with a cowboy who rides the wild broncs. She describes her flirtation with the cowboy, their dances together, and their engagement. She alludes to their sexual relationship as well, in a humorous double entendre:

> My love has a gun that has gone to the bad,
> Which makes poor old Jimmy feel pretty damn sad,
> For the gun it shoots high and the gun it shoots low,
> And it wobbles about like a bucking broncho.[81]

In the end, the cowboy lover leaves, reneging on his promise to marry. The song concludes with a warning almost identical to that in "The Wild, Rippling Water":

> Now all you young maidens, where'er you reside,
> Beware of the cowboy who swings the rawhide,
> He'll court you and pet you and leave you and go
> In the spring up the trail on his bucking broncho.[82]

The theme of premarital sex and abandonment was repeated in "I'll Give You My Story." According to folksinger Rosalie Sorrels, this song originated in the West, becoming most popular in Idaho and Utah. "I'll Give You My Story" bemoans the fate of the pregnant, single woman, deserted by her lover:

> I'll give you my story,
> I'm heavy with child;
> You said when we parted
> You'd be but a while.[83]

The vanished lover never returns, and the unwed mother-to-be is left to contemplate her future:

> I grieved when we parted,
> I cried night and day;
> Now all of my sorrows
> Have passed away.[84]

The last two lines are ambiguous, and somewhat ominous; did the narrator abort the baby or has she simply gone numb? Like "The Wild, Rippling Water" and "Bucking Broncho," "I'll Give You My Story" depicts the physical and emotional consequences of premarital sex, that is, the risk of unwed motherhood.

Ranching communities in Sweetwater County reinforced such folk wisdom by emphasizing the social consequences of premarital sex. Single women were admonished to protect their reputations. Indeed, a double standard of sexual morality prevailed, in which the woman was held responsible for a couple's behavior together. "He's as good as the girl he is with" was the saying Jerrine Stewart Wire remembered.[85] This Victorian moral standard took the place of chaperones as a social control. The consequences of flouting this standard were dire. Women who "allowed" sexual activity to happen became outcasts in a tight-knit community where everyone knew everyone else's history.

The double standard encompassed sexual assault as well as consenting sexual relations. Jerrine Stewart Wire's memory of a sexual assault during her teens was telling. Jerrine grew up on a ranch in Burnt Fork from 1909 through the early 1920s. As a young woman, she was sexually assaulted by a neighbor while fishing alone several miles from her parents' homestead. Jerrine never told her parents about the incident because she was convinced it would destroy her reputation. Sixty-odd years later, she described what happened:

> I went fishing one time, and when you fish out here there are streams that move along, they are coming down out of the mountain and they are running along at a pretty good clip. And they make a lot of noise so you can't hear what is going on. . . .
>
> I was sitting there fishing and one of our neighbors came up behind me and took a notion to see what I was made out of. I didn't hear a thing until all of a sudden he had ahold of me and he pulled me over backwards and I lost my fishing rod and my fish, and he proceeds to see if he can undo me a little bit. I guess he was wondering what I had underneath my shirt. I started beating and kicking. . . .[86]

Jerrine fought off her attacker and ran home.

> My family all said, "Where is the fish and where is the fishing rod and what's with you?" And I never told them . . . because I knew if I did I would be ostracized.[87]

So powerful was the threat of community judgment and social exclusion that women like Jerrine were afraid to report sexual assault. Jerrine knew that she would be held responsible for her neighbor's sexual attack, and she did not question this attitude. "He's as good as the girl he is with."

Jerrine had learned early, from her mother, that if a single woman and man had sexual contact, the woman became a pariah. This lesson came home through her mother's work as a midwife. As a child, Jerrine knew that her mother, Elinore Stewart, did not discriminate among those she helped in childbirth. In her capacity as midwife, Elinore attended ranch wives and unwed mothers alike.[88] At home in Jerrine's presence, however, Elinore made a point of snubbing unwed mothers. "She often took a stand in front of me," Jerrine said, "that she would not have taken if I weren't there."

> I remember there was a girl in our neighborhood who got herself in trouble. . . . She was so proud when the baby was born, like all new mothers are. They want everybody to see that pretty thing that they helped to make. . . . She walked about four and a half, maybe five miles [to the Stewart ranch] carrying that big, fat, pretty baby . . . to show my mother . . . and my mother wouldn't even let her in the house.
>
> . . . But she would have, if it had just been the two of them there. . . . She was afraid I might think she gave it her stamp of approval. . . . I thought it was too bad that girl had walked for hours and then had to walk all the way back.[89]

For Jerrine, the incident was a vivid lesson in the social consequences of unwed motherhood. Elinore Stewart had made it clear to her daughter that the unwed mother was subject to public shaming and exclusion from community. The unwed father was never mentioned. Perhaps Victorian morality was strongly emphasized precisely because premarital sex was an occasional reality, as suggested by Jerrine's memory of the discrepancy between her mother's work as a midwife and the lesson she taught her daughter.

Recalling these events sixty years later, it never occurred to Jerrine to hold men responsible for sexually active or sexually aggressive behavior. She attributed no responsibility to her unwed neighbor's partner; the single mother had "got herself in trouble." Nor did she attribute responsibility to her attacker at the fishing stream. Instead, she placed it upon herself—"he took a notion *to see what I was made out of*" [emphasis mine]. Jerrine Wire's experience suggests that despite the lack of supervision, the ranching community exercised powerful social controls on courtship, holding single women responsible for prevention of premarital sexuality. Single ranch women, then, were both physically and socially vulnerable in unsupervised situations. The stable and homogeneous community that made chaperones unnecessary also held the threat of public shame and social isolation for those who veered from its rules. In rural areas where everyone knew and judged each other by a double moral standard, single women's reputations hung in the balance.

Neither mining nor ranching communities in early-twentieth-century Sweetwater County embraced the courtship style represented by the New Woman. While the New Woman of newspaper stories lived on her own and saw whomever she pleased, Southern Slav women in coal towns lived in family settings and answered to family authority. While the New Woman of newspaper features gained worldly experience, implying sexual expression while single, ranching mothers emphasized to their daughters the harsh social consequences of unwed motherhood. And while New Women among urban, immigrant working classes flocked to unchaperoned public amusements, Southern Slav women in southwest Wyoming courted under the watchful eyes of parents, relatives, employers, matchmakers, and sometimes, boarding house keepers.

In mining towns and on ranches, then, courtship highlighted the nature of community in single women's lives. The involvement of parents and matchmakers in courtship and the high rate of endogamy among first-generation Eastern Europeans reflected their efforts to build and maintain ethnic community in the midst of transient, ethnically mixed neighborhoods. By contrast, the relative cultural homogeneity and stability of native-born ranching settlements gave rural courtship a different flavor. A shared Anglo heritage and development of long-term relationships between neighbors bred trust among ranching families. In this atmosphere, residents were less anxious to create community, and rural courtships were more casual as a result. Still, casual and unchaperoned did not mean "free." In the isolation of rural settlements, Victorian sexual mores common to ranchers' nineteenth-century, middle-class Anglo heritage persisted. Indeed, the secure sense of community that fostered unsupervised courtship was double-edged, for it threatened single women with exclusion if they violated its standards. The double moral standard was nearly as effective as chaperones in discouraging single women from sexual expression.

Contrasts between coal town Southern Slav and rural native-born courtship thus demonstrate the importance of local economy, settlement patterns, and ethnicity in women's lives. That is, courtship was deeply situational: eastern urban mores were not unknown in these places; they simply did not fit the needs and values of southwest Wyoming ranching and mining communities.

In a larger sense, courtship provides a window on single women's roles within informal social networks that framed and sustained community, whether moral or ethnic. Through their charge to maintain sexual control, single ranch women bore responsibility for preserving moral consensus. Through their choice of spouse, Southern Slav women bore responsibility for expanding networks of reciprocal kin ties. In both cases, these obligations discouraged single women from exploring the freedoms of New Womanhood—such as sexual experimentation or autonomous choice of spouse. Finally, through their part as advisors to Southern Slav women, parents and matchmakers played a significant role in promoting mutuality within their own ethnic group. In short, both the ranchers' experience and the Southern Slav example indicate that courtship activated informal social networks as important to building community as were the more formalized institutions like fraternal lodges. The Southern Slavs' influence on choice of spouse, like the ranching community's use of judgment and isolation as controls on courtship, suggest not only the power and significance of informal social networks in single women's lives, but also the significance of single women in the life of the community.

If the southwest Wyoming frontier shaped courtship in distinctive ways, it also placed unique pressures on marriage. The challenges of relocation and the seasonal nature of ranching and mining often changed the structure of households. When household membership changed, the balance of power within families shifted too. Relations between husbands and wives reverberated with the demands of a ranching and mining economy.

CHAPTER FOUR

"My Wife Just Doesn't Like It Here and I'm Going to Let Her Go Back": Marriage and Patriarchal Authority in Transition

Ann LeVar Powell's parents married in Croatia in 1911. In 1913 Mr. LeVar left his home to seek work in America. He planned to try the copper mines of Butte, Montana, or the coal mines of Wyoming and Colorado. LeVar thought he would send for his wife and two children within the year, once he found steady work and saved money for their travel. But everything took longer than he thought. During his first two years in the United States, LeVar worked with his brother on the railroads in Ohio and Illinois. In 1914 he headed west and wound up in Superior, Wyoming, mining coal. Over the next several years, he moved among the mining camps, working for the Union Pacific. Finally, in 1921, LeVar sent for his wife and children. It had taken eight years for husband and wife to be reunited.[1]

Marital separations were but one symptom of economic struggle on the mining and ranching frontiers. Settlement in southwest Wyoming placed families at the mercy of seasonal economies; miners experienced periodic layoffs, ranchers, months without income before harvests. At the same time, liberalization of homestead law provided compelling economic opportunities to women. Such conditions reverberated within marriage, as did the process of relocation itself. The record from Sweetwater County suggests that long separations caused by immigration, changes in household structure upon resettlement, and husbands' prolonged absences on the ranching frontier all had the effect of disrupting family relations. In the spaces created by such disruption, some wives renegotiated the balance of power with their husbands. That is, some carved out a new autonomy maintained by separate households. Others began redefining their husband's mandates as joint decisions. Still others accepted patriarchal authority within the marital partnership but exercised more influence over children and other kin.

In a review essay on family history, Judith Smith called for investigation of the ways that gendered divisions of responsibility have placed women's and

Marriage and Patriarchal Authority in Transition

men's interests in conflict within the family.[2] The balance of power between spouses became a particularly salient issue in the case of frontier families, as migration removed couples from familiar social moorings and subjected them to new challenges.[3] Contrary to the romantic notion that adversity bonded families, westward migration wreaked havoc on family cohesion.[4] On the mid- and late-nineteenth-century Overland Trail, the stresses of migration, accidents, disease, and economic struggle fragmented families; spouses separated and parents lost control of children.[5] On the turn-of-the-century Rocky Mountain frontier, one in three marriages ended in divorce. There, women's petitions for divorce alerted jurists to high rates of desertion, failure to provide, and spousal abuse.[6] On the Great Plains during the early twentieth century, certain European cultural traditions sustained patterns of domestic violence, violence that was aggravated by the difficulties of survival on a semi-arid frontier.[7] In short, westward migration sometimes devastated marriages.

But what of those marriages that never came to desertion, violence, or divorce? The record of intact marriages in Sweetwater County suggests that there were more subtle fluctuations in frontier family life as well. Marriage functioned as a "meeting ground" for the separate worlds of men and women, where adaptation to new conditions sometimes demanded new patterns of familial cooperation, household structure, and work.[8] These adjustments both shaped and reflected shifts in the gendered social positions of women and men.

First-generation married couples on Sweetwater County's industrial and rural frontiers often endured separations necessitated by economic constraints. Like Mr. LeVar, European husbands typically crossed the ocean alone to establish themselves before bringing their wives and children. While the LeVar's eight-year separation was unusually long, two-, three-, and four-year periods apart were not uncommon. Bertha Savo Husa Witka's parents did not see each other for three years, Mr. Savo leaving Finland for America in 1899, Mrs. Savo following in 1902. Helen Korich Krmpotich's parents endured a five-year separation, Mr. Korich immigrating to the United States from Serbia in 1901, Mrs. Korich joining him in 1906. Louise Luzan Leskovec's parents lived apart for five years as well, Mr. Luzan immigrating to Rock Springs from Slovenia in 1905, Mrs. Luzan arriving in 1910.[9] Between 1900 and 1910, European spouses who immigrated separately spent an average of three and one-half years apart.[10]

Long separations were less common among the second generation of foreign-born couples. Immigrant daughters Helen Korich Krmpotich, Margaret Plemel Metelko, Dorothy Pivik, Ann LeVar Powell, Elsie Oblock Frolic, Louise Luzan Leskovec, Bertha Savo Husa Witka, and Eleanor Eggs Gaensslen all remembered the years their parents spent apart but experienced no such separations in their own married lives.[11] In short, prolonged separations between foreign-born husbands and wives were a function of migrating from Europe to Wyoming. It could take years for an entire family to immigrate, as husbands scouted ahead for work while wives and children waited in the old country.

Ranching couples, too, sometimes parted for months at a time. Among rural homesteaders, it was not relocation that separated husbands and wives. As we have seen, most native-born ranchers emigrated to Wyoming in intact family units.[12] Once settled, however, ranching men often were forced to leave the homestead in search of contract work to supply income between harvests. Typically, they hired on with road construction and irrigation projects, or worked seasonally for livestock outfits at roundup and branding time.

Annie Birzilla Caldwell married Norris Austin in 1915. They homesteaded on the Green River, raising a truck garden, chickens, and experimenting with dry farming. But the dry climate and heavy clay soil made farming difficult. The Austin's harvests did not support their household. Consequently, Norris left the homestead to pick up jobs where he could: "He had to go out different places and work. . . . once he went up to Big Island and built sheep corrals for the Green River Livestock Company. . . . And then he would go out and help put up hay for different people down the river."[13] Once in a while, Annie Austin accompanied her husband on a work trip. When he got a job building ditches in Kemmerer, Wyoming, Annie hired on as cook for the work crew.[14] Most of the time, however, Norris and Annie endured seasonal separations while Norris worked on herding, haying, or construction.

Long separations sometimes changed wives' relationships with their husbands. Studies of the effects of marital separation on American women, due either to westward migration or to wartime, have shown that married women living apart from their husbands became increasingly independent. Some discovered self-reliance as they managed a family business on their own; others took a more assertive role within their marriage once their husbands returned; still others ended a bad marriage.[15] Peacetime separations on the Sweetwater County frontier, resulting from husbands' searches for work, had similar results.

Caroline Adams Dugdale Wade was a teenager when she emigrated with her parents from Utah to Wyoming during the early 1870s. After a brief marriage to William Dugdale, which ended in divorce, she married John Wade, a cattle rancher, in 1882. Together they homesteaded 329 acres in Burnt Fork, Wyoming. Between 1883 and 1905 Caroline Wade gave birth to eight children and worked the ranch with her husband.[16] In 1906, when Caroline was forty-five, the Wades sold their ranch and bought three separate properties near Urie, Wyo-

Marriage and Patriarchal Authority in Transition

ming. Caroline homesteaded one property, John another, and they leased the third. After nearly five years of homesteading apart from her husband, Caroline opted for legal separation from him. In 1911 the Wades separated and Caroline moved to Green River with her three youngest daughters, leaving her sons to work the Urie ranch. Caroline prospered in Green River, managing the Big Horn Hotel.[17] In 1916 she sold the Urie ranch and used the proceeds to buy herself a home in town. From 1916 until her retirement in 1935, Caroline lived in Green River and worked at the Union Pacific Beanery, a popular cafe.[18]

Caroline Adams Dugdale Wade's life history suggests that the Wades' five years apart changed their relationship. Before then, Caroline had lived in what her biographer called "the traditional lifestyle of subservience to her husband."[19] But after five years on her own at the Urie ranch, Caroline initiated a series of independent moves, including legal separation from her husband, self-supporting employment, sale of the Urie ranch, and finally, purchase of her own house in town.

Not all women made such dramatic changes in their lives and marriages. For some, the effects of separation from their husband were more subtle. Ann LeVar Powell alluded to changes in her parents' relationship when she said, "Mother hadn't seen him for eight years. He had changed. . . . He was a youngster when he left; now he was a man."[20] The LeVars had been newly married teenagers when Mr. LeVar left Croatia for the United States. When they rejoined each other, both had become independent adults. Significantly, Ann LeVar Powell remembered her mother's independence of mind when the couple reunited in Superior, Wyoming. Mrs. LeVar "hated Superior. . . It was a barren landscape."[21] She told her husband she wanted to return to Croatia and demanded that he withdraw money from the bank to send her back overseas. Mr. LeVar tried to evade her request by "forgetting" to go to the bank. According to Ann LeVar Powell, her parents' war of wills continued "for two or three years."[22] Finally, Mr. LeVar relented. He promised to go to the bank and withdraw money for his wife's return to Europe. But this time friends waylaid him en route and asked about his errand. According to his daughter, he said,

> "Well, I'm going to the bank to get money, my wife just doesn't like it here, and I'm going to let her go back." And they said, "Oh, you're crazy if you let her go back!" So they got him drunk and . . . he never got to the bank before it closed.
>
> And my mother was so angry. . . . She said that was a turning point; her desire to go back sorta waned after that.[23]

Only when faced with the combined judgment of her husband and his peers did Mrs. LeVar back down. According to daughter Ann, Mrs. LeVar's desire to keep the family intact also played a role in her decision to stay: "Paul was born, and then John was born, and then with four kids she didn't think she'd ever want to go back. . . . When she [had been] over there and my Dad was here, she said that was no life either."[24] Though Mrs. LeVar ultimately agreed to remain in Superior, significantly, her daughter remembered several years of conflict surrounding that decision. Mrs. LeVar had lobbied her husband repeatedly about returning to Croatia. Ann LeVar Powell's memory of her parents' war of wills suggests that after eight years an ocean apart, Mrs. LeVar had rejoined her husband with increased willingness to assert herself, even when it caused conflict.

Similarly, Louise Luzan Leskovec's mother, after a long separation from her husband, opposed him over family migration plans. Mr. Luzan left Slovenia for the United States in 1905. In 1910, he wrote to his wife, asking her and the children to join him in Rock Springs as soon as possible. "Send the boy first," he wrote, referring to their fourteen-year-old son. But after five years apart from her husband, Mrs. Luzan felt unwilling to relocate on such short notice. Nor did she want her teenage son to make the crossing alone. "No, I'm not going to send him over," she wrote back. But the boy, too, had his own mind, and insisted on going. In March 1910 the Luzan's oldest son traveled to Rock Springs and joined his father in the mines. Meanwhile, Mrs. Luzan received a second letter from her husband, more adamant than the first. This time, daughter Louise recalled, "He wrote to my mother, told her to make up her mind that she has to come here because he was tired of staying at boarding houses . . . [and] he would like his family with him."[25] Perhaps, like Mrs. LeVar, Mrs. Luzan placed family unity above her individual needs. In any case, she prepared to leave Slovenia after receiving the second letter. By April 1910 Mrs. Luzan and the remaining children had immigrated to Rock Springs.[26] Though Mrs. Luzan had, eventually, complied with her husband's wishes, she had not hesitated to argue against his plans for her own and her children's immigration. Indeed, Mrs. Luzan's opposition to her husband's immigration plan suggests that she had become accustomed to making decisions affecting herself and the children on her own. Doubtless she had made many such decisions during her husband's five-year absence.

Caroline Dugdale Wade, Ann LeVar Powell, and Louise Luzan Leskovec's stories suggest that long separations between husbands and wives sometimes changed the balance of power within marriages. In Caroline Wade's case, five years of ranching without her husband precipitated her metamorphosis from "traditional subservience" to independence. Homesteading became her route to autonomy; she emerged a property-holder, married yet living apart from her husband, and supporting herself with wage work. Less dramatic but equally significant were the metamorphoses of Mrs. LeVar and Mrs. Luzan. After years apart from their husbands, both women developed a proprietary attitude toward themselves and their children. Having made family decisions without their husbands present, each woman grew accustomed to self-assertion within the partnership. Both wives complied with their husband's resettlement plans only after expressing opposition and weighing the alternatives, including the value of keeping their families intact. In this way, each woman had become a force to be reckoned with, redefining her husband's mandates as joint decisions.

Just as long separations sometimes changed marital relations, immigration itself sometimes brought dramatic changes to married women's household structure. Ann LeVar Powell's mother moved from an extended family farm in Croatia to a two-room, single-family unit in Superior, Wyoming. Later, the LeVars moved to a four-room company house in which they kept boarders. Between 1911, when she married, and 1921, when she immigrated to Superior, Mrs. LeVar lived with her husband's parents in a small farming village in Croatia. According to daughter Ann LeVar Powell, her mother's living arrangement was customary among Croatian farm families during the early 1900s: "When a boy got married, the bride came and lived with the in-laws, and they all lived in one house."[27] Social relations within such households followed a traditional pecking order:

> The oldest son's wife had priority. . . . She was the first daughter-in-law. And my mother [Mrs. LeVar] was the second one, so she always was sort of in the background.
>
> . . . She said that after my father left, they didn't treat her as well. The first daughter-in-law got treated much better. And then the third daughter-in-law [the youngest son's wife], she wouldn't even stay there; she ran away.[28]

Mrs. LeVar held a middle position in the social order at her in-laws' household. Her mother-in-law ran the household, while the daughters-in-law worked outdoors. "When a boy got married," Ann LeVar Powell explained, "the in-laws gained another farm hand. She [Mrs. LeVar] went out and worked in the fields."

> The mother-in-law did all the cooking and managing the household, and when the babies were born, she took care of them, too. The mother-in-law would take them outside to their mothers when they had to be nursed.[29]

Within early-twentieth-century rural Croatian culture, then, married women like Mrs. LeVar customarily moved in with their in-laws; they had no household of their own. They labored in the fields and lived by their mother-in-law's household rules.

"My Wife Just Doesn't Like It Here"

Moving from Europe to Wyoming changed the structure and social relations of Mrs. LeVar's home life. From the deferential position of second daughter-in-law in an extended family unit, she moved to the position of wife in a nuclear family unit. Freed from the in-laws' pecking order, Mrs. LeVar took charge of her own household. She found domesticity in the new country to be a mixed blessing. On the one hand, "she was used to . . . working the land," recalled daughter Ann, and "she didn't like having to stay in and cook and never get outside." On the other hand, Mrs. LeVar now enjoyed "the mother-in-law's role that she had so envied in the old country."[30] She had become the senior woman in her household.

If, as Ann LeVar Powell indicated, Croatian farm wives customarily lived with in-laws before joining their husbands in America, then these women experienced significant change in family and household relations when they immigrated.[31] Immigration changed their household position from daughter-in-law in the old country, to wife and senior woman in the new country. This is not to say that such women lived in the privacy of nuclear family households in America. Many of them kept boarders or periodically housed adult siblings. The crucial change was their release from the pecking order of the in-law household to the autonomy of their own household.

In responding to open-ended questions about their own and their mothers' lives, none of these women explicitly related changes in household structure to the shifting balance of power between husbands and wives. Yet the anecdotal evidence clearly points in that direction. It stands to reason that the increased household authority of Croatian immigrant wives—as senior women within a pared-down family unit in the United States—may have contributed to their willingness to challenge their husband's unilateral decisions.

One measure of wives' decision-making power within marriage was family size. Though the evidence is difficult to interpret, a few significant patterns emerge. Most striking is the fact that among one hundred oral history informants of both sexes, none of the men addressed the issue of family limitation, whereas the women did. This suggests that the decision to have fewer children was a female initiative. At the same time, women informants were, in general, reticent about sexuality and reproduction. Nonetheless, a few offered explanations of why family size concerned them. Economic survival and personal health emerged as women's only articulated reasons for having fewer children. But if the "whys" of limiting family size remain sketchy, one thing is clear: over time, Sweetwater County women had fewer children.

In 1886 twenty-year-old Ann Ramsay moved with her parents to Almy, Wyoming. There she met and married William Lee. In 1889 the Lees moved to Rock

Marriage and Patriarchal Authority in Transition

Springs, where Mr. Lee worked for the Union Pacific Railroad. Between 1889 and 1904, Ann Ramsay Lee gave birth to eight children.[32] Her two daughters, Mary and Margaret, married and settled in Rock Springs; but unlike their mother, the daughters each had only two children.[33] Ann Ramsay Lee and her daughters' brief histories illustrate the decrease in family size over two generations of women in Sweetwater County. First-generation women tended to have large families with five to ten children. Second-generation women had smaller families, with two to four children.

The oral history record supports this impression. First-generation Southern Slav immigrants mentioned in these histories had large families: Helen Korich Krmpotich's mother and Mary Buchan each had five children; Ann LeVar Powell's mother had seven; Dorothy Pivik's mother had eight; Elinore Bastalich Tolar's mother had nine.[34] And Margaret Plemel Metelko, a second-generation Southern Slav-German, said of her mother, "It seemed like [she] had a child every year."[35] Oral histories and memoirs of native-born women suggest the same pattern. Ruth Ellen Day Wright, first-generation emigrant from Kansas, had five children; Caroline Dugdale Wade and Maggie Kinney, first-generation emigrants from Utah, had eight and six children, respectively.[36]

The oral history record further indicates that family size decreased among second-generation women. Second-generation Southern Slav immigrants Dorothy Pivik and Mary Jesersek Taucher each gave birth to only three children; Louise Leskovec and Elinore Bastalich Tolar each raised only two. Likewise, second-generation Swedish immigrant Bertha Witka bore only two children. Her peer, Anna Semos, had no children of her own, though she did adopt and raise one nephew.[37] Again, the narratives of native-born women suggest a similar pattern. Second-generation Green River native Louise Graf had one child; second-generation Rock Springs natives Bertha Stevens and Annie Shinazy each bore only three children.[38]

Census data reinforces the impression that family size decreased over two generations. According to the 1880 Sweetwater County census, women had an average of 4.4 children.[39] This figure represents an approximation, since the 1880 census included neither adult children who lived away from home, nor the total number of births per woman. For purposes of this discussion, then, birthrates drawn from the Sweetwater County census refer to the average number of surviving children at home, unless otherwise stated. According to these estimates, family size decreased steadily. From an *estimated* 4.4 children per mother in 1880, family size dropped to 3.5 children per mother in 1900, and to 2.7 children in 1910.[40]

Were these families limited by choice or reduced by circumstance? Two possible circumstantial influences on family size are infant mortality and age at marriage. Did shrinking birthrates correspond with the rising age at marriage? Presumably, women who married later had fewer fecund years, hence fewer children. Or did second-generation women only appear to have fewer children because fewer infants survived?

The latter is unlikely because high infant mortality was common to both generations. Elinore Stewart left a poignant record of her baby's death in "The Memory Bed," from *Letters on an Elk Hunt by a Woman Homesteader*. In 1910 Elinore lost her second child, Jamie, to a disease she called "erysipelas."[41] The baby died when only a few months old. Over the next four years, Elinore had three more children, all of whom survived.[42] But she had felt keenly the death of that second child. "For a long time, my heart was crushed," she wrote.[43] To heal her grief, Elinore planted a "memory bed" of flowers in remembrance of the baby she had lost: "Under the east window of our dining room we have a flower bed. We call it our memory bed because Clyde's first wife had it made and kept pansies growing there. We poured the water of my little lost boy's last bath onto the memory bed. I keep pansies growing on one side of the bed in memory of her who loved them. In the other end, I plant sweet alyssum in memory of my baby."[44] Elinore maintained the garden as long as she was able, until a mowing accident felled her in 1926.[45] Elinore Stewart's memory of her baby's death echoed the losses of many women on the Sweetwater County frontier.

Narrative evidence suggests a high infant death rate among the first generation. Eight out of twenty-one narratives about Sweetwater County women who bore children during from the 1870s through the 1890s reported one or more infant deaths per family.[46]

Census data from 1900 and 1910 suggest that infant mortality remained high in the second generation as well. Beginning in 1900, the census enumerator recorded not only the number of surviving children in each household, but also the total number of children ever born to each woman. Differences between the two figures are striking. There were almost always fewer surviving children than there were births.[47] Green River resident Margaret Riley was typical. Age forty at the time of the 1900 census, she had given birth to six children, but only four survived.[48] Like Margaret Riley, many second-generation women lost one or more children to disease or accident. In 1900 the average number of births per mother was 6.0, while the average number of surviving children at home was 3.5.[49] In 1910 the average number of births per mother was 4.7, while the average number of surviving children was 2.7.[50]

Finally, narrative evidence from the period 1910–1929 further indicates that infant mortality remained high among the second generation. Rock Springs resident Anne Pryde, for example, lost an infant shortly after birth in 1914. Rock Springs resident Annie Shinazy lost one of her children to infant death in 1919. Louise Leskovec lost her first daughter to spinal meningitis in 1922. And Rock Springs resident Lavinia Karg lost her fourth child to infant death in 1926.[51] In short, infant mortality remained a common theme in narratives throughout the period 1910–1929. And if infant mortality remained high across two generations, then it does not explain the decrease in family size.[52]

Another circumstantial explanation for the decrease in family size could be the rising age at marriage. We have seen how the average age at marriage for women rose from twenty in 1880, to twenty-one in 1900, to twenty-two in 1910.[53] A cohort analysis of the period 1880–1910 further showed that among second-generation women, more waited until after age twenty-four to marry for the first time. In 1880, for example, only 22.7 percent of women married for the first time after age twenty-four. By 1910, 36 percent did so.[54] If more second-generation women married later, it stands to reason that they had fewer children because they had fewer fecund years during their marriage.

This theory assumes that women continued childbearing throughout their fertile years. And there is evidence that some women did. Rock Springs resident Anna Crofts, for example, bore thirteen children at one-, two-, and three-year intervals from 1873 to 1897—from the time she was twenty until she was forty-four years old.[55] But others stopped bearing children long before they reached menopause. Rural bride Minnie Hepp Greub was typical. Married at age twenty, the Piney Creek homesteader gave birth to four children between 1890 and 1898. Minnie Greub stopped bearing children at age twenty-eight, though her marriage and her health remained intact though old age.[56] Similarly, Rock Springs resident Bertha Stevens bore her last child in 1923, at age twenty-six. Her sister, Annie Shinazy, bore her last child in 1922, at age twenty-seven.[57] In short, neither first- nor second-generation women uniformly continued childbearing throughout their fecund years. Age at marriage thus had little bearing on family size.

Circumstantial influences, then, such as infant mortality or age at marriage, do not explain the decrease in family size. Instead, the evidence suggests that second-generation women practiced deliberate family limitation.[58] Narrative evidence about rural midwives further supports this impression.

In ranching communities, midwives dispensed knowledge about reproduction. Most rural communities had a midwife—an experienced, though not necessarily professionally trained woman who attended women in childbirth. A woman affectionately known as "Auntie Bollin" was midwife to the homesteading community of Hillsdale from 1909 to 1927. One neighbor said of Auntie Bollin: "She had no special training but possessed natural ability. . . . She was called into homes where help was needed in case of sickness or to help deliver the new baby. . . . She kept a suitcase packed so she would be ready at a moment's notice, day or night. . . . She was often away from home for a week or more, as she would stay to help care for the family until the mother could do it."[59] Between 1910 and 1927, Auntie Bollin delivered fifty-three babies and did not lose one.[60] Similarly, Elinore Stewart ministered to women in the ranching community around Burnt Fork from 1909 to 1926. According to her daughter Jerrine, Elinore advised women about birth control. Women whom she tended in childbirth would sometimes ask how to prevent pregnancy. Elinore recommended abstinence or the calendar method.[61]

If family limitation was deliberate, why did the second generation choose to have fewer children? Here, the narrative evidence becomes sketchy, making it difficult to say, conclusively, why the second generation had smaller families. Certainly Sweetwater County mirrored a national trend toward smaller family size. The birthrate for all white women in the United States declined steadily during the late nineteenth and early twentieth century. The average number of children born to white women fell from 4.2 in 1880, to 3.6 in 1900, to 3.2 in 1920, to 2.5 in 1930.[62] In Sweetwater County, estimated family size fell from 4.4 children per mother in 1880, to 3.5 in 1900, to 2.7 in 1910.[63] Daniel Scott Smith first called attention to family limitation as a form of female self-assertion within marriage.[64] And one could ascribe married women's increasing autonomy to that kaleidoscopic social trend, the emergence of New Womanhood. But the term New Womanhood works best as a form of periodization rather than causation. Though deliberate family limitation among Sweetwater County women can, indeed, be seen as a form of self-assertion within marriage, the reasons behind such behavior are more difficult to discern.

In their oral histories and memoirs, women spoke of sexuality and reproduction reluctantly, with reserve, or not at all. They willingly reported how many children they had, but offered little explanation why. In an interview with second-generation Croatian Ann LeVar Powell, for example, I asked why her generation had had fewer children. She referred obliquely to larger social trends; then, in a friendly way, brushed aside the question: "Oh well, that was just the direction everyone was going in then, smaller families." She then changed the subject.[65] In an even more cryptic aside, Pat Huntley LeFaivre offered the following story about her second-generation Tyrolean Italian mother, Magdalena (Lena) Anselmi Huntley:

Marriage and Patriarchal Authority in Transition

PHL: Mother told me on the eve of my wedding that her Godmother had told her on the eve of her wedding: "You don't have to take all the children God sends you." That's all she [Mother's Godmother] said, and she left it to Mother to figure it out.

I: Did your mother explain to you what was meant by it?

PHL: No, Mother repeated the same words to me, and that's all she said. Other than that, the subject was never discussed.[66]

Lena Anselmi Huntley gave birth to only two children during her lifetime.[67] Her story is both startling and mysterious. Lena Anselmi Huntley was a devout Catholic who limited family size, with her godmother's blessing. Yet the particulars of her decision to do so remain shrouded in silence. The question of how she reconciled family limitation with Papal edicts against birth control remains unanswered.

Scholars have explored fertility behavior as a measure of cultural assimilation among immigrant groups. In a comparison of late-nineteenth- and early-twentieth-century Italian peasant families in southern Italy with those who immigrated to the urban United States, sociologist Paul Campisi argued that those in the United States gradually adopted American urban family size norms; that is, family size decreased. Campisi read this drop in birthrates as an expression of assimilation, as succeeding generations embraced American culture.[68] But in a study of Italian immigrants in Buffalo, New York, during the same period, Virginia Yans-McLaughlin countered that declining family size among Italian immigrants represented an adaptation of European tradition to American realities, a "flexible tradition," rather than wholesale adoption of American values.[69] Whether smaller families reflected assimilation of American culture, or "flexible" continuity of European culture, Campisi's and Yans-McLaughlin's divergent interpretations suggest the difficulty of reading fertility behavior as a measure of cultural identity among immigrant groups. As John Briggs observed, fertility behavior has varied from group to group, depending upon which village or region immigrants came from, and which economic or cultural conditions they encountered in the United States.[70]

Sweetwater County immigrants from Germany, Austria, Finland, and the Southern Slav countries described a European upbringing in farming villages characterized by large families.[71] Yet none of these informants perceived family size in America as a symbol of cultural identity. When first- and second-generation immigrant women were asked how they preserved ethnic tradition in the new country, they described home-based family rituals involving European food, song, decoration, and holidays.[72] When these women addressed strategies for assimilation, they focused on learning English, attending school, and finding white-collar work.⁷³ In short, none of the foreign-born women interviewed described family size as an expression of cultural identity.

They did, however, allude to family size as an economic issue and as a health issue. One story from the working-class community in early-twentieth-century Rock Springs revealed the economic motivation behind concern with family size. Mary ——— married two years after immigrating to Rock Springs from rural Austria shortly before World War I. At age twenty, she had her first child. One year later, she had another, and a year after that, another. "I was twenty-two, I got three kids," she said. "My husband wasn't too anxious to provide. . . . He liked to drink and gamble."⁷⁴ Mary began taking in laundry to earn income for the household. Laundry was strenuous work. If Mary continued to become pregnant every year, she would be unable to maintain a laundry business. And she worried about feeding and clothing the three children she already had. So Mary stopped having children. With a spendthrift husband and a physically demanding job, family limitation was a practical choice aimed at economic survival.

In addition, several second-generation women commented that their mothers had been worn down physically by the rigors of bearing large families. Lena Anselmi Huntley, second-generation daughter of Tyrolean Italian immigrants, saw her mother's health eroded by six pregnancies. When Lena was seventeen years old, her mother died, leaving Lena, the eldest daughter, to raise her five brothers and sisters. Lena quit school and took over her mother's responsibilities as homemaker and caretaker for her younger siblings. Significantly, Lena's sacrifice to the demands of family reciprocity at this stage of her life would be transformed into self-assertion within her marriage. Having lived through her mother's early death, having shouldered the childrearing responsibilities left in her mother's wake, Lena determined to have only two children of her own. In so doing, Lena avoided repeating the sacrifices of her youth to the demands of raising a large family. In so doing, she also chose against her mother's pattern of sacrificing one's health to the demands of unlimited childbearing.⁷⁵

Similarly, one of Louise Leskovec's most vivid memories was of quitting school at age twelve to care for her younger siblings at home while her mother recuperated from a difficult birth.⁷⁶ Ann LeVar Powell echoed such memories in an account of her mother's pregnancies. Powell linked frequent childbearing with the risks of miscarriage: "Almost immediately [after immigrating to America], Mother began having children, and it seemed like there was one of us born every year after that. Seven in our family, and several miscarriages."⁷⁷

For working-class women, pregnancy and childbirth on the urban frontier carried risks. Working-class women usually gave birth at home and rarely saw doctors for prenatal care. If something went wrong with a pregnancy or delivery, hospital care was often too expensive.[78] Hence the incidence of miscarriages and slow recuperation after difficult births.

Occasionally, working-class families called a doctor to attend a home birth. But even a doctor's presence was unreliable, as Louise Leskovec discovered when it came time to give birth to her first child: "We called the doctor the night that I got my pains. When I got sick. And we couldn't get him, he was just very busy. . . . Matt called him about 9:00 . . . and he didn't come 'til three or four in the morning. . . . He had another call to another coal camp for another birth, so he came about fifteen minutes before the baby was born, and my mother was with me."[79] Similarly, Rock Springs resident Beatrice Ketchum remembered giving birth at home, attended by an unreliable doctor who "had a bad, bad habit of being drunk quite a bit."[80]

For rural women, medical help was even farther away; some homesteads were as much as sixty miles from the nearest town. Even a midwife or relative could not always be summoned, if, for example, roads became impassable with mud or snow. Jerrine Stewart Wire remembered her mother giving birth alone in their homestead cabin during the winter of 1913, ill-assisted by her husband Clyde. Jerrine was too young to know what to do, and so her mother

> didn't have any help. . . . He [Clyde Stewart] got so nervous thinking he was there alone with that predicament that he was just shaking, thinking that he couldn't do anything. . . . [The baby] was blue when he was born; he was born under a coil [with the umbilical cord wrapped around his neck]. He wasn't breathing and my mother said to my father, "Smack him and get him started."
>
> "I can't hit that little thing." So she had to take him and smack him. [The baby began breathing.][81]

Like Elinore Stewart, rural women sometimes gave birth at home, unassisted by a midwife or doctor. Awareness of the risks involved and of the inaccessibility of medical help sobered daughters like Jerrine Stewart Wire. Years later, describing why she wanted to leave ranch life, Jerrine remarked that she had not wanted to go through childbirth in isolation, as her mother had.[82] Jerrine Wire, Beatrice Ketchum, Louise Leskovec, Ann LeVar Powell, and Lena Anselmi Huntley's stories suggest that the risks associated with childbirth, lack of reliable medical help, and memories of their mothers' health problems associated with frequent pregnancies influenced some second-generation women to have fewer children.

A composite picture, then, of intact marriages in Sweetwater County during the late nineteenth and early twentieth century would include long engagements and older brides. Patriarchal authority within the home would be somewhat eroded by the expansion of economic opportunity for women in the form of homesteading, and by economically motivated separations between husbands and wives. Married immigrant women, depending upon their country of origin, might find new power in a pared-down household unit. And married women, both native and foreign-born, would bear fewer children over time, suggesting increased negotiation with husbands over family limitation as well.

The exigencies of relocation, then, and the economic demands on families posed by seasonal occupations such as ranching and mining sometimes shifted the balance of power between spouses, as wives increasingly asserted their interests. Paradoxically, then, the economic uncertainty and flux that shaped courtship along more conservative lines had the opposite effect on women's place within marriage. For even as courtship activated community obligations that checked female autonomy, marital adaptations in the same environment sometimes expanded women's decision-making power. This is not to say that married women on the Sweetwater County frontier routinely made unilateral decisions or acted individualistically. As suggested by Caroline Dugdale Wade, Ann LeVar Powell, and Louise Luzan Leskovec's stories, conditions in southwest Wyoming sometimes pitted wives' individual preferences against the interests of their husbands. When this happened, the evidence suggests increased assertion on the part of wives, leavened by continued sensitivity to the needs of the family group. Indeed, within Sweetwater County marriages, the individualism of New Womanhood was less a matter of ideology than circumstance. Moreover, such circumstantial independence emerged within the context of responsibility to family—often a more powerful community of interest.

Like household relations, the world of work bounded women's everyday lives. In ranching communities and coal towns alike, married women held responsibility for feeding and clothing their families and maintaining their households. In both settings, women's household work also generated income, through keeping boarders or selling surplus garden, dairy, or livestock products. But the demand for and the meanings of work varied from one setting to the other. First-generation coal town women would find a ready market for commercialized housekeeping, while office work and retail work would attract their daughters. Rural women, on the other hand, would find few wage-earning opportunities outside the home. Changes in their work patterns were more subtle. Over time, women on ranches walked an increasingly fine line between their own and men's work. How ranch families made sense of this forms an intriguing story.

CHAPTER FIVE

Group Partnership and Cowboy Myth: The Gendering of Ranch Work

"The heavy work of the ranch naturally falls to the men," wrote Wyoming settler Mrs. B. B. Brooks in 1899, "but I think most ranch women will bear me out in saying that unless the women . . . be always ready to do anything that comes along, . . . the ranch is not a success."[1] Mrs. Brooks's statement conveys the transitional nature of women's ranch work at the turn of the century. On the one hand, gender-based divisions of labor were understood: the "heavy work" fell to the men, the household work to the women. Such boundaries echoed the nineteenth-century ideology of separate spheres. On the other hand, Mrs. Brooks expected to cross over into men's work when needed, to make the ranch "a success."

This broad definition of female responsibility foretold a blurring of gendered work roles, which intensified as the twentieth century progressed. By itself, this is not news. Historians have documented the gradual overlap of men's and women's work on late-nineteenth- and early-twentieth-century homesteads.[2] But the nature of this transition has not been fully explored. Narratives from Sweetwater and neighboring counties during this period suggest the processes by which women and men shaped and absorbed such change. Changes in ranch women's work precipitated subtle processes of rationalization and ideological adjustment.

Ranch women articulated an ethic of group partnership that normalized transgression of gender boundaries. That is, even as their daily lives increasingly required crossing over into men's work, women minimized the import of such crossover by describing it as service to family—a familiar touchstone of female gender identity. In addition, ranch families adopted popular mythology about the cowboy in ways that sharpened distinctions between genders. Cowboy myth maintained one category of exclusively masculine work, thereby limiting the scope of ranch women's expanding influence. In these ways, ranch women approached role change conservatively. Both the social construction of crossover work as family duty and the preservation of cow camp as a vestige of separate spheres deflected the egalitarian implications of ranch women's adaptations to frontier life.[3]

To fully understand such change, in both the activity and consciousness of women, one must return to some basic questions about divisions of labor in late-nineteenth- and early-twentieth-century rural Wyoming. Precisely what was understood to be "women's work" on a ranch? What values did women place on this work? To what extent did women do "men's work" on a ranch? What meanings did women attach to this work? Finally, how did the scope and meaning of rural women's work change over time?

Sylvia Eppler left a vivid account of homesteading on the high plains. Her story was one of daily and weekly chores, the most consistent and pressing reality of ranch life. The work of running the Eppler homestead resembled that of most Sweetwater County ranches in that ranching involved labor-intensive, subsistence work well into the early twentieth century. The Epplers, for example, supplied their own fuel and water:

> For fuel, we burned lots of "sheep chips" that made a hot fire, an unpleasant smell, and lots of ashes to be carried out.
>
> . . . All the water had to be carried in from a water barrel outside the house. [Water barrels were filled at the nearest spring, river, or creek, allowed to freeze overnight, then rolled up to the house.][4]

The Epplers grew most of their own food and processed it themselves:

> Every spring, a big vegetable garden was planted, and there was a lot of work to do. . . . A hoe was used in the corn and bean patches. The potatoes were dug with a digger, then picked up by hand, loaded in the wagon, and stored in the root cellar. We also planted pumpkins and squash. These vegetables were canned or stored for winter use.
>
> . . . Baking was a big chore for Mother, who had to make bread enough to fix lunches for James, Russell, Orval, Norman, Mary and Ralph.
>
> . . . Dad always butchered our meat and he would get our neighbor, Theodore Smith, to help scald and scrape a big hog. It was all cut up ready to cure the hams, and side pork for bacon was smoked with corn cobs.
>
> Mother would make sausage with homegrown sage, then fry it down and can it in jars. She also made mincemeat and head cheese.
>
> . . . Lard was rendered and put into a large crockery jar and put in the root cellar.[5]

They produced most of their own clothing and some of their own household items as well:

> Mother did all the sewing for her family of thirteen children.... It took a lot of overalls, shirts, dresses, and coats, which she made.
>
> ... The soft white feathers [of poultry] were saved for new pillows.... Nothing ever went to waste.[6]

Livestock were raised as cash crops, the proceeds used to buy supplies that the Epplers could not produce:

> We raised chickens, turkey, geese, and ducks that were picked dry and dressed for market.
>
> ... [We would] go to Hillsdale after groceries, mail, and coal.... It would take a whole day to make the trip in with eggs buried in a bucket of oats to be taken to the Olsen Grocery and traded. [Dressed poultry were also traded, for flour, sugar, coal oil, and shoes.][7]

Between 1880 and 1910, 90 percent of rural households in Sweetwater County were ranches.[8] Like the Epplers, most rural women of this region and time period were engaged in labor-intensive, subsistence work.

Electric cream separators, electric washing and sewing machines, electric stoves and irons, and hot and cold running water remained foreign to plains agricultural households well into the early twentieth century. In a study of U.S. Department of Agriculture reports on rural families in plains states from 1910 to 1940, Katherine Jellison found that most ranch women did not have access to modern household technology during this period because families tended to prioritize business needs over women's needs. Spare money went toward farm machinery, such as tractors, rather than household appliances. Consequently, most rural plainswomen remained dependent on subsistence technologies even after modern technologies had become available.[9]

A few technological developments reached Sweetwater County ranches during the second two decades of the twentieth century. Some women, for example, replaced their tub and washboard with hand-crank washing machines. As Eden Valley homesteader Lenora Wright described them:

> The early models were large wooden tubs standing on legs or supports. A manually operated wheel with a handle on one side turned the gears. A wringer was also attached.
>
> ... It saved hours of back-breaking labor ... [but] there was much work to turn the loaded washer and the wringer. Water still had to be hauled in, heated, and added to the tub.[10]

For starching and ironing, heavy irons were heated on top of the coal-burning stove. More than one iron was used; as one cooled, it was taken back to the stove and another one picked up by a removable handle. "I often think," wrote Lenora Wright, "of the many miles Mother walked on washday and ironing day."[11] By the 1920s, some ranch women acquired gas-powered irons, which eliminated time spent heating and switching the old heavy cast-irons.[12] Despite these advances, doing the family laundry remained a labor-intensive chore, and still required an entire day's work.

In addition, by the 1920s, some ranches used gas lamps and lanterns, which burned more cleanly than coal oil and kerosene. And a few ranchers bought small generators, which supplied enough electricity to light their houses and barns. But these generators usually did not supply enough electricity to run appliances like an electric vacuum cleaner, washing machine, or cream separator. Jesse McMaster Faris, young wife on a cattle ranch south of Green River City during the 1920s, remembered using a hand-crank separator: "I had all those cows to milk. . . . The hardest thing for me to do was carry it all in, and separate it, because we had a hand-crank separator, and I'd have to stop and fill up the old bowl, and go to it again—cranking."[13] Rural electrification on a scale that would support household appliances did not reach most Sweetwater County ranches until the 1950s when the Rural Electrification Association (REA) came to outlying areas such as Eden Valley.[14] In short, despite some modernization with manual washing machines, gas irons, gas lamps, and generators, women in rural Sweetwater County continued to keep house as well as produce food and clothing at the subsistence level throughout the 1920s, much as their forebears had in the 1880s.

In the subsistence economy of ranching, divisions of labor were based on gender. By custom, women did "inside work" and men did "outside work." That is, women did the household work of cooking, cleaning, laundering, and producing clothing and food. Raising and processing food made up a substantial part of ranch women's "inside work." Indeed, the term "inside work" had a broad interpretation, since much of women's food-growing activity took place outdoors—tending vegetable gardens, and raising poultry and dairy cows. The term "outside work," however, referred to men's chores like building fence, chopping wood, shoveling manure, plowing, threshing, and herding.[15]

Women's household work was essential to rural family economies. In a pathbreaking study of household work on Colorado homesteads from 1895 to 1920, Susan Armitage coined the terms "maintenance" and "sustenance" work. Maintenance work referred to cleaning, washing, and cooking—chores that maintained a household. Sustenance work referred to home production of food and clothing that made cash expenditure unnecessary. Armitage observed that ranch families' absorption into the wage economy was slower than commonly thought because sustenance work reduced the need for cash income. By producing goods for home consumption, as well as surplus goods for sale or barter, ranch women's household work often made the difference between survival and bankruptcy.[16]

Research on rural families has suggested that women's vital economic contributions raised their status. Historians argue that during the mid- and late nineteenth century, as farm families made the transition from subsistence barter to commercial capitalism, the commercial value of women's home production enabled them to "loosen the bonds" of patriarchal family authority.[17] Similarly, recent research on homesteaders in the early-twentieth-century West holds that sharing of the economic burden between husbands and wives generated "a large measure of mutuality" between them, somewhat equalizing gender relations.[18] Taken together, such studies imply that wives' essential contributions to the rural family economy reinforced a gradual liberalization of women's roles. Research on crossover work further supports this assumption. Historians concur that by the late nineteenth century, women on frontier homesteads filled in for absent men, plowing, chopping wood, or herding stock when necessary.[19] Several concluded that with the erosion of separate spheres, women who handled traditionally masculine jobs "tended to become increasingly self-reliant and independent" and to see themselves as the equals of men.[20]

Ranch women's narratives from rural Wyoming, 1880–1929, offer a revealing test of historians' assumptions about rural women's work. First, these narratives support the hypothesis that women derived status from the economic value of home production. But their sense of accomplishment and standing was rooted in an ethic of group partnership, rather than in individual achievement or in the exercise of power relative to men. Sweetwater ranch women were well aware of how their work as producers sustained family members and hired hands, either directly or through earned income. They drew social standing and recognition from their essential role in the community of labor and production that was the ranch. A successful ranch raised the status of all its members.

Second, southwest Wyoming ranch women confirmed that by the early twentieth century, crossover into men's work had become routine—except in the case of work with beef cattle. Cowboying evolved as a male province, with a gendered mystique that excluded women. Women might work as reserve labor, herding sheep, but rarely were they called to cowcamp. Most significant, those few women who did work with beef cattle expressed individualistic notions of status. Indeed, the difference between the meanings of women's home production—a feminine expression of group partnership—and the meanings of cowcamp—an expression of masculine individualism—reveals links between cowboy myth and the gendering of ranch work. This distinctly "western" phenomenon separated Sweetwater County ranch women from their eastern agricultural peers.

The first clue to ranch women's perceptions of their work was that they distinguished between their role as housekeepers and their role as producers. Armitage's division of subsistence labor into "sustenance" work and "maintenance" work paralleled ranch women's own feelings about their chores. Though both were essential contributions, women placed different values on maintenance and sustenance work. Sustenance, or producer, work was a source of pride; maintenance, or housecleaning, a source of frustration. Expression of these values, in turn, reflected late-nineteenth- and early-twentieth-century narrative and folk convention. Published memoirs about westward migration were shaped by received ideas of what a pioneering story should be. Though the details varied, depending upon time period and location, the narrative convention emphasized triumph over adversity. Overland narratives used incidents like fording rivers, hunting bison, and meeting Indian threats to illustrate the courage, stoicism, and resourcefulness of the pioneers.[21] Likewise, Rocky Mountain pioneer narratives presented Indian encounters, vigilante activity, and harsh winters as challenges that proved their endurance.[22] Great Plains pioneer narratives a generation later focused on the harsh climate as the obstacle that tested their mettle, and underscored the spiritual rewards of agricultural persistence in an arid land.[23] In each case, mastering hardship was the common theme; westering narratives celebrated triumph over adversity, and muted frustration and complaint.

Published memoirs from Sweetwater County observed the same conventions. Ranchers and homesteaders from southwest Wyoming also wrote success stories of hard work and survival, highlighting their productivity in a harsh climate. Elinore Stewart, for example, after homesteading in Burnt Fork from 1909 to 1913, proudly recounted her experiments with home production in a harsh climate:

> I have experimented and found a kind of squash that can be raised here, and that the ripe ones keep well and make good pies; also that the young tender ones make splendid pickles, quite equal to cucumbers. I was glad to stumble on that because pickles are hard to manufacture when you have nothing to work with. Now I have plenty. They told me when I came that I could not even raise common beans, but I tried and succeeded. . . . Experimenting along another line, I found I could make catchup, as delicious as that of tomatoes, of gooseberries. . . . Gooseberries were very fine and very plentiful this year so I put up a great many.

... I have raised enough chickens to completely renew my flock, ...
and have some fryers to go into the winter with.[24]

Stewart's memoir typified those of Sweetwater County ranch women in two ways. First, it expressed ingenuity and determination in the face of challenging conditions. In this respect, Stewart's memoir adhered to the narrative convention of depicting pioneer persistence. Second, it reflected homesteaders' recognition of the value of women's work as producers for home consumption.

Ranch women who produced surplus goods for market also recalled with pride their contributions to the family economy. Elinore Stewart's 1913 description of the results of her work included the fact that income from sale of her homemade butter had bought a year's supply of gasoline and flour.[25] Eden Valley rancher Minnie Webster also detailed her profitable home production, and what those profits bought. Raised on a ranch in Eden Valley during the early 1900s, Minnie married Adolph Sitzman in 1921. Together the Sitzmans homesteaded a ranch of their own in the same valley during the '20s. Minnie raised poultry to sell locally:

I started to raise turkeys the first summer we were here. ... I started with fifty and built my flock to twelve hundred. ... I sold them all in Rock Springs to ... Ben's Food Liner, Union Mercantile, Wyoming Meat Market, and the Union Pacific Coal Company Store.

... I didn't get rich but made enough to buy the present land that we live on.[26]

Earning money to buy land was a concrete and lasting contribution to the family ranch. Likewise, Jesse McMaster Faris sold milk so that she and her husband could expand their homestead:

We had 160 acres. That was the amount given in a homestead, and later we bought 120 more acres. I milked cows to buy it.[27]

Thus Elinore Stewart, Minnie Webster Sitzman, and Jesse Faris expressed pride in their work as producers, noting how it contributed to the success of the ranch.

To say that ranch women's memoirs were influenced by a narrative convention that affirmed survival and forbade complaint is not to deny them honest expression or to cast doubt on their stories. What becomes significant is how they illustrated these conventional themes of survival. While the narrators of Overland Trail, Rocky Mountain, and Great Plains memoirs chose anecdotes about dangerous rivers, Indian threats, prairie fire and drought, or vigilante activity to illustrate their endurance, Wyoming ranch women chose anecdotes about their work as producers to illustrate their victories. Hence, while ranch women's memoirs may have been shaped by a stoic, success-oriented narrative convention, their choice of topics to express triumph over adversity was their own. That they chose to detail their sustenance work suggests that they derived self-esteem and social recognition from their role as producers.

When ranch women did mention maintenance, or cleaning tasks, they described the activity but not their feelings about it. Lenora Wright was the exception, prefacing her description of laundry with the comment, "Washday was one day I wanted to hide, but never did."[28] Wright was speaking of herself as a child, helping her mother. Adult women rarely expressed frustration or aversion to the laborious, repetitive tasks of cleaning. Rather, they described them briefly, in tones that conveyed duty and resignation. Sheep rancher's wife, Doris Bailey Luman, for example, described how maintenance work changed seasonally as household membership changed. Normally, ranch women cooked and cleaned for an average of 5.4 people.[29] During harvest, branding, or shearing times, a household could expand to four times that, as seasonal work crews arrived. On the Luman ranch, sheep were sheared every spring in late April or early May, before lambing. This meant hiring a shearing crew. Doris Luman remembered her supper table crowded with almost twenty extra hands every spring: "There were about twelve to fifteen shearers and they brought with them about three wranglers and a wool tromper, and so with our herders and us, we hardly ever had less than twenty to cook for and that's what I did."[30] Maintenance work thus became more burdensome seasonally, but Doris Luman concluded her description of this pattern with a laconic "and that's what I did"—in keeping with the convention of endurance without complaint. As rancher Phyllis Luman Metal put it, "When things got the roughest, you were supposed to make a joke of it. And you were *never* supposed to complain."[31] Were ranch women really such saints? Folksongs suggest otherwise.

Folksongs expressed feelings considered inappropriate to a memoir, inappropriate to express out loud. Folklorist Alan Lomax maintains that folksongs functioned as outlets for complaint, anger, sorrow, love, or revenge fantasies that were unacceptable in daily life. According to Lomax, the moral precepts of Puritans and Calvinists became the folk mores of pioneer America. Hardship, for example, was a cross to bear without complaint—except in folksongs, where one could sing, carp, and moan about things "too disturbing to be more openly stated by the singer and his community."[32] With ranch family members relying upon each other's labor, any one person's rebellion at work threatened the fabric of daily life, the survival of the ranch. Given this reality, ranch wives continued to do their chores each week, but probably found vicarious relief in songs of complaint about housework.

The Gendering of Ranch Work

Housework songs used comic exaggeration to register complaints about the drudgery of cleaning. Comic songs allowed singer and listener to identify with the complaint, and at the same time, to distance themselves from it, since the song, after all, was an exaggeration. "The Washing Day" addressed laundry, one of ranch wives' most tedious jobs. Subtitled "A Ballad for Wet Weather," this song was popularized in minstrel shows during the early 1900s. It was a comic song, exaggerating the meanness of one wife driven to ill temper by washday. The first verse set the scene:

> The sky with clouds was overcast
> The rain began to fall;
> My wife, she'd whipped the children
> And raised a pretty squall
> She bade and with a frowning look
> To get out of the way;
> Oh, the deuce a bit of comfort here
> Upon a washing day!

The second verse insisted that this woman normally was cheerful—until washing day destroyed her spirits:

> Kate, she is a bonnie wife
> There's none so free from evil,
> Unless upon a washing day,
> And then she is the devil!

The chorus repeated the husband's lament:

> For 'tis thump, thump, scrub, scrub,
> scold, scold away
> The de'il a bit of comfort here
> Upon a washing day.[33]

In each succeeding verse, washday destroyed family life, marital peace, and friendship, as the wife became a horrible "scold" until her laundry was done. Ranch wives who heard this song very likely enjoyed its celebration of bad temper on washday.

Another popular folksong about housework was "The Housewife's Lament." Originally written during the 1860s by Mrs. Sarah Price of Ottawa, Illinois, the song spread west after the Civil War. By the late nineteenth and early twentieth centuries, "The Housewife's Lament" had become well known throughout the western states.[34] This song emphasized the frustration of cleaning, which never had lasting results, but always had to be repeated, again and again and again. The opening verse presented a discouraged housewife, sweeping mud from her doorstep:

> One day I was walking, I heard a complaining,
> And saw an old woman the picture of gloom.
> She gazed at the mud on her doorstep, 'twas raining,
> And this was her song as she wielded her broom.
> Chorus:
> Oh, life is a toil and love is a trouble,
> Beauty will fade and riches will flee,
> Pleasures they dwindle and prices they double,
> And nothing is as I would wish it to be.

On this self-pitying note, the song continued with a litany of complaint:

> In March it is mud, it is slush in December,
> The midsummer breezes are loaded with dust,
> In fall the leaves litter, in muddy September,
> The wallpaper rots and the candlesticks rust.
> (Chorus)
> There are worms on the cherries and slugs in the roses,
> And ants in the sugar and mice in the pies,
> The rubbish of spiders no mortal supposes,
> And ravaging roaches and damaging flies.

Succeeding verses stretched the futility of housecleaning to comic exaggeration:

> With grease and with grime from corner to centre,
> Forever at war and forever alert,
> No rest for a day lest the enemy enter,
> I spend my whole life in a struggle with dirt.
> (Chorus)
> Last night in my dreams I was stationed forever,
> On a far little rock in the midst of the sea
> My one chance at life was a ceaseless endeavor
> To sweep off the waves as they swept over me.

The closing verse added bitter irony to the housewife's futile struggle against dirt:

> "Alas! 'Twas no dream; ahead I behold it,
> I see I am helpless my fate to avert."—

She lay down her broom, her apron she folded,
She lay down and died and was buried in dirt.[35]

Black humor colored the final verse—why clean house when we all return to dirt anyway? "The Housewife's Lament" thus did everything a pioneer narrative could not do: complain, wallow in self-pity, and give up hope. Indeed, its list of frustrations and its dark humor probably helped many a ranch woman cope with mud season.

Notably, there were no western folksongs about the joys of maintenance work. Housekeeping songs like "The Washing Day" and "The Housewife's Lament" focused only on frustration and depression engendered by repetitive cleaning chores. Perhaps ranch women's maintenance work, like modern housecleaning today, was taken-for-granted labor, with no permanence and little reward.

If maintenance work formed an unrecognized contribution, it was, nonetheless, essential to the family economy. Cooking and cleaning eliminated the need for hiring a housekeeper or boarding out. Indeed, hiring a housekeeper was too expensive for most rural men. Between 1880 and 1910, among rural men without wives or adult female relatives, only 1 percent hired a housekeeper. Instead, 30.7 percent opted to board out with a family; and 68.2 percent lived in all-male households where they faced the labor-intensive work of cooking and cleaning in addition to their wage-earning jobs.[36] The presence of a woman in the family, then, saved her male relatives the expense of boarding out, or spared them the costs in time and energy of "doing for themselves." While historically we may appreciate the value of maintenance work, ranch women themselves did not dwell on it.

The absence of spirited and detailed descriptions of housekeeping in most memoirs, and the presence of complaints about housekeeping in folksongs, thus suggest that maintenance work, while economically valuable, was not viewed by ranch women as a source of pride and status. Again, it seems that women's role as producer of food, clothing, and salable surplus was most highly valued.

The meaning of ranch women's sustenance work is further clarified when compared to attitudes about their crossover into men's work. Sweetwater County ranchers described a gradual overlap of gender roles over time. In the 1880s a ranch woman's crossover into men's work was rare, occasioned by emergency; by the 1900s, it had become unremarkable.[37]

One 1882 diary, for example, described how women helped with herding emergencies during a sheep drive. LeVancia Bent, an unmarried woman, lived with her sister and brother-in-law, Emmeline and George Squires. In the summer of 1882, when LeVancia was forty-nine years old, she and Emmeline accompanied George's outfit on a sheep drive from Evanston, Wyoming, to Kearney, Nebraska. George was trailing eight thousand head east to their winter range. Normally, Emmeline and LeVancia did not accompany the herders, but in this case they did so in order to visit relatives. Once the outfit reached Kearney, the two sisters planned to travel on to Illinois to winter in their hometown.[38]

On the trail, while the men tended the sheep, LeVancia and Emmeline cooked, washed, and set up and took down the bedding. But in a herding emergency, the women pitched in. LeVancia described one such incident in her diary entry of August 6, 1882, Ham's Fork River: "About forty sheep rushed into the river to drink, and couldn't pull themselves out of the mud. It was very dark, the wind blowing terribly. One of us held the lantern, while the others kept the sheep back from rushing in after their brethren."[39] Only the emergency need for extra hands, then, drew LaVancia Bent and Emmeline Squires into "outside work" on the trail.

A generation later, it was unremarkable for ranch wives to occasionally ride herd when their husbands were short of help or behind schedule. On the Bob Luman sheep ranch, Doris Bailey Luman took charge of the household or "inside work." But every spring when storms threatened to soak the herd during shearing time, Doris helped move the herd into "sweat sheds" where their wool stayed dry. "You can't shear sheep that are wet," she said, so "sometimes Bob would come in and say stop your work in the house and go get your horse and help the herder bring in the sheep . . . and I'd be late with my evening meal."[40] Bob Luman counted on his wife as reserve labor during shearing season.

Aside from being "on call" as herders, many ranch women did routine "outside work" as well. Early-twentieth-century ranch women reported mowing hay, building ditches, and shoveling manure as part of their workday. Jesse McMaster Faris remembered hauling manure to build irrigation ditches with her daughter Wilma: "In the spring . . . we hauled the manure from the corral to build up the dikes and dams for irrigating. For many days Wilma and I shoveled and hauled thirteen wagon loads of manure a day with a team of horses. Oh boy, we were tired. Then we went home to cook supper and milk all the cows."[41] While ranch wives often helped men with the outside work, the reverse was rarely true. Jesse Faris and Doris Luman both mentioned returning from an outside job to confront unfinished household work unassisted by their husbands.

Jesse Faris and Doris Luman were not unusual. Accounts of women regularly handling inside and outside work appear in oral histories from the early 1900s. Verla Richie, growing up on her parents' Muddy Creek Ranch during the second decade of the twentieth century, described her mother's work routine: "Be-

The Gendering of Ranch Work

sides all the housework and taking care of us kids, Mamma packed in all the wood and water. When Dad moved the cattle out for the winter, he went with them, and Mamma and us kids stayed at home. Jep and Norm [younger brothers] were real tiny, but Mamma was always very capable in seeing that what had to be done outside was done. There was always stock to feed, and she'd just bundle us up and take us with her."[42] In short, second-generation ranch women frequently were responsible for "outside" as well as "inside" work.

In most cases, early-twentieth-century ranch women viewed the crossover into men's work as a routine, albeit periodic, responsibility. Verla Richie described her mother's attitude toward crossover work as one that emphasized group cooperation: "To her the work and obligations of the ranch, and the things that were to be done on it were just part of life. . . . Dad and Mamma raised us this way. When you have something to do you should do it, and if there were things to be done and the people who were to do them weren't there, you should go ahead and get them done anyway."[43] Clearly, Mrs. Richie viewed her "outside work" as a family responsibility, something any able-bodied family member would do to make the ranch a success. Through an ethic of group partnership, ranch women normalized their crossovers into men's work. In this way, "outside work" gradually lost its gendered meaning.

Indeed, for women, the meaning of "outside work" is best understood in terms of their identity as contributors to a successful ranch. A group work ethic prevailed, with notions of success stemming from group achievement. Like home production, women framed "outside work" in terms of interdependence rather than individual accomplishment. Ranch women expressed a sense of group partnership with husbands and children. Verla Richie said it best: "If there were things to be done, and the people who were to do them weren't there, you should go ahead and get them done anyway."[44] Marie Jordan Bell echoed this theme when she described filling in for absent ranch-hands during World War I:

> That was the first year of the war and all the men from the ranch had gone to fight. Dad didn't want me to go to college. He said, "I need you here so badly." And I knew he did.
>
> . . . I said, "I'll stay here 'til you're through haying."
>
> So I stayed and helped put up the hay. . . . That made me a month late [starting college], which was a little hard, but if you want to do something bad enough, you can do it.[45]

In delaying college for the sake of the family hay harvest, Marie Bell expressed this sense of group partnership. Similarly, Jesse Faris's description of haying conveyed a sense of group partnership with her husband and daughter: "I mowed, Wilma did the raking, and Will did the sweep. . . . I wouldn't trade those years for anything."[46]

Marie Bell made it to college despite some delay, and Jesse Faris seems to have appreciated the satisfactions of group partnership; but for some, responsibility to a family ranch created painful choices. Obligation to family moved Jerrine Stewart to end her relationship with her fiancé when her parents needed her help on the ranch during the post–World War I economic recession. While attending the University of Colorado at Boulder on an art scholarship during the late 1920s, Jerrine had fallen in love with a fellow art student. He, too, came from a ranching family. Just about the time they were considering marriage, his elderly parents requested his help on their ranch. If Jerrine married him, she would go with him to work his parents' ranch. But her father sent word that he needed her help as well, particularly since her mother was slowly recovering from a serious mowing accident. Times were hard in rural Wyoming, and the Stewart ranch was struggling. As Jerrine remembered,

> I told him [her fiancé], . . . I absolutely cannot turn my back on [my mother and stepfather]. . . . This man [her stepfather, Clyde Stewart] . . . gave me a home when I had no home, and now in his old age I am going to walk away and leave him in debt up to his ears? . . . He couldn't possibly run the place alone. I will not leave him [and my mother] and if it means that we will have to part then we will have to part.
>
> He [Jerrine's fiancé] said, well, I can't leave my father in his old age with a big dairy herd to handle, and my two sisters living with him. I can't leave him. And if you can't come with me, we will have to part.
>
> So we did. And I cried.[47]

Jerrine felt that her first responsibility was to respond to her parents' need for her labor on the ranch. Her fiancé felt the same responsibility toward his family. Neither of the two families at that time could afford to hire help to replace family labor. And so in this case, the ethic of group partnership made ranch family solidarity more important than romantic love, for both Jerrine and her fiancé.

Even the most personal choices, then, could be painfully shaped by women's commitment to sustain the family ranch. Indeed, Jerrine's choice suggests the strength of the group work ethic that characterized ranching families. Doubtless it reflected the very real challenges of survival on the high plains desert. In this context, doing outside work had more significance as an expression of commitment to family than as a test of gender identity.

Only one type of men's work elicited a different response from ranch women. That was cowcamp. While sheep ranching dominated agriculture in Sweetwater County, it was cattle ranching that captured people's imagination. By the first

The Gendering of Ranch Work

decade of the twentieth century, cowboy myth had been popularized in mass culture through Erastus Beadle's dime novels, best-sellers like *The Virginian*, and traveling Wild West shows such as that led by retired outlaw Buffalo Bill Cody. And westerners themselves were not immune to such myth. Bruce Siberts, a cowboy who rode herd from the 1890s through the 1920s, wryly compared life before and after the cowboy was romanticized: "I had a liking for the girls, but when I went into town with my rough clothes on, they wouldn't pay any attention to me. . . . Owen Wister hadn't yet written his book *The Virginian*, so we cowhands did not know we were so strong and glamorous as we were after people read that book."[48] Within his lifetime, Siberts saw the cowboy transformed from working stiff to hero in the American mind. With an individualistic code of honor, and without family ties, the nomadic cowboy became a male role ideal.[49]

Links between cowboy myth and masculinity carried over into ranch work. Even after the open-range phase of herding had ended, when stock growers settled on family ranches and cattle-raising had ceased to be a nomadic lifestyle, the occupation retained a masculine identity. Women ranchers who capably herded sheep or drove oxen were rarely called to help herd cattle. Because work with beef cattle had become interwoven with a compelling ideal of masculinity, cow-punching seems to have been the one kind of "outside work" resistant to women's participation as reserve labor.

Even the exceptions proved the rule. Charlotta Hartley Albert grew up at the turn of the century on her parents isolated Horse Creek ranch. The oldest two children were girls, one of them Charlotta. Because her father needed a cow-hand, she rode herd with him, but only until her younger brother matured enough to take her place. "I was Father's cowboy until Grover was old enough," she explained.[50] The fact that Charlotta referred to herself as "Father's cow*boy*," and that her younger brother took over as soon as he was able, reinforce the impression that ranchers saw work with beef cattle as a distinctly masculine occupation.

Indeed, the few women who worked as cowhands were not accepted as women. They were incorporated into cowcamp only as quasi-men, indistinguishable from "the fellers." Elsie and Amy Cooksley's narratives illustrated their identity as "fellers" in cowcamp. In 1914 Elsie and Amy Cooksley came from England to Sheridan, Wyoming, with their parents. The family established a cattle ranch. Ages fourteen and seventeen, Amy and Elsie routinely helped both parents as needed. They also worked with their father in cowcamp, but noted how unusual it was: "We were the only girls that ever rode with the roundup. I don't know why, unless its due to the fact that Dad sent us out to take care of our own stock and we got started doing it. . . . Nobody else did."[51] Indeed, cowcamp had such a strongly gendered meaning that Elsie and Amy were accepted only as "one of 'the boys'" by the other cowhands. Amy Cooksley Chubb said,

> Well, here's an illustration. We were holding the herd one time while half the men had their dinner. We saw a lady and her daughter drive up to the wagon for dinner. When the wagon came around, sometimes the neighbors would come for a chuck wagon dinner.
>
> Our relief came out and told us we could go eat. One of the fellers that was helping hold the cattle said, "No way! I'm not going in there and eat with those women. I don't mind Amy and Elsie and the rest of the boys. But I'm not going in with those women.[52]

In short, cowcamp was understood as masculine territory; Amy and Elsie Cooksley were accepted within it only as quasi-"boys."

Cowcamp had become so associated with masculinity that the few women who herded cattle found themselves reclassified as males. When Marie Jordan Bell helped her father with a roundup in southeast Wyoming shortly before World War I, her grandmother objected, convinced that the experience would masculinize Marie: "Grandma . . . scolded Mama because I was out with the boys riding. . . . She told Dad that she thought he was making a boy out of me."[53] During the early twentieth century, then, those few women who worked as cowhands were aware of their anomalous position as women in a man's world.

Because cowcamp was so exclusively defined as male territory, it existed in a realm apart from the occasional "outside work" that women accepted and valued as part of their responsibility to a successful ranch. Indeed, cowcamp's anomalous position in the world of ranch work caused those few women who worked as cowhands to value this work differently. They valued it as an individualistic accomplishment—a masculine prerogative, rather than as an expression of group partnership, the traditionally feminine virtue of service to family.

Consider the example of Phyllis Luman. Luman grew up during the second and third decades of the twentieth century on her parents' sheep and cattle ranch in the Green River Valley, where she cooked, cleaned, and gardened. Phyllis also had helped herd and sort sheep during lambing season. She described both household work and sheep herding as routine chores.[54]

Then, at about age sixteen, Phyllis decided she wanted to work with the cowboys during branding. Her father was skeptical. "You don't know what it's like up there [in cowcamp]. All the ranchers send their meanest broncs up there. I don't think you can ride their horses. They have no time to be coddling you girls." Phyllis took her father's words as a challenge, and insisted on going, with two female cousins. "All right," her father said, "But I'll bet you don't last two days."[55] Phyllis found cowcamp to be extremely hard work, but she and her cousins stuck it out:

> When the herd was rounded up, they told us girls to ride herd while they roped the calves and took them over to the fire where the irons were getting hot.
>
> . . . At noon they let that herd go and we rode back to camp as fast as we had come. There were steak and potatoes, sourdough biscuits, and coffee. Then we got a fresh mount and headed back as fast as we had ridden forenoon to round up another herd.
>
> Once again we rode herd while they branded. Then back to camp. I was so stiff and sore, I could barely walk.
>
> . . . Dawn came as soon as I had closed my eyes, and we did the same thing the next day—and the next and the next.
>
> We rode with them for seven days . . .
>
> We made it. We had stayed. At the end of the time, we were proud of ourselves. It was the hardest time I ever spent in my life, but I never had felt so good about myself. When I finally got back to the ranch, there was a glint of pride in my dad's eyes. Nobody knew better than he did what cowcamp was like.
>
> At last I had been allowed to be part of the culture which was my heritage.[56]

Clearly, Phyllis savored her work in cowcamp as a personal achievement. Cowcamp was no ordinary responsibility, no routine family chore.

Because cowcamp had been romanticized as a masculine ideal, Phyllis enjoyed the mystique of the exceptional woman in a man's world. Her father had doubted her ability as a female to function in that world, warning her that the cowboys would have "no time to be coddling you girls." Women were not trusted as reserve labor in cowcamp; Phyllis's father had assumed she wouldn't "last two days." Consequently, when Phyllis proved herself a cowhand, she saw "a glint of pride" in her father's eyes. She had done the unexpected: she was a female cowboy, literally an oxymoron, culturally an anachronism.

Cowpunching, then, stood out among "outside work" with a mystique of its own. Long after open-range herding had faded, cowboys on fenced ranches shared in the legendary identity of those before them who had ridden the open range. The cultural significance of the cowboy as an exemplary masculine type probably contributed to ranchers' resistance to women as reserve labor in cowcamp. And so work with beef cattle was charged with questions of gender identity in a way that other outside chores were not: Could a woman do it? Did she belong there? Should she even try it?

Indeed, the status Phyllis Luman drew from cowcamp was individualistic, rather than an expression of group partnership. Her labor was not essential to cowcamp; it could have functioned without her. In defying her father's skepticism, she set up a personal challenge and won. Disproving conventional wisdom about female abilities through individual effort, was, to Phyllis, a personal victory. "I had never felt so good about myself," she said, for she had overcome the assumed limitations of her gender. Not only did Phyllis Luman derive individualistic status from her stint in cowcamp, but the world of cowcamp also brought cultural status. It was cowcamp, not housekeeping or herding sheep, that symbolized "the West." It was cowcamp that moved Phyllis Luman to say, "At last I had been allowed to be part of the culture which was my heritage."

Finally, Phyllis Luman, Marie Bell, and the Cooksley sisters' stories suggest that daughters had more role flexibility than their mothers. Superficially, children's work roles resembled those of their same-sex parent. By custom, girls helped their mothers with "inside work," boys helped their fathers with "outside work."[57] But some daughters crossed gender lines in their childhood role as helper. These young women carried into adulthood a legacy of work role flexibility, which further redefined the boundaries of womanhood.

Many ranch women reported working with their mothers as soon as they were able. Verla Richie recalled: "My earliest memories are helping Mamma do the chores like milking, churning butter, [and] taking care of the chickens.... I also had to do dishes when I was quite young."[58] Similarly, Jerrine Stewart helped her mother Elinore with cooking, cleaning, and tending the poultry, dairy, and kitchen garden.[59]

Like their mothers, daughters did men's work as well. As young children, some played at doing men's work without a thought to their gender. Verla Richie, for example, played at wrangling and herding: "I used to play I was rounding up wild horses or going on beef drives. Sometimes I'd get on a stick horse and run wild, and pretend I was gathering up a whole desert of horses to bring them in because I was fascinated with the corralling of wild horses off the desert."[60] Girls who accompanied their fathers on "outside" chores got ideas for their childhood games. Doris Bailey, for example, modeled games on her father's winter cattle-feeding routine: "In the winter I had a little wagon which could be converted into a sled, and my father made me a little hay rack, it was the cutest little hay rack, and I'd go fill it up with hay and scatter the hay all around, and I'll bet I ran one hundred thousand miles with that wagon, feeding my imaginary cattle."[61] By making her a play hay rack, Doris's father was grooming her to help with that chore when she got older. "When I got older," Doris said, "I always helped my father with . . . [feeding] the cattle."[62] Doris's father enlisted her help because she was the oldest child in the household. According to Doris, "For most people on ranches, the oldest always helped outside. . . . I was the oldest and if Dad had something for me to do outside, that was OK. . . . When I was ten years old, we broke the ground on our ranch, and I drove four horses on the gang plow."[63] Similarly, Verla Richie went from "play" to "real" outside work as soon as she became a capable rider and team drover: "I don't think I started haying until I was thirteen years old, but when I did I drove a team because tractors weren't being used then. It took us about forty-five days to do all of the haying."[64] Jesse Faris's daughter Wilma and Elinore Stewart's daughter Jerrine also helped their parents with haying, mucking stalls, clearing rocks, building irrigation ditches, and other outside work.[65] Beatrice Jack grew up on a sheep ranch near Green River City during the early 1900s. As a teenager, she traveled to sheep camp when school let out, herded all summer, and returned home when school started again in the fall.[66]

At first glance, it seems plain that second-generation ranch women—daughters raised on frontier homesteads—were more involved in men's work than their mothers. But changes in ranch women's work roles had as much to do with a woman's life cycle as with a change in attitude over generations. After all, these daughters had mothers who did outside work as well. What made some daughters *more* involved in outside work than their mothers was their freedom from responsibility for inside work. Mothers could not avoid inside work, since it was their primary responsibility. But "tomboys" could spend all day helping their fathers, or several weeks working outside at other ranches for money, as long as their mother had enough help from other children.[67]

Consequently, daughters' involvement with inside and outside work varied according to temperament. As a girl, Doris Bailey liked working outside, while her sister preferred working inside:

My sister liked helping my mother, and to her a horse was just something to go somewhere on.

. . . I had nothing to do with the house—that held no enjoyment for me at all. . . . So I guess you'd say I was an outdoor gal.[68]

In short, girls' work-role flexibility reflected their status as children. The adult woman of the house could not abandon her household responsibilities in order to do outside work on a regular basis. Her daughters, on the other hand, had more leeway. If one sister helped in the house, that freed the other to work outside, as was the case with Doris Bailey and her sister.

The fact that daughters had more role flexibility raises the question of generational changes in attitude. That is, how did daughters translate their versatility on the ranch into their adult lives? Did their work roles as adults differ from those of their mothers?

Narratives that follow two generations of ranch women indicate that some daughters extended work-role flexibility into adulthood in ways that their mothers had not. Marie Jordan Bell, Barbara Fox Davis, and Jerrine Stewart Wire's life stories suggest a liberalization of their work roles as married women, which stemmed from their role flexibility as daughters. All three women represent the second generation, which came of age during the second and third decades of the twentieth century. Their mothers represent the first generation, which came of age during the late nineteenth century or early 1900s.

Marie Jordan Bell grew up on a ranch on Chug Creek, Iron Mountain, Wyoming, during the first two decades of the twentieth century. Like most ranching daughters, Marie helped her mother with inside work, her father with outside work. Early on, however, she showed a preference for outside work: "I certainly liked to work out more than work in the house. And I'm sure Mama thought I should be helping her sometimes when I wasn't. But she never objected to me riding so much and helping my dad."[69] Indeed, while Marie's mother "did not ride," Marie rode as often as possible. As a young woman, her father would send her out to ride after stray cattle.[70] In 1917 Marie left the ranch to attend college. In 1921 she graduated and married rancher John Bell. Together they built one of the largest cattle ranches in southern Wyoming. John "loved the business end of it," Marie "loved the ranching."[71]

Throughout her adult life, Marie Bell continued to herd cattle and break horses, just as she had as her father's helper. Marie Jordan Bell, then, translated her childhood versatility on the ranch into adult work roles more broadly defined than those of her mother. For although Marie took responsibility for household work during her married life, she maintained involvement in outside work as her primary focus. No reserve labor, Marie Bell was a "top hand" throughout her married life.[72]

Barbara Fox Davis's lifelong involvement in men's ranch work was even more pronounced. Born in 1909, Barbara Fox grew up on a spread just over the Wyoming border, in northern Colorado.[73] Like Marie Jordan, Barbara Fox inclined toward outside work on the family ranch: "I went with my father right from the start. My older sister would help in the house, but I tagged along with Dad. An older brother and I did a lot of the riding."[74] As a girl and young woman, then, Barbara Fox rode the lines, fixed fence, and drove the hayrake.

In 1925 she married rancher Sam Davis. For a wedding present, Barbara's father gave her two registered Herefords. She bought two more, and started her own herd with four head of cattle. Her husband, meanwhile, started his own herd with only three to four head as well. "When we first started," he said, "I kept what I made and she kept what she made."[75] Thus began the pattern of their marriage.

Barbara and Sam Davis each kept separate herds and managed their respective cattle businesses independently. They kept separate bank accounts and dealt independently with livestock merchants. As Barbara described it,

[I run] my registered herd. . . . My husband runs a grade herd. [Generally a registered herd's offspring are sold as breeding stock; a grade herd's offspring are sold for slaughter].

. . . [I] sell my stock. . . . And I want to do it. I don't want to do the work and then let Sam have the fun of selling them.

. . . 'Course, Sam helps promote my cattle. He likes them. I do his, too. If I find a buyer and I think he's interested in Sam's cattle, I'll show them if he's not around. But [Sam] sets his price, . . . and I set my price.[76]

Not only were their herds separate, but Barbara contributed equally to the family income. "I take in just about as much as he [Sam] does," she said.[77] And she used proceeds from the sale of her livestock both to support her choice of outside work and to improve the ranch. Once she began to prosper, for example, Barbara hired a cook so that she and her daughter could work in the fields and ride after cattle. Her earnings also went toward the ranch as a whole: "Like, in the house, I built on [paid for] this room."[78] Finally, though Barbara Davis expressed the ethic of group partnership common to ranching families—"we help each other ride and so forth"—she also said, "I guess I have been an independent woman." In short, Barbara Fox Davis continued her childhood familiarity with men's work into married life, as a full-time stockgrower and businesswoman.

Jerrine Stewart Wire also chose adult work roles different from those of her mother. Like Marie Bell and Barbara Davis, Jerrine grew up on a ranch doing both inside and outside work. As a young woman, Jerrine, too, preferred outside work. Every summer during her teens she worked with young men on hay crews to raise money for college. But unlike Bell and Davis, Jerrine did not continue ranching in her adult life. Rather, she rejected the economic insecurity, isolation, and arduous work that she perceived as a rancher's lot. After graduating high school, Jerrine attended the University of Colorado at Boulder on an art scholarship. Halfway through her second year, illness forced her to leave. She returned to her parents' ranch, feeling defeated. The next fall, Jerrine returned to art school, only to be called back to the ranch to help her aging parents. For the next five years, Jerrine remained on the ranch, duty-bound, but chafing to leave. Finally, at age thirty, Jerrine left the ranch to marry Frank Wire and the couple moved to Pennsylvania. There Jerrine taught art in the local schools.[79] Though Jerrine ultimately rejected ranching, she translated her versatility on the ranch into a prescription for wage-earning work and self-expression as an artist-educator within married life.

Marie Bell, Barbara Fox, and Jerrine Wire's life stories suggest that some second-generation ranch women continued the role flexibility begun as daughters into their adult lives. All three married and raised children. Yet none made inside work their primary focus, as their mothers had. Instead, each developed adult responsibilities that reflected their individual skills and preferences. Their choices reflected a sense of entitlement and capability, which very likely stemmed from their broadly defined work experience as ranching daughters. In this way, the loosening and overlap of gendered work roles intensified over generations. Daughters who had had a choice of work roles while growing up carried a broader perception of women's work roles into their adult lives, and encouraged their daughters to do likewise. By the mid–twentieth century, even cowcamp drifted toward becoming routine outside work for women.[80]

As a whole, then, ranch women's narratives from Sweetwater and neighboring counties confirm that Victorian divisions of labor lost force by the turn of the century, and did not carry over into early-twentieth-century ranch life. While the doctrine of separate spheres may have shaped the work of middle-class white women of the mid–nineteenth century, by the early twentieth century, ranch families demonstrated a looser definition of gendered work roles, in which women's role as reserve labor included all ranch chores except the male preserve of cowcamp.

Central to this transition was the ethic of group partnership articulated by ranch women. Ranch women drew recognition and social standing from the economic value of their household production, which comprised a large part of women's or "inside work." They also expressed pride in their willingness and ability to cross over into men's or "outside work" when necessary. But they did not see such crossovers as a vehicle for redefining gender identity. Quite the opposite: by placing crossover work under the umbrella of group partnership, ranch wives deflected its implicit challenge to gender ideology. Instead, ranch wives' identification with their accomplishments, both "inside" and "outside," emerged as expressions of service to family, a traditionally feminine behavior.

Cowcamp was the exception to this rule. Working with beef cattle was one form of outside work in a class by itself. Romanticization of the cowboy in early-twentieth-century American culture gave cowcamp cultural resonance as an expression of masculinity. Consequently, for women who crossed this boundary, work with beef cattle represented an overt challenge to gendered conventions. Thus, those few women who worked cowcamp during the early twentieth century either gave up their feminine social identity to become occupational men, or derived individualistic status as anomalous women in a man's world. The masculinity of cowcamp suggests both the power of western myth in westerners' lives and the deep connections between occupational identity and gender identity. Indeed, it is striking that ranch culture clung to at least one compelling symbol of gendered work roles from an earlier era. In this way, ranch families framed women's role change conservatively, blurring gendered boundaries in practice, while maintaining gendered worlds in their minds.

Generational differences account for at least part of this paradox. Daughters had more latitude in their work choices than did their mothers. While daughters were expected to learn women's work, their actual roles fit the demand for labor on the ranch, regardless of gender. The differences between mothers' and daughters' work on a ranch reflected different levels of family responsibility. One was either a wife in charge of whole areas of ranch sustenance, or a child in a helping role.

And daughters' role flexibility was not without future repercussions. By the mid-twentieth century, some second-generation ranch women translated their childhood versatility with men's work into adult roles different from their mothers'. Some of them made outside work their full-time job, rather than an incidental responsibility. Still, it was not until an interview conducted during the 1970s that Barbara Fox Davis identified the potential in crossover work for redefining woman's place. "I guess I have been an independent woman," she said. By that time, the concept of female independence had gained enough social currency to be openly acknowledged.

If early-twentieth-century ranch wives framed their changing work role in conservative terms, eschewing individualistic accomplishment for group partnership, and emphasizing the traditional feminine behavior of service to family, some single women homesteaders were not so constrained. To the single woman, homesteading opened opportunities both for family service and for individualistic ambition. Indeed, homesteading meant property ownership; and property ownership, in turn, signaled changes in a woman's economic and social standing. Those who wrote about their experience as single women homesteaders for popular audiences would freely explore the gendered implications of filing a claim.

CHAPTER SIX

Single Women Homesteaders and the Meanings of Independence: Places on the Map, Places in the Mind

Marie Jordan Bell grew up on a ranch at Chug Creek, Iron Mountain, Wyoming, during the early 1900s. Shortly before World War I, she filed a claim on land adjacent to her parents' ranch:

> I took out a section homestead when I was around sixteen. It wasn't too far from the house, up in the meadow by a tiny stream. Dad fixed up a little old house for me and I homesteaded. I lived there for three years, except for the time I was in school. That was how long it took to prove up.
>
> It wasn't much. I just had a bed and a little stove, and I think I had a mirror hanging in it and one little window. But I was sort of proud of it. I had a little garden up there.
>
> Dad kept that land. He paid me so much lease on it every year and I finally said, "Well I'm not going to use it, so why don't you just take it." He wouldn't do that, but he said, "I'll give you a thousand dollars for it."
>
> With that thousand dollars I fixed up part of our house after I was married.[1]

Marie Bell's account of her land claim expressed the three motivations most common to single women homesteaders in early-twentieth-century southern Wyoming. First, she noted that her father leased her claim, and eventually bought it from her. Like Bell, many single women filed claims to enlarge their family's property. Second, she netted a thousand dollars from the experience, and used it to improve her own home after getting married. Like Bell, some single women filed claims as investment properties, earning a profit from the sale of their claim. Finally, Marie Bell remarked on feeling "sort of proud" of her

---

Originally published as "Single Women Homesteaders and the Meanings of Independence: Places on the Map, Places in the Mind" in *Frontiers: A Journal of Women's Studies*, 15, no. 3 (1995). Copyright © 1995, Frontiers Editorial Collective.

homestead claim. And like Bell, some single women drew satisfaction from the economic and social status associated with land ownership.

Romanticized as intrepid pioneers, and spotlighted as models of female liberation, single women homesteaders deserve a careful second look. Their story in Wyoming reveals the variety of meanings which property ownership and independence held for women.[2] What makes this story particularly intriguing are the seams between homesteading as concrete reality and homesteading as a literary metaphor for gender role change. Robert Hine wrote that the American West has been "part economic and social fact, part myth."[3] Homesteading fell into that compelling region where the mythic West—an opportunity for reinvention of the self—was grounded in actuality.[4] The availability of public lands offered the very real prospect of land ownership to any U.S. citizen able and willing to earn title. Land ownership in the West, in turn, embodied mythic qualities of renewal, the chance to redefine one's identity and one's place in society. This reinvention of self had significant resonance for women during the early twentieth century, as Victorian mores gave way to modernity. That is, western women wrote about homesteading for readers nationwide, in ways that spoke to the challenges of New Womanhood. Indeed, the story of single women homesteaders in the early twentieth century reveals gendered facets of the West as both a place on the map, and a place in the mind.

To unravel the weave of economic reality and social meaning that was homesteading, one must comb both the records of single women homesteaders and the symbolic expression of this phenomena that surfaced in popular literature. During the second two decades of the twentieth century, a woman's homesteading genre emerged in mass-circulation magazines. These published stories spanned desert and plains across several states, yet shared a remarkable consistency of theme. They celebrated female independence, and they presented homesteading as a vehicle for transforming gender identity.

Yet the unpublished record from Wyoming during the same period gave women homesteaders a more complex face. Records of land transfer and personal narratives from Sweetwater and neighboring counties during the first three decades of the twentieth century provided a cross-section of actual experience, which clarified the meanings of homesteading for women, meanings that sometimes contrast with its uses as a literary metaphor. Homesteading was like a fault line in the terrain of opportunity for single women—the drift of one side toward group cooperation and service to family; the other, toward individual ambition and economic independence.

Legally, "filing a claim" meant applying to the Department of the Interior for ownership of a 160-, 320-, or 640-acre section of public lands. "Proving up" meant earning title to one's section by meeting the federal requirements for distribution of those lands. Depending upon the law under which one filed a claim, such requirements included residency and improvements like irrigation, silvaculture, or construction of a permanent dwelling.[5] Homesteading, then, meant acquiring legal title to property formerly owned by the federal government.

Contemporaries also used the term "homesteading" to mean ranching. Ranching in early-twentieth-century Sweetwater County typically combined commercial agriculture with a subsistence family economy. Ranchers raised sheep, cattle, or a cash crop for market, while home production of food and clothing supplanted income from livestock or crops.[6] But not all homesteaders were ranchers. That is, some earned title to public lands, but made their living in nonagricultural occupations. Such distinctions are essential in unraveling the meanings of homesteading for women. As the unpublished record will show, one must distinguish between individual autonomy and a subsistence family economy; between claiming land and ranching for a living.

If homesteading had two meanings, "independence" implied at least four different conditions. First, to ranch families, independence meant economic viability as a family unit through acquisition of enough land to raise livestock and feed a household. Second, for unmarried women on family ranches, independence could also mean decision-making power within a group enterprise. Widows and daughters who inherited management of a family ranch exercised such leadership. Third, for single women not engaged in a family agricultural venture, the independence associated with homesteading meant economic self-support. Such women made a living on their own, often in nonagricultural occupations. And fourth, to women who wrote about homesteading for a literary audience, independence meant the expression of individualistic, egalitarian values.

One settler in particular came to embody these values. She was Elinore Pruitt Stewart, author of *Letters of a Woman Homesteader*. Stewart ranched in Burnt Fork, Wyoming, a rural hamlet in the southwest corner of Sweetwater County, from 1909 until her death in 1933. Stewart's *Letters* and three sequels were serialized in the *Atlantic* magazine in 1913–14, 1915, 1919, and 1923. During the late 1970s, these stories were rediscovered and reprinted in book form.[7] *Letters* described Stewart's experience as a widowed washerwoman convinced that land ownership was the key to upward mobility and self-reliance. Any woman who worked hard at homesteading, Stewart declared, could achieve "independence . . . and a home of her own in the end."[8] The *Letters* open in 1909, shortly after Stewart has quit a low-paying job as a laundress in Denver in order to file on land in Wyoming. The *Letters* close in 1913 with an entry subtitled "Success," in

1. High plains desert near Green River, Wyoming. "A miserable lonesome country here," where soils resisted cultivation, forage for livestock grew sparse, and irrigation required corporate organization.

(*Opposite top*) 2. Union Pacific Company Store. Paying miners in company scrip forced them to buy at the company store, one way the Union Pacific tried to consolidate influence in Sweetwater County.

(*Opposite bottom*) 3. Eggs-Spinner-Gaensslen clan, gathered to celebrate Louise Spinner's marriage to George Graf. In the extended kinship network of Spinners, Eggs, and Gaensslens, family ties were business ties.

(*Above*) 4. Eleanor Eggs. Backed by her parents' capital, Eleanor Eggs opened a millinery business in Green River.

5. Mine Safety wagon in Superior. "It was a dangerous day today . . . in the mines."

6. Mr. and Mrs. Felix Taucher. Slovenian immigrant Mary Jesersek Taucher met her spouse with the help of employers and boarding house keepers.

(*Opposite*) 7. Annie and Norris Austin, 1908. Rural couples were often separated for months at a time while husbands searched for wage work between harvests.

(*Above*) 8. Stewart homestead. The wing extending to the far left lay on Elinore Stewart's claim; the remainder of the house lay on husband Clyde Stewart's claim.

9. Margaretta Kemp, secretary to the clerk of court in Rock Springs, 1921.

10. Female clerks in Rock Springs Commercial Store, 1912. Second-generation immigrant women with American educations moved into downtown jobs. From left to right, Signe Carlson, clerk; Mary Guy, bookkeeper; and Mary Subic, clerk.

which Stewart claimed: "This year I set out to prove that a woman could ranch if she wanted to. . . . Many of my neighbors did better than I did, . . . but *I did it* [emphasis mine]. I have tried every kind of work this ranch affords, and I can do any of it."[9] In short, *Letters* celebrated the newfound autonomy of the single woman homesteader.

Historians' treatments of Elinore Stewart have been a bellwether of changing perceptions about single women homesteaders. Citing the *Letters*, scholars initially presented single women homesteaders as exemplars of female independence, proof that the frontier experience liberalized women's roles.[10] They read Stewart uncritically, accepting her *Letters* as the accurate account of a woman who homesteaded on her own. This is understandable, given that Stewart's *Letters* had been published as autobiography, beginning with their appearance in *Atlantic Monthly* in 1913.[11] Publication of the *Letters* in book form reinforced the impression that Stewart's narratives could be taken as fact. For example, the 1982 edition of *Letters* included cover copy that read, "Here are presented the . . . true-to-life letters of a woman who took up homesteading." The 1988 edition included a foreword in which Wyoming essayist Gretel Erlich confirmed that, "during the four years spanned by these letters, Elinore Stewart . . . proved up on her own homestead."[12] Such comments added verity to Stewart's presentation of herself as a model of female independence. But there is more to the story. Recent research suggests the primacy of group effort rather than individual independence in accounting for the successes of single woman homesteaders. In a study of mid-nineteenth through early-twentieth-century frontierswomen, Susan Hallgarth observed that "the spirit of cooperation explains the particular meaning independence held for them [single women homesteaders]. For the clever people who built their house covering the corners of each piece of land, or those who joined forces to share expertise, cooperation meant protection and encouragement as well as shared labor."[13] Indeed, the theme of group cooperation guides the most recent interpretation of Elinore Stewart's homesteading experience.

Historian Sherry Smith researched Stewart's life in Wyoming and compared her findings with Stewart's version of homesteading in *Letters*. Smith found discrepancies between Stewart's vision of herself as an independent homesteader and the reality of her life in Burnt Fork. For example, in 1909, while working as a housekeeper on Clyde Stewart's ranch, Elinore Rupert did, in fact, file a 147-acre claim adjoining the Stewart ranch. But one week later she married Clyde Stewart and was no longer a "single woman homesteader." Rather, she was ranching in partnership with her husband, having filed an adjacent claim to enlarge the family holdings. In 1912 Elinore Stewart relinquished her claim to

Ruth C. Stewart, Clyde's widowed mother, because land law forbade a married couple from sharing a residence while homesteading adjacent properties. Ruth Stewart proved up on the claim, then sold it back to Elinore and Clyde. In short, though Elinore Stewart presented herself in the *Letters* as a successful single woman homesteader, in actuality her claim represented a cooperative effort between family members to accumulate enough land to support a ranch. Elinore Stewart filed the claim adjacent to Clyde's and cultivated a large vegetable garden on it; Clyde Stewart provided the livestock, implements, housing, and some of the capital and manpower to make the necessary improvements; and Ruth Stewart ensured that the claim would remain legally within the family's control.[14] Thus Smith found in Elinore Stewart's life a model of group cooperation and interdependence, rather than individual independence. For Elinore Stewart, in actuality, the "independence" associated with homesteading meant self-employment within a subsistence family economy, rather than work as a domestic in the households of others. For the Stewart family, independence meant acquiring control of enough acreage to support a household. In either case, it did not mean individual self-sufficiency.

Smith's and Hallgarth's studies underscore the point that ranching required both the work and the legal existence of several cooperating members. It was not a lone woman's occupation. How, then, do we reconcile the evidence of group cooperation with the published stories of individual independence?

Again, research on Elinore Stewart points the way. Both Smith and Stewart's biographer, Suzanne George, observed that Elinore Stewart used homesteading as a literary vehicle to address larger cultural issues of her day. Stewart drew upon epistolary tradition to structure her narratives, creating fiction that linked the promise of land ownership with traditional ideals of individualism, and extended these possibilities to women.[15] Ultimately, Smith's and George's analyses demonstrate that Stewart added a significant female voice to western literature, and a significant western voice to contemporary gender role definition.

Indeed, what we now know about Elinore Stewart's literary and homesteading careers can be magnified and elaborated on the wider screen of Wyoming records and contemporary popular literature. The evidence from Sweetwater and neighboring counties indicates that both the liberation and cooperation theses hold merit. First, the record shows that numerous single women, like Marie Bell and Elinore Stewart, filed claims to enlarge a family ranch. In these cases, filing a claim reflected the ethic of group cooperation, which bound women to a family enterprise. Second, Wyoming homesteading records also include single women who filed claims nowhere near family holdings, and who supported their claims with income from nonagricultural occupations. For these women, it was *sale of the claim* that earned them economic independence. In this respect, homesteading presented a unique opportunity for single women, since investment in land could yield more cash than most occupations open to women at that time. But the place where homesteading most dramatically proved liberating for women was in the pages of popular magazines. During the second two decades of the twentieth century, a female homesteading genre swept popular literature, which spoke metaphorically to the challenges of New Womanhood. Elinore Stewart, it turns out, was only one among many who were part of this literary phenomenon.

Officially, the Homestead Act allowed one claim per family head.[16] On the arid plains of Wyoming, however, one claim was "hopeless" to support a ranch.[17] It took substantial acreage to pasture a herd, as well as grow winter hay for stock feed and crops to feed a family.[18] Consequently, families worked around homestead law by having qualified members file adjacent claims, in order to accumulate sufficient land. Records of property transfer from Sweetwater and Sublette Counties consistently reveal this pattern. Property histories from the upper Green River Valley,[19] for example, contain numerous entries like the following:

The Wilhelm Place, North Piney:
> Wilhelm came here in 1900 and took up land on Horse Creek. He also obtained rights to adjoining land on Green River through his wife's filing, later his second wife and a daughter filed.[20]

Similarly, the entry for "Walter Ball's Ranch" reads,
> Lot Haley and his sister-in-law Margaret Cunnington took up land here in 1900. Frank Nickolson took land here in 1907. He married Margaret Cunnington.[21]

And the entry for "The Sommers Place (Horse Creek)" reports that,
> In 1908, J. E. McAlister, May McAlister [brother and sister], . . . Pearl V. Sommers and A. P. Sommers [brother and sister] filed [adjacent claims] on land here. In 1911, May McAlister and A. P. Sommers were married, and together purchased the other places and built up a fine ranch.[22]

In each of these cases, a single woman filed on land adjoining the claim of her fiancé, parent, or brother, thus combining forces to accumulate property. As long as a woman was unmarried at the time that she filed a claim, she could continue to prove up on it, even if she married after filing the claim.[23] And so sisters and brothers, daughters and parents, fiancés and their future spouses often filed adjoining claims to create a sizable holding.

Wyoming homesteaders' narratives reinforce the pattern suggested by property records. Fern Dumbrill Spencer homesteaded with her parents in Thornton, Wyoming, sometime between 1910 and 1920. In her memoir of ranch life,

Spencer described how her older sister Olive "took up a homestead, too, so that father would have more land to work with."[24] Similarly, in a memoir of early-twentieth-century settlement near Worland, Wyoming, Peggy Kirkbride reported that her ancestors, "Sarah, Mabel, and Mary Kirkbride, daughters of Mr. and Mrs. Alex D. Kirkbride, claimed homestead land adjacent to the family holdings."[25] Marie Bell's narrative, cited at the beginning of this chapter, told the same story. In short, single women often filed claims within a family context, working with relatives to accrue needed range, so vital on the arid plains. In this context, single women homesteaders demonstrated cooperation, not individualism; they filed claims to support a family enterprise rather than to establish solo property ownership. By prioritizing their claim as a contribution to the family ranch, these women echoed the ethic of group partnership that ranch wives had so clearly articulated.

Evidence regarding agricultural work and expenses further indicates that single women homesteaders rarely ranched on their own. Not only were several claims needed to make a ranch successful, but the work and the costs of ranching were too much for any single person. Despite the term "free land," homesteading was neither cheap nor easy. Homesteading costs in the late nineteenth and early twentieth century began with a filing fee of anywhere from $15.50 to $25. Next came a surveyor's fee to locate the claim and mark its boundaries, anywhere from $30 to $100, depending upon the size and location of the claim. On some claims, one had to purchase water rights. These, plus the appropriate maps and notary fee could amount to an additional $22. Under the Carey Act, settlers homesteading land within a large-scale irrigation project paid the state of Wyoming 50 cents per acre, and the irrigation developers $20 or more per acre for water rights. A 160-acre claim under these conditions would cost $3,280. Finally, buying title to land in lieu of proving up cost $1.25 per acre under the Homestead Act, and $1 per acre under the Desert Land Act. For 160-acre or 640-acre claims, the cost of buying title reached $200 or $640, respectively.[26]

Then there were travel expenses; food, farm, and building supplies; and livestock. Sylvia Eppler came to Laramie County in 1914 with her parents to homestead. Her parents' preparations included renting an entire railroad car ("immigrant car") so that they could bring enough livestock and supplies to last until their first harvest: "Mr. Eppler [Sylvia's father] came in the immigrant car bringing four horses, two cars, and some chickens. Also in the car were barrels of cured meat, canned fruit and vegetables. Mrs. Eppler and the children came by passenger train."[27] Though single homesteaders may not have needed four horses, or an "immigrant car," they would have at least needed food to last until the first harvest, and perhaps passenger train fare.

"Improving" a claim was costly as well. Building a cabin, cutting and sinking fenceposts, stringing barbed wire, digging a well, plowing fields, and developing an irrigation system required additional supplies, and often, hired help. Clyde Stewart, for example, spent $500 on improvements while homesteading his claim in Burnt Fork.[28] In short, homesteading was difficult to do alone, both physically and financially. As one would-be single woman homesteader concluded in 1918, "Practically, you must have considerable capital, both of time and money, to prove up on a homestead claim."[29]

Despite the expenses and work, a few single women homesteaders did make their living by ranching. As a rule, however, these were women who took over the family ranch when their parent or spouse died. A handful of unmarried daughters and widowed women appeared in the 1880, 1900, and 1910 Sweetwater County census manuscripts as "stockgrowers" and family heads. Their households invariably included male family members whose occupation read "ranchhand."[30] In other words, these women—though single and homesteading—did not ranch alone. Like Margaret Cunnington, May McAlister, and Olive Dumbrill, they operated a joint venture with close relatives.

The Barrett Sheep Company provides a good example of single and widowed women homesteaders who ran the family ranch. Mary Armsbury, born in Ireland in 1840, married Patrick Barrett sometime between 1858 and 1864. During the early 1860s, the Barretts emigrated from Ireland to Canada, and then to Buffalo, New York. Here, Mary Barrett's first daughter and namesake, Mary, was born, sometime between 1863 and 1865. In 1867 the Barretts moved to Green River City, Wyoming, where Patrick set up a general store, supplying emigrants on their way to Salt Lake City and Oregon, and miners on their way to South Pass City. With the coming of the Union Pacific Railroad to Green River City in 1869, Patrick Barrett's business thrived.[31]

By 1880 the Barrett family had grown. In addition to Patrick, Mary Sr., and Mary Jr. (then age thirteen), the household now included three brothers and two sisters.[32] Sometime during the 1890s, the Barretts filed a homestead claim near Green River City and began raising sheep. Barrett sheep herds ranged along the Green River drainage, south to the Browns Park country of northern Colorado. Shortly before 1900, Patrick Barrett died. In 1900 the Sweetwater County census reported Mary Barrett, age sixty, widowed, as a "stockgrower." Her daughter Mary, age thirty-three, and son Edward, age twenty-five, also were listed as stockgrowers. The youngest daughter, Hattie, age twenty-three, also lived at home. The other children had moved away.[33]

The census enumerator in 1900 listed Mary Barrett Sr. as head of the household. This is significant because female parents in households with adult children were not automatically listed as household heads. More typically, an adult son would be listed as the household head and his widowed mother as a dependent.[34] But in this case, the census enumerator listed the widow Mary Barrett as "head," despite the presence of an adult son, twenty-five years old, in her household. From this, we can infer that Mary Barrett Sr. acted as head of the family and ran the ranch. Here, then, was a widowed woman homesteader, who managed the family sheep ranch with the help of two adult daughters and one adult son.

By 1916 Mary Barrett Sr. had passed away, leaving the sheep business to her children. Mary Barrett Jr., now age forty-nine, had remained single and taken over the management of the ranch. An article noting her success as a wool grower appeared in the *Rock Springs Miner* on July 15, 1916: "There are few women in the state of Wyoming who are as successful as Miss Mary Barrett, who conducts the affairs of the Barrett Sheep Company. Miss Barrett has been identified with the livestock industry of . . . Sweetwater County for a number of years, and each passing year is marked with further success."[35] Mary now worked the ranch with her brothers James and Patrick, while siblings Edward and Hattie had married and moved away. According to the *Miner*, the Barrett Sheep Company prospered under Mary's direction: "Shearing of her flocks was completed at Fossil last week, and 60,000 pounds of fleece was marketed at top price, understood to have been considerably over thirty cents a pound. Miss Barrett makes her headquarters in Green River, but travels over both Sweetwater and Lincoln counties, personally supervising everything in connection with her constantly increasing business."[36] Mary Barrett ran the family sheep ranch until 1928, when she fell ill with "pernicious anemia." After hospitalization in Salt Lake City and two years of failing health, she died in 1930. The *Green River Star* observed Mary Barrett's death with an article about her career as a wool grower. She was praised for her business successes, described as a "highly respected citizen of Green River," and noted as "one of the early pioneers."[37]

Mary Barrett Jr. typified single women who made their living by ranching. Her parents began the ranch by filing the original homestead claim when Mary was a young girl. By the time she had reached her twenties, her parents had established a sheep herd. By the time Mary's father died, she, her brothers, and her mother were experienced "stockgrowers." By the time her mother died, Mary had the expertise and the inclination to take over ranch management. With the help of two brothers, she spent most of her adult life running the Barrett Sheep Company. A single woman homesteader, Mary Barrett Jr. drew on family labor, property, and assets to grow and sell wool. Thus, unmarried women stockgrowers did not ranch "on their own." Rather, like the elder and younger Mary Barretts, they managed a family business.[38]

While successful ranching required a group effort, homesteading as a real estate investment could be done alone. Records of property transfer from Sweetwater and Sublette Counties indicate that single women homesteaders sometimes developed land claims as investments. The history of the "Fish Creek Place" in the upper Green River Valley was telling: "This small tributary of the South Piney was homesteaded . . . in 1907, and Alice Sellon had a desert claim. Charles Budd bought [this] place. . . . The Frank Mann place at the head of Fish Creek was taken up by Hattie Sellon and Jennie Budd, who then sold the land to Frank Mann."[39] Alice Sellon, Hattie Sellon, and Jennie Budd all took advantage of homestead law to invest in land for resale. In the same ranching valley, Nellie Yates filed a claim on the Green River near Daniel, Wyoming, in 1908, then sold it to Mr. and Mrs. A. P. Sommers in 1911.[40] North of Daniel, Stella McKay filed a claim along South Cottonwood Creek in 1916, then sold it to Jigg Ball in 1923.[41] Narratives of homesteading in neighboring counties echoed this pattern. Peggy Kirkbride's description of settlement near Hillsdale, Wyoming, included three single women, Minnie Hidy, Bessie Fox, and Blanche Lyons, all of whom filed claims, proved up, and then "sold to local stockmen."[42] Similarly, Helen Coburn, a single homesteader, filed a claim in Washakie County in 1905, proved up, and sold it at auction in 1908.[43]

While proving up, investment homesteaders supported their claim with income-earning work off the claim. Homesteaders Helen Coburn and Mary Culbertson supported their claims near Worland, Wyoming, from 1905 to 1908 by nursing and teaching.[44] Others financed their claims with jobs as stenographers, bank clerks, and horse trainers.[45] For these women, property investments enhanced their economic independence, since income from real estate often matched or exceeded the average wage available to women. In Wyoming, for example, between 1893 and 1917, the most common occupation for single women homesteaders, schoolteaching, earned an average of $51 per month. This salary, for a term varying from three to nine months, yielded from $153 to $459 per year.[46] Between 1900 and 1920, sale price of a quarter-section claim with title varied from $300 to $500, while the sale price for a whole-section claim with title went as high as $1,000.[47]

Strictly speaking, sale of one's claim did not always generate a profit, if all expenses and labor during the three- to five-year residency period were figured in. Nonetheless, land sale did generate cash income that would have been impossible to earn by wage work alone. Indeed, because most investment homesteaders supported themselves with wage work, proceeds from the sale of their claim could be set aside as savings. For entrepreneurial homesteaders like the Sellon sisters, Jennie Budd, Stella McKay, and Nellie Yates, proceeds from the sale of their claim yielded a tidy nest egg.

Property sale, then, could increase the economic independence of single women who developed claims as investments. In this way, homesteading did contribute to the liberalization of women's roles, in that it provided an opportunity for capital accumulation unequaled in other occupations available to women on rural frontiers. Neither lone ranchers nor cooperative members of a family ranch, the entrepreneurial homesteaders were, quite simply, real estate speculators. For these women, property became an individualistic asset, a means of advancing their personal fortunes.

Links between homesteading and the liberalization of women's roles appeared most vividly, however, in the pages of popular magazines. The publication of Elinore Stewart's "Letters" in the *Atlantic*, in 1913 and 1914, suggests that women homesteaders had an enthusiastic literary audience.[48] In 1915 the *Atlantic* serialized Stewart's sequel, "Letters on an Elk Hunt, by a Woman Homesteader." In May 1919 the *Atlantic* followed with "Return of the Woman Homesteader," and in 1923, with "Snow: An Adventure of the Woman Homesteader."[49]

But Elinore Stewart was not the only one supplying homesteading stories to an eager public. Neither was she the only writer to present homesteading as an answer for single women wanting to improve their lot. Between 1913 and 1928, magazines such as the *Atlantic, Sunset, Collier's, Overland Monthly,* and *Outlook* published over thirty articles by women about homesteading.[50] Historian Stanford Layton attributes the popularity of this theme to a "back-to-the-land" movement that signified nostalgia for the closing frontier and implied criticisms of urban industrial society.[51] But Smith's characterization of Stewart as a voice for female enterprise is equally apt, for the popularity of homesteading stories by women *also* spoke to early-twentieth-century gender role change.[52]

The woman homesteading genre appeared in popular literature at a time when women's roles, at least within the culture of white America, were in transition. By the second decade of the twentieth century, the separate spheres of Victorian society had blurred, and conventional wisdom urged women toward developing personal autonomy in a heterosocial world. With more women entering the workforce outside the home, more women entering higher education, and the professionalization of social work and nursing, urban women increasingly worked in proximity with men. At the same time, the commercialization of leisure, decreases in family size, and the emergence of a separate youth culture encouraged women toward a more youthful, adventurous ideal, and offered a variety of escapes from domesticity. Gradually, as Freudian psychology was popularized, concepts of "individual fulfillment" replaced collective social reform as yardsticks of female progress. And, as women's demand for civil equality intensified, individual achievement in a male-identified, heterosocial world became the new model for female advance. In short, the brash, kinetic flapper replaced the Victorian matron as a symbol of womanhood.[53]

In this context, homesteading became a compelling metaphor for female transformation. The woman homesteader of popular literature tested herself against traditional assumptions about her gender and discovered new strengths. Literary homesteaders presented their experience as a vehicle for developing emotional self-reliance, economic autonomy, and political clout. They also defined their successes in terms of solo achievement. In these ways, homesteading writers spoke thematically to the challenges of female role change, as New Women increasingly defined themselves in individualistic, egalitarian terms.

In 1913, for example, the *Independent* featured "The Lady Honyocker," by Mabel Lewis Stuart. Stuart was a single woman "honyocker," a slang term for beginning homesteader derived from a Russian word that meant "one who is new at his business." Stuart used the term proudly, and described the benefits of homesteading on the Dakota plains: "Girls who come out to the claim broken down in health find they can do things which before they would have thought impossible."[54] Stuart then listed feats of physical prowess and emotional stamina: single women homesteaders chopped wood, killed snakes, lived alone fearlessly, successfully raised crops, and initiated social service work in their communities.[55] Single women homesteaders were, according to Stuart, heroic examples of female self-reliance: "The independence and freedom, together with the added responsibility of managing one's own affairs, are irresistibly and healthfully enthralling. . . . [Her] courage and sprightly independence are winning for the pioneer girl the applause of the truest modern chivalry."[56] For Stuart, the physical frontier served as a metaphorical frontier, where women achieved autonomy and competence, valued qualities in the brave new world of modern gender roles.

An article in *Collier's* the same year echoed Stuart's enthusiasm for homesteading as a proving ground for single women. Joanna Gleed Strange reported on single woman homesteaders in her investigation of "The Last Homesteads" on the Rosebud and Pine Ridge Indian Reservations in South Dakota. In 1912, three thousand sections were opened to white farmers on reservation lands. Homesteaders flooded the region, among them, "any number of young women [who] are living alone on their claims during the time necessary to prove up."[57] To illustrate the aptitudes of single woman homesteaders, Strange quoted one "girl from Omaha" who had successfully developed a claim for three years: "'Like it?' repeated the girl from Omaha. . . . 'Like it?' Why nothing could make me go back. . . . I love it. I have my little shack fixed up with my own things, and last year I raised twelve different kinds of vegetables and the best hay in the country."[58] Like Elinore Stewart, the "girl from Omaha" described her year's harvest as proof of her competence, while her enthusiasm implied the benefits of a vocation that allowed both self-employment and self-support. It is not too far a leap from the rural economic independence of "the girl from Omaha" to the individualistic self-definition of the New Woman.

The theme of single women proving themselves capable in unorthodox ways was repeated in an article by Metta Loomis, "From a Schoolroom to a Montana Ranch," in *Overland Monthly* in 1916. Loomis, who left a teaching job in Iowa to homestead in Montana, began her story by noting, "It is an undertaking for a man to cut loose from the anchorage of a comfortable salary and stake his future on a homestead, but for a woman to venture such an undertaking requires more than ordinary fortitude."[59] Loomis implied that for a woman to venture homesteading was to exceed the expected limits of her gender. And the willingness to take risks in occupational choice and behavior was a theme that probably spoke to the fears and aspirations of many a New Woman who worked outside the home, or demanded better conditions on the job.

Like Elinore Stewart, Mabel Stuart, and "the girl from Omaha," Loomis also touted the advantages of homesteading for single women. She cited improved health and the rewards of property ownership and economic productivity:

> I know of no other way by which in five years time I could have acquired such riotous health, [and] secured much valuable property. . . .
>
> . . . I proved up on May 22, 1915. . . . I own my farm which I value at $30 an acre. . . . I have 170 acres planted in to wheat, twenty acres to oats, [and] eight acres to alfalfa. . . . The prospect is that we will have record crops. I have four fine brood mares, a riding pony, a two-year-old colt, three one-year-old colts, . . . [and] a cow and a calf, besides some fifty chickens. I have a fine barn, a chicken coop, and a root cellar. I also have a wagon, a carriage, harness, and farm implements.[60]

Loomis's detailed description of her property values and assets conveyed both the knowledge and the pride of a successful businessperson. Prosperity and economic independence were clearly hers. Self-definition in terms of business acumen and individual material accumulation echoed classic American male success stories; and without apology, Loomis appropriated these prerogatives for her gender. Doubtless, her story of economic independence appealed to New Woman readers who struggled to make ends meet on a salesclerk, stenographer, or cashier's paycheck. For Loomis, the intangible benefits of property ownership and economic autonomy were "joy in living, . . . hope and buoyancy."[61]

Similarly, Gladys Belvie Whitaker celebrated the inner strength she developed as a result of homesteading. In 1920 *Overland Monthly* published Whitaker's account of her first year on a 280-acre claim in Kern, California. Like the other literary homesteaders, Whitaker dwelt on the satisfactions of property ownership: "As I climbed down [from nailing shingles on her cabin roof], the sense of possession came strongly—that sense of ownership which is so much a part of us. It was all mine—I owned a house and land."[62] But material possession was not the only benefit for Whitaker. She expressed a new sense of self-possession, gained from weathering hardship and solitude. In the following passage, Whitaker described how serenity gradually replaced loneliness and fear on her isolated homestead:

At times the loneliness of the plains became unbearable, and even encroached upon my sleep. Then I would wake suddenly, sob hysterically, and fall asleep again.

. . . Time passed . . . [and some time later], riding to the ranch house through the soft blackness [of evening], I watched the stars gather brightness. To the creaking of the saddle leather and jingle of the bridle chain, I sang. . . . Perhaps I felt then, more strongly than ever before, that goals cannot be achieved without great struggle, and that reward is as warming and softening as the end of a day in "Lonesome Land."[63]

Whitaker thus highlighted the theme of self-reliance, discovering within herself the ability to appreciate solitude. Homesteading taught Whitaker emotional as well as economic independence. Metaphorically, this, too, was part of the prescription for New Womanhood, as single women moved beyond the boundaries of family supervision.

As well as economic independence and emotional self-reliance, the literary homesteaders mined their experience for access to political equality. In 1921 *Sunset* ran an article by Kate Heizer, "Via the Homesteading Route," which articulated connections between property ownership, self-reliance, and improved political status. Heizer filed on land in the Uinta Basin of Utah, just over the Wyoming border. There she developed a successful farm. Like Stewart, Stuart, "the girl from Omaha," Loomis, and Whitaker, Heizer alluded to the satisfactions of mastering a new vocation: "There are many experiments to be made in testing the productive qualities of new land. Different methods of cultivation are eagerly discussed. . . . I have ninety acres in alfalfa now and I am studying agriculture."[64] But Heizer added: "There is something that comes to a settler on land more gratifying than the satisfaction of slowly and surely acquiring a competency. This something—I speak from personal knowledge—is the realization of being an important factor in the community, one whose voice has weight, a person to be consulted about matters of public interest."[65] For Heizer, it was homesteading that improved her political status. Moreover, her newfound public stature was not dependent on Victorian public identities like that of wife, mother, teacher, or social worker. Rather, her public stature derived from nontraditional sources for women: independent property ownership, vocational competence outside the domestic realm, and economic self-support. For the New Woman reader, the idea of being a person in the community whose "voice ha[d] weight" very likely echoed recent demands for civil equality through the suffrage and the Equal Rights Amendment. In this way, too, literary homesteaders spoke to the direction of gender role change.

We have seen that the literary homesteaders attributed a variety of rewards to staking a claim—challenge, renewal, accomplishment, political sway. But, overwhelmingly, the genre emphasized emotional and economic independence through risk-taking in an unfamiliar world. In stories like those of Stewart, Stuart, "the girl from Omaha," Loomis, Whitaker, and Heizer, "proving up" on a homestead became a metaphor for proving that a woman could function competently outside traditional limits ascribed to her gender. For a New Woman, such limits might have included family authority, domesticity, or economic dependence—all of which the literary homesteader cast aside.

Indeed, these stories read like initiation myths, in which the protagonist faces a challenge, meets it successfully, and thus earns a new place in the community. As in initiation myth, the literary homesteaders pushed their own limits, and thus emerged with a broader sense of their own capabilities. Over and over, the phrases "I did it. . . ," "I produced. . . ," "I own . . ." punctuate these narratives. In this respect, the literary homesteaders supplied readers with a female version of individualism. Their milieu was the frontier, traditionally viewed as a male domain. In short, the single woman homesteader of popular literature functioned as a metaphor for the New Woman making it in a man's world. Given the changes in women's roles during the first three decades of the twentieth century, the themes of risking unfamiliar conditions, developing economic independence, and learning emotional self-reliance surely spoke to a generation of women readers who went forth without the security of separate spheres.

The unpublished Wyoming record, then, indicates that homesteading was like a fault line in the terrain of opportunity for single women, marking two very different kinds of enterprise. Numerous single women filed claims to enlarge a family ranch. These homesteaders echoed the ethic of group partnership articulated by ranch wives. At the same time, some single women filed claims as investment properties. Most of these women supported themselves in nonagricultural occupations, then sold the claim for profit as soon as they proved up.

The investment homesteaders, taken together with the literary homesteaders, suggest the varieties of female independence. While the literary homesteaders rooted self-reliance in the experience of developing a claim, the investment homesteaders saw economic independence in the sale of their claim. For them, ranch property was not an end in itself, but rather, a means of capital accumulation. They homesteaded as a form of real estate speculation, not ranching. Theirs was an entrepreneurial rather than agrarian independence.

For those homesteaders who did file with intent to ranch, the theme of female independence takes yet another meaning. While the literary homesteaders emphasized solo achievement, the ranching homesteaders succeeded only within a group. Ranch members were interdependent, relying on each other as a community of labor and resources. If these women exercised independence, it meant decision-making power within a group enterprise. Ranch managers like Mary Barrett demonstrated such leadership. But authority within the group should not be confused with self-sufficiency or solo achievement—fictional themes popularized by the literary homesteaders.

Finally, the literary homesteaders' use of "proving up" as metaphor for proving female competence beyond domesticity linked the western phenomena of homesteading with the nationwide trend toward gender equality in early-twentieth-century American culture. At times, historians present the American West as a world apart from life in the rest of the nation. Some make this artificial separation in order to limit research to a manageable scope. And certainly there are compelling arguments for the uniqueness of the American West as a geographic, ecological, and cultural entity. But we cannot lose sight of the connections between concrete experience in the West and cultural expression nationwide.

Homesteading in the early twentieth century functioned as an economic opportunity in the West alone, but as social metaphor nationwide. As urban women increasingly asserted their rights to higher education, paid labor, and political voice, rural women in the West capitalized on opportunities for land ownership, and literary homesteaders bridged the two with popular tales of female empowerment. The published stories of single women homesteaders created a western version of New Womanhood, with images of independent women who succeeded in the heterosocial world. This theme spoke to women throughout the country, at a time when many sought to redefine their role in increasingly individualistic, egalitarian terms. The case of single women homesteaders thus adds gendered dimension to the symbolic West in the American mind.

If rural Wyoming offered symbolic as well as economic possibilities through homesteading, urban Sweetwater County held no such romance. Mining towns wheeled on the fluctuating coal market; women's work patterns there reflected cycles of industrial expansion and recession. How women carved a place for themselves in such towns forms a complex story of class, ethnicity, regional economy, and changing social mores.

CHAPTER SEVEN

From *Klenickso* to Main Street: Town Women's Work

The summer of 1880 found Alice Paterson, a twenty-one-year-old English immigrant, working as live-in servant for the Oliver Smith family of Rock Springs. Smith was a prosperous, middle-aged merchant from Massachusetts; he and his wife had one daughter. Alice Paterson had traveled with her parents from England to Wyoming in 1874. Since then, her parents had moved to lower elevations in Boone, Iowa, for her mother's health. Alice had elected to stay in Rock Springs.

On summer mornings, Alice rose early, carried water to the "shanty" behind the house, and lit the cookstove there. She used the shanty for cooking and laundry, so that the main house remained cool as the day wore on. After serving breakfast to the Smiths, Alice began the day's work. In addition to preparing meals, on Mondays she baked bread for the coming week. Tuesday was washday; and Wednesday, she ironed the clean shirts, dresses, tablecloths, linens, and curtains. Thursday, she sewed and mended; and Friday, she swept and washed the floors, beat the carpets, changed the bedding, and dusted. On Saturdays, she worked outdoors in the kitchen garden. When Sunday came, Alice attended the Episcopal church and prepared meals for the Smith family as usual; what remained of the day was her own. For these housekeeping tasks, Alice earned room, board, and a small wage.[1]

Alice Paterson typified single women wage-earners in Sweetwater coal towns during the late nineteenth century. Like Alice, 72.7 percent of single women in the county worked as domestic servants in 1880.[2] In town, 61.5 percent of single female servants, like Alice, worked in private, middle-class homes.[3] In short, domestic service was the most common form of wage work for single women at this time.

Fifteen years later, married and then widowed, Alice Paterson Kierle owned and managed the Commercial Hotel in Rock Springs. She made sure that the hotel was regularly listed in the *Wyoming State Business Directory* and advertised in local newspapers as well.⁴ Under her direction, the Commercial earned a reputation as "the leading, and in fact only first-class hotel" in town. Alice Kierle ran the hotel until her retirement in 1916.⁵

Alice Paterson Kierle's progress from domestic servant in 1880 to hotel proprietor in 1905 foreshadowed a shift among wage-earning women in Sweetwater coal towns from home-based work to downtown jobs. At the same time, her career encompassed commercialized domesticity in two forms: housekeeping for private, nuclear families, and hosting lodgers. But if Alice Kierle was a representative woman in 1880, she had become an anomaly in the world of commercialized domesticity by 1905. Few women ran establishments on the scale of the Commercial Hotel, a downtown inn that drew honored guests like the Governor of Wyoming.⁶ Instead, most paid housekeepers after the turn of the century in Sweetwater County were working-class wives who kept boarders in their family household, and single, working-class women of the same nationality who helped them. Indeed, the demand for commercialized housekeeping increased during the first two decades of the twentieth century, as the expanding coal industry drew workers from Europe to southwest Wyoming. Hundreds of single men and married men whose wives had remained behind came to Sweetwater mining towns, needing rooms, meals, and laundry service.⁷ What, for men, was an extractive industry frontier, became, for women, a service industry frontier.

Nationwide, domestic servants declined in both numbers and status during the early twentieth century. In 1870, for example, 60 percent of all wage-earning women in the United States worked as domestic servants. By 1910, only 25 percent did so, and by 1920, the proportion had dropped to less than 16 percent.⁸ Domestic service became less and less desirable as new job opportunities for women emerged during the early twentieth century. The professionalization of social work, teaching, and nursing during the Progressive Era added prestige to these occupations, since licensing requirements established recognition of skill and training. New ranks of female office workers claimed a similar level of respect because their working conditions were clean and genteel, and their jobs required some education. Department store clerks developed pride in their position, for even though their wages often dipped below those of factory hands, they attached importance to their contact with the public, which required careful dress and cultivated manners. Factory hands, in turn, valued their respectability in comparison to waitresses, whose morals were thought questionable. Finally, both factory workers and waitresses were proud of their independence relative to domestic servants—who worked without specified hours, lived at the beck and call of their employers, accepted payment in-kind rather than in wages, and thus claimed little time or money of their own.⁹

Sweetwater County mirrored the national trend in women's work patterns, with important exceptions. As in the nation, the number of household servants declined over time. In 1880, 25.6 percent of all wage-earning women in Sweetwater railroad and coal towns worked as domestic servants. In 1900, the proportion had fallen to 17.6 percent; by 1910, it was only 11.1 percent.[10] Over time, then, fewer and fewer women in Sweetwater County took jobs in domestic service.

At first glance, this seems paradoxical. If commercialized housekeeping was on the rise in Sweetwater County, why did domestic service decline? The answer lies in the shifting demographics of Sweetwater railroad and coal towns. As the working-class population expanded and the middle-class population shrank, the locus of household service changed from private, middle-class homes to working-class homes that kept boarders. Indeed, the early-twentieth-century increase in commercialized domesticity was rooted in working-class households that kept lodgers, not in private, middle-class homes that hired servants. This change would have profound repercussions for employer-servant relations.

In Sweetwater coal towns, demographic change was dramatic after the turn of the century. The ethnic, working-class population rapidly expanded as coal production in Wyoming doubled between 1898 and 1910, then tripled by 1918.[11] Southern and Eastern Europeans flocked to southwest Wyoming coal towns in response to the demand for labor. In 1880, 47.8 percent of the Sweetwater County population came from Europe; this proportion rose to 58.6 percent in 1900, then to 62.7 percent in 1910.[12] After the turn of the century, the working-class population steadily increased, while the middle-class population gradually decreased, both numerically and proportionally. Working-class people comprised 40 percent of the railroad and coal town population in 1880; this proportion rose to 53.8 percent by 1910.[13]

The growth of the working-class population outpaced that of the middle class because Sweetwater coal towns remained essentially single-industry towns; business did not diversify to the extent that took place in large metropolitan centers elsewhere. Corporate trade, government bureaucracy, educational institutions, and social welfare agencies that expanded the white-collar classes in large cities did not proliferate in Sweetwater coal towns. And so the middle-class population, with its demand for servants in private homes, did not keep pace with working-class demand for lodging with families who kept boarders. In 1880 nearly two thirds of household servants in Sweetwater County, like Alice Paterson, had worked for private families in middle-class homes. By 1900, the situation was reversed: fully two thirds of household servants now worked for families in working-class homes who kept boarders.[14]

Croatian immigrant Elsie Oblock Frolic remembered her immigrant mother's description of her first job in Rock Springs. A single woman who spoke no English, Mrs. Oblock [maiden name unknown] found work and housing as a domestic servant with a Croatian family who kept boarders. According to Elsie Frolic: "My mother, she came here when she was about sixteen years old. . . . And coming here she started working out as a, at that time we used to call them a *klenickso*, which is equivalent to a girl working in a home where they had people boarding, and they used to do the washing and the cooking and things like this."[15] By the turn of the century, then, the *klenickso* was replacing the maid who served a middle-class, nuclear family. By 1910, household servants in working-class families that kept boarders comprised fully 85.7 percent of all domestics in Sweetwater County.[16] Qualitatively, this meant the difference between servant-class status in a private, middle-class home and quasi-familial status in a working-class home.

Expansion of the coal industry and subsequent demographic change brought about a shift in employer-servant relations—from "domestic service," a hierarchical, class-conscious relationship based on economic exchange, to "helping," a peer-class relationship grounded in local ethnic community networks.[17] Oral histories from Southern Slav immigrants suggest that single, working-class women in early-twentieth-century Wyoming coal towns who worked in domestic service among their own ethnic group gained valuable social supports in the process.

In 1910 Louise Luzan immigrated with her mother and siblings to Rock Springs. There they joined her father in a three-room company house. Very quickly, her mother began keeping boarders. When Louise was twelve years old, her mother was severely weakened by a difficult birth, and Louise dropped out of school to help her mother at home with the boarders. By the time her mother regained strength, nearly two years had passed, and Louise was embarrassed to return to school, having fallen behind her peers. Instead, Louise's mother directed her to a job in the home of a Slovenian acquaintance who took in sewing. Louise was to help with the household work in return for instruction in sewing. But the sewing apprenticeship never materialized. As Louise recalled: "She had only one machine; [I] didn't get to the machine; she didn't like to change threads and all that. . . . I ended up mostly doing housework."[18] When it became clear that Louise's "apprenticeship" would never progress beyond routine household work, the Slovenian employer placed Louise's future on a par with that of her own children. She encouraged Louise to leave household service and resume her education: "She [Louise's employer] says, 'I have a family. . . . I'm a-goin' send, educate, my children, and I want you to go.' She says, 'Louise, you do the right thing if you go back to school.' So . . . I did."[19] In her concern for Louise's future, Louise's working-class employer revealed a quasi-familial relationship between the two. Like a caring relative, Louise's employer placed the importance of Louise's education ahead of her own need for household help. And so Louise returned to high school and graduated within three years. Describing her time in household service, Louise remembered her employers' support and direction: "They were good to me. . . . I was very happy that I did [return to school]."[20] Louise Luzan's story suggests that single, immigrant, working-class women in domestic service for working-class families of the same nationality experienced a peer-class relationship of mutuality and quasi-familial guidance. In this way, domestic service within the working-class community doubled as a supportive social relationship.

Indeed, among Southern Slavs in Rock Springs, domestic service was inseparable from the web of informal social networks through which women sustained their families and others of their ethnic group. Informal networks of support between working-class Southern Slav women in industrial Sweetwater County echoed patterns of mutuality between neighbors in the old country. Mary Jesersek Taucher, for example, remembered working in the old country for a neighboring farm family in return for room and board, at age seven, when her widowed mother was struggling to make ends meet.[21] Similarly, Mrs. Luzan not only placed her daughter, Louise, with a Slovenian seamstress, she also reached out to single Slovenian women who arrived without kin. The story of Mrs. Luzan's placement of newcomer Mary Jesersek is telling. It reveals both Mrs. Luzan's role as informal employment agent for her countrywomen, and the quasi-familial relationship that developed between Mary and her employers.

When Mary Jesersek arrived alone in Rock Springs, only to find that she did not want to marry the young stranger who had proposed to her by mail, it was Mrs. Luzan who guided her toward alternatives. After listening to Mary's dilemma, Mrs. Luzan advised her, "You don't have to get married. I could get you a place to work."[22] Mrs. Luzan then introduced Mary to the Suvicks, a Slovenian couple who kept boarders. "Mr. Suvick," Mary recalled, "said, 'Stay with us.'" Mary accepted the Suvick's offer, and told her fiancé: "That wedding is off. I want to go to work."[23] The next day, Mary began work for the Suvicks, where she cooked and cleaned for room, board, and $10 per month.

Mary remembered the Suvicks as a lifeline, for they offered her work and a home, alternatives to a dubious marriage. By the time she eventually married, Mary had lived with the Suvicks for two years. She described them with affection: "They were really nice people."[24] Like surrogate parents, the Suvicks had taken her in, steered her away from a rash decision, and provided a stable home base. For Mary Jesersek, both Mrs. Luzan and the Suvicks had supplied social and emotional support in a world where she faced major decisions without benefit of guidance from kin. Her story suggests that single working-class women benefited from the mutuality that pervaded household service within the working-class community among servants and employers of the same nationality. Both Louise Luzan and Mary Jesersek enjoyed quasi-familial status in their employer's household, a peer-class relationship within which their well-being and their futures were considered, even nurtured.

Becoming part of a household and sharing in its systems of reciprocity was one way that unmarried women found a place in the community. Indeed, domestic service was an unmarried woman's occupation. Between 1880 and 1910, 95.2 percent of female servants in Sweetwater County were either single or widowed.[25] This is not surprising, for housekeeping remained labor-intensive in Wyoming mining towns throughout the early twentieth century. Even in thickly settled neighborhoods, women kept chickens, dairies, and kitchen gardens.[26] In short, a married woman with her own household to maintain would not have had time to do another family's housework, much less live in.[27]

Married women could, however, take in boarders. And the vast majority whose families needed income chose this route. Between 1880 and 1910, 88.1 percent of income-earning married women in Sweetwater coal towns kept boarders.[28] According to one Rock Springs couple, even throughout the 1920s, "everybody had boarders."[29]

But if keeping boarders was a constant among married women in Sweetwater County, the shifting class base of railroad and coal towns altered the profile of these women over time. In 1880 the average woman who kept lodgers was a middle-class settler, born in the United States, married to a farmer, rancher, or small businessman. At this time, 52.9 percent of married women keeping boarders were native born, and 65 percent were middle class.[30] With the expansion of coal mining at the turn of the century, the face of commercial housekeeping changed. As the Union Pacific increasingly recruited European labor, the foreign-born working-class population burgeoned. By 1910, 74.2 percent of married women who kept boarders were foreign born; and 69.7 percent were working class.[31] The average woman who took in lodgers was now a European woman married to a day laborer, miner, or railroad hand.

Most striking, however, was how widespread the practice of keeping boarders had become. By 1910, 52.3 percent of all foreign-born married women, and 51.4 percent of all working-class married women in Sweetwater County took in lodgers.[32] These figures suggest the predominance of commercialized domesticity in southwest Wyoming mining towns. The early-twentieth-century mining boom became a service industry bonanza for working-class women. In company towns like Rock Springs, Superior, Reliance, and Megeath, men outnumbered women by two to one. With almost two thirds of these men unmarried, there was great demand for bachelor housing.[33] Indicative of this demand was a rise in the average number of boarders per household, from three to four between 1900 and 1910.[34]

Married women capitalized on the demand for bachelor housing by designating extra space within their household for as many lodgers as the family could handle. Louise Luzan Leskovec recalled her mother's enterprising allocation of space in their four-room company house: "We had only four rooms and that was a kitchen and one room a bedroom for my folks, and I slept on the floor all the time, and then there was . . . a dining room, and we had benches around there and cots on each side, and then there was about five cots in the men's room."[35] Married women like Mrs. Luzan could incorporate housekeeping for boarders into their daily routine. If a woman had children old enough, she could enlist their help cooking and cleaning for lodgers. Dorothy Pivik remembered her mother assigning her a share of housekeeping responsibility for bachelor miners at their home: "It seemed like mother . . . always had bachelors and we had to clean for them."[36] Reluctant daughters notwithstanding, married women who kept boarders contributed as much as 25 percent of the family income.[37]

For women from rural villages in Eastern Europe, keeping boarders was the new expression of an old ethic, that of family reciprocity. In the old country, every member of the household was obligated to contribute labor or income to the maintenance of the whole.[38] But in late-nineteenth-century rural Eastern Europe, renting household space to lodgers had not been part of this pattern.[39] Rural households in Eastern Europe customarily had been limited to nuclear families, occasionally enlarged by an aging parent,[40] or by married adult children who helped with farm labor.[41] In short, women's economic contributions in the old country had centered on home production rather than commercialized domesticity. In Sweetwater mining towns, keeping boarders became the practical expression of Eastern European married women's customary share of responsibility for economic support of the household. Just as they had raised crops or made clothing in the old country to minimize cash expenses, Eastern European women in Sweetwater coal towns now took in lodgers to generate cash income.

Keeping boarders was crucial to the working-class family economy in Sweetwater mining towns. With periodic layoffs, miners had no protection from unemployment. The only compensation was that slack times were somewhat predictable. During the summer, when demand for coal dropped, production fell back, reducing the work week from six days to only one or two days. Some miners were laid off altogether until winter.[42] Men responded to unemployment with a variety of strategies. Some left Sweetwater coal towns every summer in search of work elsewhere. A few filed homestead claims on the high desert and used the claims to hunt rabbit, sage hen, and deer, or to attempt gardening the arid soil.[43] Still others pooled money with families of the same nationality to order a railroad car full of grapes. Participating families would divide the grapes among themselves and gather in communal work parties to make wine. They would keep some for home consumption and sell the rest.[44] Louise Luzan Leskovec of Rock Springs remembered her parents discussing the necessity of keeping boarders as a hedge against her father's seasonal unemployment: "My dad told my mother she would have to start keeping boarders because work was awfully hard to get. . . . When the mines were working slack, it was hard to find employment anywhere."[45] Invariably, then, working-class families also relied on income from boarders to see them through slack times at the mines.[46]

If keeping boarders had value as a source of family income, it also met social needs in the larger community.[47] In a study of immigrant families in Pennsylvania coal towns, JoAnne Schneider argued that keeping boarders was understood as a social obligation within the working-class, ethnic community. As Schneider explained it, "The eastern European community included a number of people who needed to be boarded, and households contributed their part."[48] Similarly, in a study of Eastern European women in industrial Connecticut, Laura Anker described the social meaning of keeping boarders. For host families and lodgers, "joint residence acted as a kind of mutual aid, extending the bonds of assistance to new arrivals."[49] Oral histories from Sweetwater County suggest that Eastern Europeans there, too, viewed boarders as both economic strategy and social responsibility.

Louise Leskovec recalled that her family took in lodgers even before they had adequate space. When she and her mother first arrived, they joined her father in makeshift housing. "We had three little rooms for the time being," she said, and crowded into these three rooms "there was [our family] . . . and then there was two other boarders right from the beginning."[50] It was only later that the Luzans moved into a four-room company house that allowed more space—such as it was—for boarders. Louise Leskovec's account of her crowded but willing family as hosts to boarders implies that keeping lodgers was a form of mutuality based on ethnic identity. "They [the boarders in the Luzan household] were mostly Slovenian, our nationality," Louise explained.[51] In some cases, having space for boarders in itself created an obligation. Referring to neighbors Mary Bogeti and Mrs. Begovich of the Number Four Mine District in which she lived, Louise commented, "They [each] used to keep boarders because they [each] had five rooms."[52] The suggestion of mandatory hospitality expected of those with larger dwellings reinforces the impression that taking in boarders was a form of social obligation within the ethnic community. Finally, Mary Jesersek and Louise Leskovec's memories of guidance from host families where they boarded underscores the theme of mutual assistance between host families and boarders of the same nationality. The Eastern European example in Sweetwater County, then, suggests that keeping boarders doubled as economic strategy and social activity that linked lodgers and host families in relationships of mutuality based on ethnic origin. As the ones responsible for keeping boarders, married women figured centrally in these informal social supports.

Given the steady demand for lodging and the lack of industrial diversification, income-earning married women in Sweetwater coal towns rarely worked outside the realm of commercialized housekeeping until the 1920s.[53] By then, their appearance on the margins of the wage workforce outside the home would mark two decades of change in the occupational structure of Sweetwater coal towns.

Changes in the regional economy of southwest Wyoming altered women's work patterns in subtle but significant ways. After the turn of the century, the coal boom spawned new businesses and institutions to meet the demands of a growing population. Banks, law offices, insurance companies, libraries, new schools, a hospital, retail stores, theaters, and even beauty parlors opened doors in downtown Green River and Rock Springs.[54] World War I accelerated this trend, bringing more workers to the region, raising wages, boosting consumer activity, and hence, downtown businesses. Gradually, a small proportion of income-earning women in Sweetwater County shifted from home-based work to downtown jobs. Initially, middle-class, native-born women and college-educated women from "old immigrant" groups took jobs in the emerging white-collar sector. By the 1920s, American-educated, working-class immigrant women also entered new occupational categories as receptionists, stenographers, telephone operators, retail managers, and sales clerks.

As well as changes in the regional economy, ethnicity, class, and educational opportunity further influenced women's work patterns in Sweetwater railroad and coal towns.[55] Social solidarity among the owning classes shaped opportunity for women in emerging retail and office jobs. Under these conditions, education and acculturation became central to immigrant women's strategies for occupational mobility. Americanization became an entrée into the white-collar world.

Crucial to the shift among Sweetwater County women from paid housekeeping to work outside the home were changes in the occupational structure of min-

From Klenickso *to Main Street*

ing towns. As the coal market boomed after the turn of the century, the Union Pacific stepped up prospecting activity and opened new mines. Towns sprung up around new mine sites, Superior in 1906, Reliance in 1910. As new mines drew more workers to the region, independent mercantiles began competing with Union Pacific company stores. In Rock Springs, Henry, Joe, and Alexander Bertagnolli's "Union Mercantile" won customers away from the company store with its name, chosen to honor union activity. Entrepreneur Joseph Anselmi also appealed to Union Pacific workers with his "Miner's Mercantile." Frank Kershisnik opened the "Rock Springs Commercial" store and won over customers by dropping prices below those of the Union Pacific Company Store.[56] In short, independent merchants found a ready consumer market.

Rock Springs, for example, showed steady commercial and municipal growth after 1900. In 1880 the town had existed only as a loose collection of coal camps with a bank and a company store. In 1884 the town incorporated; in 1898, the Wyoming General Hospital was erected; and by 1903, downtown Rock Springs boasted four general merchandise stores, three hotels, three restaurants, three drugstores, two banks, two meat markets, two barbers, a cigar-maker, and about thirty saloons. By 1908, a Carnegie Library graced the South Side, downtown, as did the Grand Opera House, host to musicals, prize fights, plays, operas, and dances sponsored by local fraternal organizations.[57] By 1910, the population in Rock Springs reached almost 6,000. Between 1911 and 1916, new schools went up, the capstone being an $80,000 high school equipped with domestic science and vocational training rooms, science labs, and a gymnasium with separate showers for girls and boys. Telephone service with one- and two-party lines became available to Rock Springs residents in 1913.[58] And by 1914, the downtown business district included three banks, fifteen general merchandise stores, ten clothing or shoe stores, fourteen hotels, seven meat markets, three theaters, and nine white-collar establishments offering insurance, legal services, or real estate. Rock Springs residents also found twenty-one specialty stores, which carried everything from tea and coffee to cigars, pharmaceuticals, jewelry, stationery, wallpaper, and paints.[59]

With the expansion of municipal services, retail stores, and business offices, new job opportunities for women appeared. Teaching, nursing, cashiering, typing, stenography, and telephone operation drew town-dwelling women into outside wage work. In 1880, only 7.5 percent of income-earning women in Sweetwater County had worked outside the home; by 1910, 18.9 percent held jobs in downtown businesses.[60] But commercial growth was not the only factor influencing women's work patterns. Oral histories from Sweetwater County indicate the importance of ethnicity, family connections, and American schooling as well, in shaping women's occupational choices.

During the first two decades of the twentieth century, American emigrants and second-generation immigrants from the British Isles and Germany predominated in supervisory positions with the Union Pacific, in town government, and in the white-collar professions. As employers, they were predisposed to hire women from among their own social circles—the largely native-born or "old immigrant" middle class who populated the South Side in Rock Springs and the North Side in Green River.[61] A glance at the names and birthplaces of women who entered the world of downtown work during the early 1900s highlights this impression. Business listings in the 1908 *Wyoming Gazetteer* for Rock Springs included the following: "Empire Theater, Mrs. Anna V. Gaunt, prop."; "Rowley, Sarah, milliner"; "Skedd, Jennie A., music tchr."; "Smith, Laura E., stenographer"; and "Wyoming General Hospital Training School for Nurses, Martha Converse, supt."[62] Similarly, the 1914 *Wyoming Directory* for Rock Springs included "Carnegie Public Library, Mrs. Mary A. Clark, Librarian"; "Neuber, Pearl, secretary, Beeman & Neuber Mercantile Co."; and "Smith, Laura E., notary public."[63] The surnames Gaunt, Rowley, Skedd, Smith, Converse, Clark, and Neuber indicate American, English, Scottish, or German ethnicity.

Evidence from the Sweetwater County census reinforces the impression that native-born women and women from "old immigrant" groups such as the Britons or Germans predominated in retail, professional, and office jobs. The 1900 census manuscript for Rock Springs, for example, yielded Bessie Taylor, Lizzie Brown, and Sarah Abraham, dry goods clerks; Mary Muir, saleswoman; Jennie Anderson, milliner; Marmis Regan, dressmaker; and Maude McCoy, stenographer. McCoy was born in Ohio; Abraham in Wyoming; and Regan in Montana, of Irish parents. Anderson and Brown were born in Wyoming, of Scottish parents; Taylor and Muir were, themselves, Scottish immigrants. The 1900 census for Rock Springs also showed six nurses working at the Wyoming General Hospital, two of whom were born in Ohio, one in England, and three in Canada, all with Scottish surnames.[64] The 1910 census manuscripts for Green River and Rock Springs included Mary Murphy, Celia Fisher, and Tessa Dean, telephone operators; Jean Jeffers, stenographer; Mary Davy and Evie Garth, bookkeepers; Nellie Whalen, store clerk; and schoolteachers Anna Bills, Mabel Sodergrun, Dora Paulson, Nellie Hasting, and Mary Bennett. Every one of these women was American-born. The exception was Mary Teresini, a store clerk whose parents came from the Italian Tyrol.[65] By far, though, the majority of women entering new occupations outside the home in Sweetwater County during the first decade and a half of the twentieth century were native-born or "old immigrants" of Irish, English, Scottish, or German descent.[66]

The predominance of these groups in white-collar occupations implies that social solidarity among them played a role in shaping opportunity. For example, "old immigrants" from Great Britain or Germany occupied a higher proportionate share of downtown jobs in 1900; they comprised 46.1 percent of single women in downtown jobs, but only 31.7 percent of the entire female population. In 1900, native-born women occupied a share of downtown jobs equally proportionate to their numbers in the county population as a whole: 50 percent of *all* women were native born; and 50 percent of unmarried, income-earning women in non-domestic wage work were native born. But "new immigrants" from Southern and Eastern Europe occupied a lower proportionate share of downtown jobs in 1900; they comprised 5.7 percent of the entire female population; but only 3.8 percent of single women in downtown jobs.[67]

By 1910, native-born women occupied a significantly higher proportionate share of downtown jobs; they comprised 92.3 percent of the unmarried female workforce outside the home, but only 57.1 percent of the female population as a whole. "New immigrants" from Southern and Eastern Europe continued to occupy a lower proportionate share of downtown jobs; they comprised 11.9 percent of the entire female population, but only 7.7 percent of the unmarried female workforce in non-domestic jobs.[68] The increasing predominance of native-born and "old immigrant" women in supervisory and white-collar positions suggests that social solidarity among the native born and "old immigrant" middle class shaped new job opportunities for women in Sweetwater railroad and coal towns. Shop owners and supervisors hired their own kind.

Family connections functioned as another entrée for young, middle-class women into the world of downtown work. Jean Jeffers, for example, may have benefited from her husband's influence as Union Pacific Railroad shop foreman when she applied to the U.P. for a position as stenographer. Similarly, Pearl Neuber, secretary to Beeman & Neuber Mercantile, probably benefited from her kin relationship to A. F. Neuber, president of the company.[69] Just as working-class immigrants found jobs through kinship ties, so too, young, middle-class women tapped family connections to enter the world of downtown work.[70]

Louise Spinner Graf's work history best illustrates the value of family connections in the local job market. Born in Germany in 1900, Louise Spinner came to Green River, Wyoming, with her parents in 1901. The Spinners were part of the Spinner-Eggs-Gaensslen clan, a prosperous German family in Green River whose business interests included the State Bank of Green River, the Green River Opera House, the Sweetwater Brewing Company, the Thomahawk Pharmacy, the Charles Eggs Shoe Store, and the Eleanor Gaensslen Millinery. The clan's municipal influence included one member as deputy county assessor, another on the county school board, and another on the county library board. Louise Spinner was a third-generation member of this family.[71] After graduating from the University of Wyoming at Laramie in 1923, Louise took a job as teller at the State Bank of Green River, a financial institution presided over by her uncle, Hugo Gaensslen. Louise worked as a bank teller for seven years, until her marriage to Mr. Graf in 1930.[72] Louise Spinner Graf's work history suggests that for some middle-class women, commercial family ties facilitated their entry into the white-collar world of Green River and Rock Springs.

To acknowledge the benefits of ethnic solidarity or family influence is not to deny these women their very real accomplishments. For white-collar work required English literacy, American education, and sometimes, skilled training. Margaret Plemel Metelko's story illustrates the combination of schooling and family connections that landed her a downtown job.

Second-generation German Margaret Plemel knew firsthand the value of education. Her mother had never learned to speak or read English well. Though born in Minnesota, Margaret's mother was "brought up by German parents in a German school. . . . At that time," Margaret explained, "you didn't go to school with the idea of going to school for twelve years. If you went to school four years, you were lucky."[73] Instead, girls of Margaret's mother's generation had been expected to quit school when their labor was needed on the farm: "In the fall, there was harvesting to be done, the garden to be dug up and canned and saved for winter time, and potatoes, and all these things that had to be done. . . . That was just the way it went. . . . Your livelihood came first, before an education."[74] Margaret's mother had cut short her own education to work on the family farm. But her father, Frank Plemel, modeled the benefits of a completed education. And a good education made for a better livelihood. Frank Plemel's family had allowed him to finish high school and then attend a Catholic seminary. But after graduating from seminary, Frank Plemel entered the business world rather than the clergy. His knowledge of several languages, including English, earned him a job at the Rock Springs National Bank as Assistant Cashier. "He was an asset to that bank," Margaret recalled. "All these people, foreign people, brought their money up there, deposited it there, because there was a man there that could write letters to Europe, that could send money to Europe for them."[75] Because of her father's white-collar position, Margaret remembered a level of material comfort and social standing that her friends from miner's families did not share: "Life was maybe a little bit more comfortable . . . because my Dad could speak better and he could help people with writing.

It was on account of him, we were elevated a little bit."[76] Margaret learned early, then, to view education and white-collar work as routes to upward mobility.

Frank Plemel encouraged his daughter to follow his example. He even went so far as to pick out the business school she attended after graduating high school. After completing her business degree, Margaret returned to Rock Springs and worked at home for a year, helping her mother with a new baby. At the end of that year, Margaret said to her father, "'Well, it would be nice to have a job.' And he says, 'Yah, I guess it would.'"[77] Frank Plemel then talked with his acquaintances in the white-collar world to help his daughter find work. As Margaret described it: "I don't know, I suppose one of the [business] men came up to the bank to make a deposit or something, and my Dad said, 'My daughter's out of school. . . . Could you give her some kind of a job? She'd like to work.'"[78] Frank Plemel's business contacts brought results. The Union Pacific Coal Company Store hired Margaret as a cashier in 1927. She worked there for two years, "waiting on the coal miners when they brought in their checks to cash," until her marriage to Louis Metelko in 1928.[79] For Margaret Plemel Metelko, then, both her training at a business college and her father's influence with Union Pacific managerial staff facilitated her entry into white-collar work.[80] Parental support for college and commercial family connections were the benefits of middle-class status that enabled some young women to move into new occupational categories.

For working-class women with neither commercial family connections nor financial means to attend college, completing an American high school education was the next best route toward occupational mobility. Single, working-class immigrant women who came to Sweetwater County as children reaped the benefits of American schooling. Italian, Southern Slav, Austrian, Hungarian, and Scandinavian children from the Number Four Mine District school in Rock Springs, for example, found that despite the fact that 90 percent of them spoke a foreign language, the teachers insisted that "all children . . . learn English, to grow up to be 'good Americans.'"[81] This training, and the availability of vocational education in Rock Springs High School after 1916, made a difference in the occupational mobility of single immigrant women from Southern and Eastern Europe. A survey of twenty-two life histories of Sweetwater County women showed that among single, working-class immigrant women, the 50 percent who graduated from American high schools thereafter moved into downtown jobs.[82]

Louise Luzan Leskovec approached her high school education as a conscious strategy for occupational mobility. When her "dressmaking apprenticeship" became little more than domestic service, she returned to high school, despite her embarrassment at having fallen behind. She caught up quickly, and in the tenth grade, took shorthand and typing to train for white-collar work.

As she became proficient in Business English and clerical skills, Louise planned to move from high school into office work downtown. Those close to her, however, had other plans. At age nineteen, during her junior year in high school, Louise's parents and boyfriend began pressuring her to marry. They expected her to marry as soon as she graduated high school.

But Louise Luzan was not ready for domesticity. She wanted to test her language and clerical skills in the workplace. Knowing that her family and fiancé would accept a delayed marriage as long as she had not graduated, Louise quit school after her junior year. The following year, 1919, she took a full-time job as a secretary in a law office. In 1920 Louise returned for her senior year in high school, graduated in 1921, and married Matt Leskovec at age twenty-two.[83]

Louise Luzan Leskovec had insisted upon office work for the occupational mobility it represented; she successfully replaced housekeeping experience with white-collar skills. These skills would prove useful when she and her husband opened a small variety store during the early 1920s. The Leskovecs ran this business together until the Great Depression forced them to close in 1931.[84] For Louise Leskovec, the expansion of white-collar opportunity was not, by itself, enough to jog her out of the pattern of commercialized housekeeping. American education was equally essential to her occupational mobility.

For working-class, immigrant women without a public school education, such occupational mobility was difficult. First-generation, single immigrant women found their lack of familiarity with the English language, or their lack of a high school education, to be cultural barriers that hindered movement into work outside the home. Mary Jesersek, for example, commented that for single Slovenian women who spoke no English, "there [were] no jobs" except domestic service. "It was the only kind of work a young girl could do."[85] Though Mary worked in household service for a kind and supportive Slovenian family, at times she yearned to work in an English-speaking household, so that she could learn the language: "Sometimes I wish[ed] . . . some people, English people, would let me come work for them. You know, I could [have] learn[ed] a lot of English ways."[86] After two years in domestic service with a Slovenian family, Mary Jesersek married Mr. Taucher, a Slovenian butcher. Within another two years, Mary had begun taking in laundry to augment her husband's income.[87] With limited knowledge of American language and culture, she was forced to fall back on home-based domestic work for income.

Mary Jesersek alluded to domestic service with an American family as a strategy for acculturation. Indeed, her remark offers a poignant counterpoint to the common pattern of domestic service within a family of the same nationality. Though such arrangements offered the comforts of peer-class and ethnic social support, they also isolated the domestic from American language and customs. Mary's case showed that limited exposure to English language and American customs also limited upward mobility.

For single European women who immigrated as adults, too old to enter Sweetwater public schools, household service for an American family sometimes functioned as a step toward occupational mobility. Learning the language and habits of an American household better qualified one to move into downtown jobs that required interaction with the public. Louise Leskovec remembered occasionally acting as translator for her mother, when her mother interacted with the downtown, English-speaking world.[88] Louise was keenly aware that as long as one needed a third party to mediate interactions with the general public, employment downtown remained out of the question. And while Louise Leskovec completed high school in order to broaden her options, Mary Jesersek, arriving in Rock Springs at age seventeen, missed the opportunity for public education. For women like Jesersek, domestic service with an American family would have provided an alternative route toward acculturation. One cannot mistake the wistful tone of Jesersek's statement, "You know, I could have learned a lot of English ways."

If Mary Jesersek's education was a story of frustration and missed opportunity, Anna Waananen Berg Semos's was a tale of success. Her work history demonstrated the use of domestic service as a resource for acculturation, followed by movement into wage work outside the home. Born in Finland in 1890, Anna Waananen immigrated alone to the United States in 1909, at age nineteen. During her first four years in the United States, Anna worked as a domestic servant for a wealthy American family in Duluth, Minnesota. By 1913, she spoke English fluently and left domestic service to wait tables at the Fay Hotel in Regina, Minnesota. In 1916, she married Gust Berg, a Finnish miner. For the next three years, the Bergs lived in Butte, Montana, where Anna trained as a barber. In 1920, the Bergs moved to Rock Springs, where Anna set up shop as a barber for the Gunn-Quealy mine. She ran a barber shop there until 1924, when the mine closed. For the rest of the decade, Anna worked at a cafe in Rock Springs.[89] For Anna Waananen Berg Semos, domestic service with an English-speaking family provided the language skills she needed to move into other occupations—as waitress, then barber. Taken together, Anna Semos and Mary Jesersek's stories reveal the trade-offs that single immigrant women without an American education faced. Those who served in same-ethnic households reaped the benefits of reciprocal social support, but had less occupational mobility. Those who served in American households acculturated faster, but may have missed the comforts of ethnic community.

The shift from home-based to downtown work among income-earning women in Sweetwater coal towns accelerated during World War I. As coal production surged, wages rose, increasing consumer activity. Miner's wages jumped from $3.52 per day in 1916 to $5.42 per day in 1917. Railroad engineers, by 1918, earned $8.50 per day. Women's wages rose as well. In 1918, female stenographer's wages rose from $1.50 to as much as $5.80 per day.[90] Nationwide, with male workers entering the armed forces, more women entered the work force outside the home, in some cases replacing men in industry. In Sweetwater County, the Union Pacific hired women to work in the railroad yards as section gangs. Women did not, however, enter the mines, as federal contracts for fuel exempted skilled crews of miners from military service. Moreover, women's work on the railroad was temporary, an emergency policy that ended at the close of the war.[91]

More lasting were the new positions in retail sales and office work, which expanded as wartime prosperity encouraged commercial growth. By 1918, Rock Springs's downtown businesses included two new communications companies, the Postal Telegraph Company and a branch office of Western Union Telephone and Telegraph Company. A new department store, the Salt Lake Salvage Company, advertised "Sell for Less," to compete with Rock Springs's fifteen other mercantiles. Four new professional offices opened, among them a brokerage house, an insurance office, and a law firm. The number of specialty stores expanded from twenty-one in 1914 to twenty-six in 1918, with new candy shops, cigar vendors, and a florist.[92]

Wartime commercial growth accelerated women's movement into occupational categories outside the home. Business listings for Green River and Rock Springs in 1918 show a number of women in newly created clerical and administrative positions. The Mountain States Telephone and Telegraph Company of Green River, for example, hired Pearl Grumer as telephone operator. The Commercial Hotel of Green River hired Mrs. W. H. Forshea as General Manager. Louis Westholder, the new florist in Rock Springs, employed Nellie Saleen as manager, and Rock Springs insurance corporation Van Deusen & Murphy added family member Rachel Van Deusen to its growing staff of insurance agents.[93] Wartime movement of women into white-collar work occurred nationwide as well. Following World War I, more women worked in office jobs than in manufacturing, domestic service, or agriculture.[94]

In Wyoming, the aftermath of World War I brought an industrial recession.

The coal market slumped. From 1920 to 1922 coal production in Wyoming fell by 3.4 million tons, resulting in massive layoffs. For the rest of the decade, the coal industry moved at half speed; between 1923 and 1927, 1,872 miners were laid off. Still, many continued to work in the mines, at reduced hours. One- and two-day work weeks became all too common, due in part to declining coal production, in part to increased mechanization. In 1928 natural gas discoveries in Baxter Basin raised hopes for a new boom in fossil fuels. But the gas deposits proved insufficient to raise Sweetwater County out of an industrial recession.[95]

Commercial businesses fared better than the coal industry in Sweetwater County during the 1920s. Though miners and their families had less money to spend during the industrial recession, consumer activity remained strong enough to support continued expansion of the retail and white-collar businesses for several reasons. First, some miners supplemented reduced incomes by taking part-time work in recently developed service industries. Auto parts stores, lumber suppliers, billiards halls, hardware stores, auto service stations, auto rental companies, cement contractors, and rubber tire vendors offered supplemental work to partially employed miners.[96] Second, in some cases, the Union Pacific allowed miners and their families to defer rental payments on company housing until the mines re-opened full-time.[97] Finally, in 1927, when the UMWA called for a strike in the eastern United States, Wyoming miners voted to remain on the job. Having won local concessions on wage rates, they deemed part-time work preferable to total unemployment. And so while the industrial recession forced miners and their families to reactivate strategies like women's home canning or men's part-time work outside the mines, their purchasing power was not crippled. Commercial activity in Green River and Rock Springs subsided from its wartime peak, but continued to thrive as the 1920s progressed.[98]

By 1925, twenty-eight women appeared in the business listings for Green River and Rock Springs, as opposed to only sixteen in 1918—a 42.8 percent increase in the number of women working downtown jobs.[99] Municipal institutions increasingly recruited women as well. In Green River in 1925, Anna Davis worked as City Clerk, Mae Brooks served as County Treasurer, and Grace Siegert clerked at the district court.[100]

Most striking, however, was the appearance of women in positions formerly held by men. Both Grace Siegert's post as court clerk and Mae Brooks' job as County Treasurer were positions previously filled by male employees.[101] Before the 1920s, among the five banks in Green River and Rock Springs, none had ever hired a woman as Assistant Cashier.[102] By the early 1920s, however, this boundary had shifted to include women. In 1923, for example, a wedding announcement for Bertha Larsen in the *Green River Star* included laudatory mention of her position as Assistant Cashier for the State Bank of Green River.[103] And in 1925, the *Wyoming Directory* included Catherine MacLaughlin, Assistant Cashier for the First National Bank of Rock Springs.[104]

By the mid-1920s, then, Sweetwater coal town women increasingly entered new occupational categories outside the home, as a result of continued commercial expansion in retail and white-collar services. While it is significant that a small proportion of income-earning women in Sweetwater County left commercialized housekeeping to enter downtown jobs, this change must be kept in perspective. The paradox of the 1920s, according to historian Alice Kessler-Harris, was that even as more women entered the workforce outside the home, gender ideology reinforced the notion that women's "real" work was homemaking. This concept was reflected in the prevalence of occupational segregation by sex. That is, occupations that could be interpreted as extensions of homemaking admitted women. Even white-collar jobs for women were understood as support services for men, who remained in charge. Wage rates in women's retail and office jobs remained low, under the assumption that income-earning women did not hold economic responsibility for themselves or their families, as male breadwinners did. Finally, young, single women were hired preferentially, but not promoted, reinforcing the assumption that women's jobs were mere stopgaps before marriage, at which point every woman would depend on a husband for economic support. The result of this confluence between gender ideology and economic structure was that nationwide, from 1910 to 1940, between 86 and 90 percent of all women wage-earners were clustered in only ten different occupations, most of them low-paying with little opportunity for advancement.[105]

And so the world of downtown work had limits. Still, within the context of occupational segregation in Sweetwater coal towns, the record is alive with evidence of female initiative. Some women in Green River and Rock Springs began to advertise their own secretarial services, preferring to work as independent contractors. LaPrele Crosby and Margaret Connor, for example, listed themselves in the 1925 *Wyoming Directory* as "public stenographers."[106] Not only were women contracting as independent office workers, the number of female entrepreneurs increased by 46.1 percent between 1914 and 1925.[107] The increasing presence of women downtown as independent contractors and small business owners suggested expression of personal ambition as well as economic responsibility. On the face of things, such women personified the dimensions of New Womanhood: they left commercialized housekeeping and staked claims on the fruits of wartime commercial growth.

But the oral history record suggests a subtler picture. Sometimes the demands of family reciprocity cut short a woman's personal ambition. Lena Anselmi Huntley's story is revealing. The second-generation daughter of Tyrolean Italian immigrants, Lena's ambition was a career in nursing. By age seventeen, she was well versed in English, doing well in school, and inquiring into nurse training programs. But when her mother died that year, it fell upon Lena, the eldest daughter, to raise her five brothers and sisters. She quit school in order to care for the youngest ones, foreclosing her ambition to become a nurse. The responsibilities of homemaking and childcare for a family of six proved too consuming to allow for nurse's training. And so Lena Anselmi Huntley never entered the medical profession. Generously, though, she supported her youngest sister's ambition, eventually sending her to nursing school—a poignant expression of the ethic of mutuality, which bound women to place the interests of the family above their own.[108]

The picture is further complicated when one considers those ethnic women who did manage to enter skilled jobs outside the home. Were these women expressing individualistic career ambitions? Again, the oral history record suggests otherwise. Louise Luzan Leskovec, Margaret Plemel Metelko, and Louise Spinner Graf each quit their white-collar jobs when they married. Moreover, when Louise Leskovec, Margaret Metelko, or Anna Semos spoke about their first downtown jobs, they emphasized their training and education and their mastery of the English language. They reflected on the difference between their hard-won competence in the public world and their own earlier struggles or their mothers' struggles with the English-speaking world.[109] In short, these women framed downtown work as an expression of acculturation, rather than as a conscious redefinition of gender. Through acquisition of language and business skills, such women kept pace with a changing economy, preparing themselves to better serve traditions of family reciprocity in their married lives. Indeed, Louise Leskovec helped her husband run a variety store throughout the 1920s. Margaret Metelko continued to work part-time for the Union Pacific Company Store throughout her married life, filling in for absent clerks every summer; her income from part-time work helped the family during lean years. Anna Semos continued work as a barber after marriage, supplementing her miner husband's income.[110] Taken together, the many stories detailing family obligation—including working-class married women's shared responsibility for household support—and the stories describing acculturation suggest that women's changing work patterns in coal towns reflected a blending of new occupational opportunity with transplanted customs of family reciprocity. Enterprising single immigrant women trained to be more versatile in the wage labor market as job opportunity diversified beyond commercialized housekeeping. Married women with such training then expressed the tradition of mutual obligation between family members in new ways, through downtown work.

Women's work patterns in Sweetwater coal towns thus form a compelling story of regional economic development, changing gender systems, and immigrant assimilation. In their gradual movement into new occupational categories outside the home, Sweetwater coal town women mirrored contemporary trends nationwide. In other ways, however, women's occupational choices in southwest Wyoming towns were quite regionally specific. That is, Sweetwater coal towns remained single-industry towns, where the female counterpart to male employment in extractive industry was employment in the household service industries. Commercialized domesticity dominated the women's labor market in these coal towns for four decades, from the late 1890s through the late 1920s.

Among foreign-born settlers, commercialized domesticity was of a richer texture than some labor historians might suggest. With the early-twentieth-century coal boom, the locus of household service changed from private middle-class homes to working-class families that kept lodgers. Within these households, domestic service met needs both economic and social. The Southern Slav example suggests that servants and employers of the same nationality shared a peer-class relationship of mutual assistance, even quasi-familial relations. In this setting, household service doubled as a valuable form of social support for single women.

Similarly, keeping boarders represented both an economic strategy and a community responsibility. Again, the Southern Slav example suggests that boarders and host families of the same nationality understood the relationship as another form of reciprocity based on shared ethnic background. The host woman earned income essential to family survival in a single-industry town; the boarder found job leads, orientation to town, and social support among his or her own kind. Immigrant women who kept boarders, then, functioned as informal agents of assimilation for newcomer Europeans. They also gave new expression to the Old World tradition of family reciprocity, replacing farm produce with income from boarders, as their contribution to household survival.

Sweetwater coal towns shared important characteristics with industrial burgs elsewhere in the United States, in that low wages, high rates of injury, and seasonal unemployment necessitated women's wage work in the family economy. But the continued prevalence of keeping boarders, even after commercial and municipal expansion opened other jobs to women, attests to the social value of this work as well. Women's paid household work was inseparable from the web of informal ties that linked first-generation immigrants to their countrymen and women in ways that sustained them through adjustment to a foreign culture.

For those women who chose the world of downtown work, initially, class and ethnicity shaped access to new occupational categories. Women who had commercial family connections or parental support for college were the first to enter white-collar work. Initially, too, the managerial and owning classes of Green River and Rock Springs hired from among their own kind, placing native-born or "old immigrant" women in retail and municipal positions. For "new immigrant," working-class women eyeing such possibilities, occupational mobility was an expression of acculturation. Not surprisingly, education became a key strategy for occupational mobility. With English language proficiency and a high school education, "new immigrant" daughters, too, moved into downtown jobs during the second and third decades of the twentieth century. And when these women married, they brought new versatility to the family economy. That is, some met their obligation to contribute to household support through downtown work rather than commercialized housekeeping. The ethic of mutual obligation between family members, then, was double-edged for women. On the one hand, it moved some immigrant women into new occupational categories as they met their wage-earning responsibilities with white-collar jobs. On the other hand, it could also subsume their personal ambitions to the needs of the group, as was the case with Lena Anselmi Huntley.

The Sweetwater County example thus demonstrates how women's work patterns were influenced by class, ethnicity, local economic base, and changing gender norms. Was there anything that distinguished the working lives of southwest Wyoming coal town women from those of their eastern, urban peers? Perhaps only that the forces of class, ethnicity, regional economy, and changing gender ideology were thrown into sharper relief by the raw boundaries of coal boomtowns. Indeed, Sweetwater County's mono-industrial towns created a setting where population growth, subsequent commercial and municipal growth, and the dearth of alternative jobs for women in light manufacturing allowed some working-class women to move from commercialized domesticity directly into white-collar work. This transition, in turn, highlighted more subtle processes of ethnic community-building, assimilation, and family reciprocity through which women defined their place.

CHAPTER EIGHT

"Grasping at the Shadow": The Paradox of Change

Louise Luzan Leskovec, Jerrine Stewart Wire, and other Wyoming women's stories reach beyond regional history. For their stories about migration, relocation, and building community also reveal processes of reconstructing social identity. "In the West," wrote Sarah Deutsch, "race, culture, and gender worked themselves out in elemental simplicity."[1] Elemental perhaps, but not simple. Women in late-nineteenth- and early-twentieth-century southwest Wyoming displayed forms of material adaptation and ideological mediation that resulted in new and sometimes paradoxical constructions of gender. A contradictory blend of broadened opportunity, on the one hand, and the circumscriptions of community, on the other hand, surfaced in distinctive ways across ethnic and regional lines among Sweetwater County women.

Ranch work, by its very nature labor-intensive, increasingly drew women outside the boundaries of domesticity. By the early twentieth century, gendered work roles in rural Sweetwater County had blurred to the point where women routinely crossed over into what was still understood as men's or "outside" work. Most intriguing about this change was the way ranch culture minimized its implicit challenge to gender ideology. Ranch women held to an ethic of group partnership, which normalized their transgressions into masculine territory as "service to family." Of course, it was that, too: successful ranches required group labor and group cooperation. But such transgressions also represented a significant drift from the cultural roots of Sweetwater County ranchers, where an ideology of separate spheres had supported patriarchal authority among mid- and late-nineteenth-century, middle-class, midwestern farm families. It is significant that southwest Wyoming ranch women found ways, ideologically, to minimize this drift. The fact that ranch women defined crossover work as nothing more than incidental family responsibility, avoiding altogether the implications for gender equality, suggests a conservatism that mediated gender role change.

"*Grasping at the Shadow*"

Equally telling, early-twentieth-century Sweetwater ranch families adopted popularized cowboy myth to demarcate one last bastion of all-male activity: work with beef cattle. Though fenced family ranches had long since replaced open-range herding, cattle herding retained its cachet as the work of single, nomadic males. Culturally defined as a masculine occupation, it remained off-limits to women even as reserve labor. The few women who entered cowcamp were known as exceptions. And when they ran herd, they were temporarily masculinized: one functioned in the world of cowhands only as a "feller" or *cowboy*. The fact that ranch culture clung so steadfastly to this vestige of separate spheres, despite the actual necessity of recruiting daughters as "fellers," also suggests a conservative attitude toward gender role change. Consider again the evidence of such conservatism from the *Big Piney Examiner*. On October 20, 1915, the *Examiner* ran an editorial titled, "Grasping at the Shadow." The piece was virulently antisuffrage, disparaging women who wanted the vote, and characterizing them as disgruntled misfits. The author went on to assure dutiful homemakers that they were not to blame for the prosuffrage "harangues" of a few morbid deviants: "Be it said to the credit of womanhood that it is not, as a rule, the woman who rocks the cradle, who wants to cast the ballot: It is not the mother who teaches her children to say 'Now I lay me down to sleep' that harangues the populace; it is not the daughter who hopes to reign as queen over a happy home that longs for the uniform of the suffragette. It is, as a rule, the woman who despises her home, neglects her children, and scorns motherhood that heads parades and smashes windows."[2] Such hostility toward suffragist women was striking in 1915 in a state where women had been voting since 1870.

Even more striking was the fact that this clipping was reprinted without comment in a volume of Green River Valley ranchers' published memoirs, edited by women of the next generation. The editor-daughters of these early-twentieth-century ranchers evinced no reaction to "Grasping at the Shadow." They simply reprinted it amid several innocuous excerpts from the same newspaper about unrelated events—the meeting of a supper club, a music teacher's new pupils, a sentimental poem memorializing a drowned boy. The editors of these Green River Valley memoirs commented at length on the drowned boy, detailing his accidental death and expressing compassion toward the bereaved family. The antisuffrage article, however, drew no comment. The memoir editors introduced it with one line, "From this same issue of the *Examiner*, the days of the militant suffragette was [sic] recognized by—."[3]

Nowhere within these thirty-five collected memoirs of ranching on the upper Green River Valley was there mention of a prosuffrage faction. Nowhere in this text did the editors, only one generation removed from those whose stories they

The Paradox of Change

printed, offer information to balance the antisuffrage article. In short, the evidence indicates that Green River Valley ranchers did not take issue with it. Instead, the antisuffrage article and its random presentation in the memoirs suggests the essential conservatism of ranch culture toward questions of gender. Though the demands of ranching moved women to broaden their work roles, they refrained from marking such change with a conscious redefinition of gender. Instead, they affirmed ideological remnants of a Victorian sexual order, deflecting the egalitarian implications of crossover work. This suggests a cautious process of social change, in which the tail wagged the dog. Gender ideology shifted slightly to accommodate the broadening of women's work roles, but in a manner that simultaneously reinforced patriarchal notions of gender difference.

The gendering of ranch work reveals one more pattern worth mention. While ranch wives cast their effort in terms of group partnership, cattlemen emerged as heroic individuals. Phyllis Luman Metal titled her memoir *Cattle King on the Green River: The Family Life and Legends of Abner Luman; A Cowboy King of the Green River Valley*, though it was as much about her, her mother, and her grandmother as it was about Mr. Luman.[4] In the historical record left by women, family life had little room for female individualism. Rather, the family, and the women in it, supported the public accomplishments of men.

Cowcamp, as a masculine occupation, was also therefore a field for individual accomplishment. The few women who worked with cattle, if not camouflaged into anonymity as "fellers," gained notoriety as individualist women in a masculine world. Female rodeo stars of the early twentieth century represented the popular manifestation of this phenomena. By 1920, national rodeos such as the Pendleton Round-Up featured three women's events: bronc riding, trick riding, and the women's relay race. The few women who competed in these professional rodeos earned notoriety as female mavericks, individualist heroines. Theresa Jordan conveyed their novelty status in her description of 1920s rodeo stars Lucille Mulhall, Alice Greenough, Fox Hastings, Vera McGinnis, and Tad Lucas: "These rodeo women were stars, celebrities, their names well-known nationwide. They were wined and dined in every city, and the top magazines and papers gave them lengthy coverage. These 'little wisps of women' who could tame the wildest bronc or hang upside down over the hooves of a galloping steed, but who still dressed in silks and satins and loved to preen for men, charmed an America in love with the Wild West."[5] In the seams between working ranch culture and the mythic West of the popular imagination, gender roles were consistent. Family women—ranch wives—drew respect and social standing as contributing members of a group enterprise. Single women—ranch daughters or rodeo stars—sometimes enjoyed individualistic status as anomalies in the masculine world of the cowboy. The feminine world, then, emphasized identification with group success, while the mythic masculine world of the cowboy was identified with individualistic accomplishment. Such values limited the liberalizing implications of female crossovers into men's work.

Over time, a few daughters who worked without fanfare as their father's "cowboy" extended such role flexibility to their adult lives. They then encouraged their daughters, in turn, to develop whatever skills they preferred, whether cooking or cowpunching. In the generations beyond the scope of this study, cowcamp gradually would lose its gendered status as a male domain.[6]

The question of individualism, the mythic West, and women's place resonated further in the record of single women homesteaders. Often presented as exemplars of female independence, single women homesteaders attached a variety of meanings to this enterprise. Many simply filed claims to augment a family ranch, echoing ranch wives' ethic of group partnership. Others inherited management of a family ranch. Though working in concert with surviving family members, these women, like the Mary Barretts, held decision-making authority within the group. As heads of families, they exercised leadership, which we can read as a kind of independence.

Some single women also filed claims as real estate investments. Their purpose was to earn money through sale of the property. These women demonstrated an entrepreneurial rather than agrarian independence. Indeed, homesteading represented a unique economic opportunity for women, in that sale of a titled claim could yield enough cash to set aside as savings, a yield unmatched by the modest wages that characterized other female occupations on the early-twentieth-century rural frontier. Homesteading, then, represented a route toward economic independence for those single women who filed claims as investment properties.

Finally, homesteading also appeared as a metaphor for individualistic accomplishment in the published writings of woman homesteaders. These tales read like initiation stories. They depict lone women who overcome obstacles and discover new strengths—self-reliance and a sense of equality chief among them. These stories mirrored the aspirations of New Woman readers, who formed an eager audience for models of female independence. "Proving up" on a homestead claim symbolized proving that a woman could succeed by herself in the world beyond the home, in the world of individual initiative rather than service to family.

Ironically, these writers "paved the way" by looking backward. They celebrated the egalitarian, individualist spirit of the New Woman, using imagery of the Old West. As a literary symbol, filing a claim was charged with agrarian vir-

The Paradox of Change

tue, democratic opportunity, and the romance of the West as a place of self-reinvention. In short, the literary homesteaders affirmed gender role change through the nostalgic device of return to a rural frontier. In the worlds created by these writers, the romance of homesteading ennobled female ambitions toward independence. This, too, suggests a conservative process of gender role change, in which women invoked popular tradition to legitimize the path of transformation.

If homesteading provided a rural Western vision of New Womanhood for literary audiences, mining town women lived an urban version of gender role change in their daily lives. Over two generations, coal town women redefined their options through the world of work. As the service industries diversified, immigrant daughters left commercialized domesticity for white-collar work downtown. Clerical and secretarial positions drew young, American-educated women out of housekeeping and into offices and retail stores. For immigrant daughters, downtown work represented successful acculturation. Young, foreign-born, high-school graduates minimized their ethnic identity, emphasizing instead their grasp of the English language and of American customs. Such achievements qualified them for white-collar work, itself a symbol of upward mobility. For second-generation coal town women, economic versatility and assimilation were part of the same equation.

Indeed, assimilated immigrant daughters, once married, put white-collar skills to use in service to the family economy. Like the ranch woman's ethic of service to family, immigrant coal town women held to an ethic of family reciprocity. In the case of immigrants from rural Eastern Europe, traditions of mutual obligation between family members included wives' contributions to household support. This tradition went through two new incarnations in Sweetwater County—from subsistence agriculture in the old country, to keeping boarders in Sweetwater coal towns, and finally, by the 1920s, to white-collar work. While this tradition took new form, the expectation that women would place family well-being first continued.

Indeed, the broadening of town women's work roles outlines only part of the story. As with ranch women's work, the story acquires depth when the meanings of such activity are considered. The work of keeping boarders, for example, gains dimension when added to definitions of frontier. Women's work in mining town service industries is scarcely addressed in most histories of the West. Traditionally, history courses on white settlement in the trans-Mississippi West were organized around male occupational roles. Professors spoke of the trader's frontier, the miner's frontier, the transportation frontier. These frontier classifications treated male economic roles more or less in isolation from the community around them. The result was that women's activity remained largely invisible. In a review essay on the teaching of western history, William Cronon, Katherine Morrissey, Jay Gitlin, and Howard Lamar noted that women's work roles in the West, such as keeping boarders or raising poultry, never became the basis for a frontier classification. We do not, for example, speak of the "chicken frontier."[7] Such omissions reflected the unexamined assumption that women's roles were marginal to the "real work" of settling the West, or that women's roles were somehow ahistorical; they did not change over time. Sweetwater County history suggests otherwise.

The mining frontier in southwest Wyoming emerges incomplete without its counterpart, the service industry frontier. Integral to the extractive economy staffed by men were commercialized domestic services staffed by women. Rooming houses, laundries, hotels, restaurants, and the countless immigrant wives who kept boarders sustained the men who worked in the mines. After the turn of the century, as the immigrant population burgeoned, keeping boarders became the most common form of commercialized domesticity.

Indeed, southwest Wyoming could be recast as a mining/commercialized housekeeping frontier, for keeping boarders was no marginal activity. Roughly two thirds of all married, working-class women did so during the early-twentieth-century coal boom. Moreover, keeping boarders met economic and social needs crucial to immigrant survival. Women who kept boarders generated income for families who could not have subsisted on miner's wages alone. In addition, they provided newcomers with same-language housing, emotional support, and referrals to jobs and marriage partners. Such guidance formed an uninstitutionalized but vital phase in the assimilation of European immigrants. The example of keeping boarders suggests the power and significance of informal systems of social and economic exchange established by women in the industrializing West.

Courtship further underscored ties between households and the larger community, in which women played a central role. Through their choice of spouse, first-generation immigrant women bore responsibility for building kin-based ethnic community by choosing a partner of the same nationality. Because ethnic community did not exist residentially, the ties of kinship created through marriage became compelling sources of support in a population vulnerable to unemployment, work-related injury, and catastrophic illness. The Southern Slav example suggests that a spouse of the same nationality extended the web of kin ties that functioned as uninstitutionalized social welfare services. Second-generation women's responsibility to expand and perpetuate such networks meant that despite their new pattern of wage work outside the home, they did not adopt the social freedoms, such as unsupervised courtship, modeled by the independent New Woman of popular literature.

If mining town courtship reinforced the evidence of women's centrality in informal networks of social and economic exchange, rural courtship further demonstrated the situationality of gender systems. The rules for single women in ranching communities reflected a set of concerns particular to their demographic homogeneity and shared cultural background. Largely native-born, middle-class Midwesterners, ranchers shared a common value system that allowed courting couples unsupervised time together. At the same time, ranchers kept alive a Victorian double standard that held women responsible for sexual control. Just as Southern Slav women in coal towns felt the obligation to strengthen kin-based ethnic ties through their choice of spouse, so single ranch women sensed their responsibility for maintaining sexual reticence.

Though the liberalizing social and sexual mores of urban New Womanhood were not unknown in Sweetwater County, such values did not fit the needs of either mining or ranching communities. Instead, each community held single women to its own more conservative standards of social and sexual behavior. Adult supervision and sexual reserve marked courtship in mining and ranching communities, respectively. In the former case, the frontier meant that it was urgent to create kin-based ethnic networks in a chaotic environment that lacked residential ethnic cohesion. In the latter case, it meant that a powerful, undisturbed network was in place; single women who violated the ranching community's Victorian standard faced ostracism. For these reasons—situational reasons relating to local economic and demographic patterns—courtship took place within an attentive community network. Thus single women in Sweetwater County negotiated more than just relationships to their beaux. In the process of courtship, they also negotiated a relationship to their community. While isolation from eastern, urban conditions played some role in all of this, it seems more likely to suggest that the East, too, was full of situations in which courtship reflected, to varying degrees, relationships of accountability between a single woman and her community, which shaped the boundaries of female behavior.

Changing marriage patterns on the Sweetwater County frontier further underscored the situationality of gender relations. Regional economic conditions reverberated in Sweetwater County marriages. Ranching and coal mining were seasonal occupations with neither steady employment nor steady income. Consequently, spouses sometimes separated for months or years at a time, while husbands traveled in search of wage work. In the wake of such separations, some wives began challenging their husband's directives and redefining them as negotiable decisions.

Ethnicity, too, affected the balance of power within marriages. In the case of Croatian women, for example, migration to southwest Wyoming changed household structure in a way that increased wives' domestic authority. Young, married Croatian women typically left an extended family farm ruled by their mother-in-law in the old country, to establish nuclear family households with boarders in Wyoming company towns, where they became the senior women of their households. Such a windfall in domestic authority may have contributed to Croatian women's increased assertiveness within marriage.

Another clue to the erosion of patriarchal authority within marriage was the gradual decrease in family size over two generations. Women of the second generation practiced deliberate family limitation. Their willingness to shape marital sexuality around concern for their own reproductive health further reinforced the impression that frontier conditions in early-twentieth-century Sweetwater County catalyzed an increase in married women's domestic authority. Thus, the record of economically motivated marital separation, changes in household structure, and smaller family size add western dimension to that constellation of gender role change that historians call New Womanhood.

A final reflection on women's processes of adaptation and self-definition on the Sweetwater County frontier: amid immigrant cultures grounded in traditions of family and ethnic reciprocity, working-class coal town women held a paradoxical position. For even as the first generation gained domestic authority within marriage, and the second generation entered new occupational categories, the ties of family and community responsibility mediated the liberalizing effects of such changes. Kin-based and informal ethnic networks might just as easily foreclose individual expression as support it. For some, meeting the obligations that sustained family and community on the industrial frontier also constrained them to marry men of their parents' choosing, or to abandon their careers of choice.

Similarly, rural women's lives reveal a contradictory blend of tradition and adaptation, individualism and community. The gendering of ranch work suggested the force of shared, ritualized memory, in the form of westerners using popular mythology about the cowboy to sharpen boundaries between men's and women's work. Together, cowboy lore and the group work ethic framed ranch families' perceptions of woman's place in neo-traditionalist terms. Using such constructs, ranch women mediated change by affirming traditional values even as they acted out new patterns. Such conservatism reflected, in part, the real

The Paradox of Change

contingencies of agro-economic survival on the high plains. Ranch family members relied upon each other as a community of labor. Perhaps the necessity of cooperation and the vulnerability of family harmony moved women and men alike to reinforce familiar systems of gender hierarchy.

While most ranch women identified with a model of group success, women homesteader-writers drew on popular mythology about the West to promote a fully independent model of womanhood. But these women, like female cowboys and rodeo stars, accepted their place as mavericks. Their individual successes bore both the taint and the promise of exceptionalism. As much as they heralded new directions for women, their status as anomalies worthy of comment signaled a larger pattern of resistance to gender role redefinition. In rural Sweetwater County, the conservatism of ranch culture limited the liberalizing effects of both homesteading opportunity and the necessity for ungendered labor.

The assumption that frontier conditions liberated women because they disrupted gender roles thus calls for reexamination. Adaptations both to coal town life and to ranching on the arid plains did move women into new occupational roles, change household structure, and reduce family size. Such changes coincided superficially with the shift toward more individualistic, egalitarian values represented nationwide by the New Woman. But on the Sweetwater County frontier, adaptations also included powerful systems of mutuality, informal networks of support, which bound women to family and community. As often as not, women's responsibilities to a larger community of interest—be it her immediate family, extended kin, ethnic group, or rural cohort—outweighed individualistic choice. Only a few female voices made visible the connection between the vaunted individualism of the West and its reality as a masculine prerogative. Though the literary homesteaders, the female cowboys, and the rodeo stars articulated the possibilities of such privilege, it would be decades before their initiatives would find parallel in everyday life.

Appendix

Demographic analysis for this study was based on a random sample of one hundred households from the Federal Census Manuscript of Sweetwater County, Wyoming, for each decennial census year—1880, 1900, and 1910.[1] I encoded the following variables for all adult men and women, defining "adult" as age fifteen or older. All variables were encoded numerically:

Household Number (1-100)
Census Year
County Subregion (rural=agricultural settlement; urban=mining and railroad towns)
Sex
Race (white, African American, Asian, Native American)
Age
Marital Status (single, married, widowed, divorced)
Place of Birth
Literacy
Occupation
Household Membership

Interpretation of these data began with the encoding process itself, for I had to transform implicit information about women into explicit categories of analysis in order to make women's experience visible. First, I delineated the varieties of women's household work. Most census enumerators grouped all varieties of women's household work under the term "keeping house." Occasionally, they wrote "none" under occupation, or left the column blank. Yet women in Sweetwater County who kept house ran the gamut from those who lived in middle-class, private homes in town, to those who lived on ranches, to those who lived in company houses with boarders. Running a private, nuclear-family household in town, working a ranch, and keeping boarders in a Union Pacific rental were qualitatively different experiences. Accordingly, I developed a code which ac-

Appendix

counted for the following variations: ranch work; nonranch, nuclear-family housekeeping; and keeping boarders. In this way, analysis of women's occupations approximated the qualitative spectrum of household work in Sweetwater County.

Second, I developed a code which described household members by their relationship to the senior woman. Census enumerators described all household members by their relationship to the household head, who, in most cases, was an adult man. Because I wanted to make women's kinship ties visible, I recognized men as household heads whenever the census listed them as such, but I described household members by their relationship to the senior woman in the household. For example, a household recorded by the census enumerator would have appeared as follows:

Carl Nelson	Head
Annie Nelson	Wife
Elisabet Petersen	Sister-in-Law
George Dahlberg	Boarder

The example cited above, using my code, would appear as:

Annie Nelson	Senior Woman
Carl Nelson	Husband (household head)
Elisabet Petersen	Sister
George Dahlberg	Boarder

Analysis of household composition thus focused on the senior woman's relationship to household members, rather than on household members' relationships to a male head of household. This made women's kin and ethnic networks visible.

Third, to account for class differences, I inferred economic and social status from occupation and property ownership. Specifically, I created three class categories, based on the household head's occupation and whether the family owned or rented their home: "Working Class" referred to members of any household headed by a day laborer, unskilled miner, railroad hand, or landless ranchhand; and in the case of female-headed households, by a waitress, cook, laundress, or keeper of boarders. Most working-class households in Sweetwater County were rentals. "Middle Class" referred to members of any household headed by a land-claiming rancher, skilled miner or railroad employee (for example, "engineer"), craftsman, small business owner, supervisor, or municipal employee; and in the case of female-headed households, by a teacher, nurse, secretary, hotel proprietor, restaurateur, or small business owner. The incidence of home ownership, mortgaged homes, and rented homes varied among the middle classes. "Upper Class" described any members of a household

Appendix

headed by a business executive, corporation owner, or professional.[2] Upper-class families generally owned their home. Using these criteria to infer the class status of each household, I then assigned to each adult woman the class status which I had ascribed to her household.

Encoding place of birth was problematic because foreign-born nationalities were so numerous in Sweetwater County that within a one hundred-household sample for each census year, many nationalities surfaced in proportions too small to be statistically significant. Instead of recording every nationality that appeared on the census manuscripts for Sweetwater County, then, I first encoded the two broad categories, native-born and foreign-born. Then I collapsed individual nations into the following regional categories:

France, Belgium
Germany, Austria, Switzerland
Eastern Europe (Poland, Hungary, Croatia, Slovenia, and other Eastern European ethnicities)
Norway, Finland, Denmark, Sweden
England, Scotland, Wales, Ireland
Italy
Greece
Japan
China

Similarly, to create statistically viable categories for native-born residents, I collapsed the forty-eight states into the following regional categories:

Northeast and Mid-Atlantic states (Maine, New Hampshire, Vermont, Massachusetts, Connecticut, Rhode Island, New York, Pennsylvania, New Jersey)
Chesapeake, Bluegrass, and Southern states (Maryland, Delaware, Virginia, West Virginia, Tennessee, Kentucky, North Carolina, South Carolina, Mississippi, Alabama, Louisiana, Arkansas)
Midwest and Northern Midwest states (Ohio, Illinois, Indiana, Iowa, Missouri, Michigan, Wisconsin, Minnesota)
Central and Southern Plains states (North Dakota, South Dakota, Nebraska, Kansas)
Far West states, inland (Montana, Colorado, Utah, Nevada, Idaho, New Mexico)
West Coast states (Washington, Oregon, California)
Wyoming

Thus I could approximate broad regional and ethnic differences, as well as differentiate between native and foreign-born settlers.

Appendix

The 1900 and 1910 census added the date of immigration for every foreign-born resident. I encoded these dates to calculate patterns of migration. By checking dates of immigration against dates of marriage, I determined which couples married before immigrating; whether they immigrated together or separately; and for those who immigrated separately, the average length of time spent apart. This proved valuable to the discussion of marital separations necessitated by the demands of relocation.

For adult women, I encoded several additional categories of analysis. One was the number of children for each mother. The 1900 and 1910 census offered up two more variables for women. First, to the number of children born to each mother was added the number of surviving children for each mother. And second, the 1900 and 1910 censuses also recorded the number of years married for each couple. I encoded these variables for 1900 and 1910, which allowed analysis of child mortality rates and of the average age at marriage for men and women.

I encoded household structure for each adult woman, using the following categories:

Primary Nuclear (parents and their children)
Nuclear Augmented (nuclear plus non-kin)
Extended (nuclear plus relatives)
Extended Augmented (nuclear, relatives, and non-kin)
Hotel

These categories facilitated measurement of the larger patterns of women's kinship networks and household enterprise, such as the proportion of women housing relatives, or the proportion of women keeping boarders. I also encoded the number of boarders per household, the number of extended kin per household, and the number of servants per household, figures which added further dimension to the picture of household structure in Sweetwater County. In addition, I encoded the incidence of female-headed households for women of all marital categories: single, married, widowed, and divorced. This revealed the most common living arrangements for women outside of marriage. Finally, I encoded all adult women's names alphabetically. This allowed me to trace specific women across time, from one census to the next.

Following the example of David Emmons's study of class and ethnicity in Butte, Montana, during the late nineteenth and early twentieth century,[3] I chose to omit statistical tables from this manuscript. Instead, the demographic analysis is fully integrated into the text. The statistics gleaned from such analyses are not the centerpiece of this study; they function directly as supporting evidence for patterns of settlement, economic development, and gender role change.

Notes

ABBREVIATIONS

AHR   *American Historical Review*
JAH   *Journal of American History*
MMWH   *Montana: The Magazine of Western History*
WAS   Wyoming Archaeological Services, Western Wyoming Community College, Rock Springs WY
WPA   Works Progress Administration, Cheyenne WY
WSAHD   Wyoming State Archives and Historical Department, Cheyenne WY

INTRODUCTION

1. "Grasping at the Shadow," *Big Piney Examiner*, October 20, 1915; reprinted in *Tales of the Seeds-Ke-Dee*, ed. Sublette County Artists' Guild (Denver: Big Mountain Press, 1963), 221–22.
2. Barbara Welter, "The Cult of True Womanhood, 1820–1860," *American Quarterly* 18 (summer 1966): 151–74; Linda Kerber, "Separate Spheres, Female Worlds and Women's Place," *Journal of American History* 75 (June 1988): 9–39.
3. Richard White, *"It's Your Misfortune and None of My Own": A New History of the American West* (Norman: University of Oklahoma Press, 1991), 613.
4. John Mack Faragher, "The Frontier Trail: Rethinking Turner and Reimagining the American West," *American Historical Review* 98 (February 1993): 106–17; and Allan G. Bogue, "The Significance of the History of the American West: Postcripts and Prospects," *Western Historical Quarterly* 24 (February 1993): 45–68.
5. Frederick Jackson Turner, *The Frontier in American History* (New York: Holt, Rinehart, and Winston, 1920).
6. Anne M. Butler, "Through a Lens Less Turnerian: Women on the Frontier," *Reviews in American History* 17 (September 1989): 417–22; Susan Armitage, "Through Women's Eyes: A New View of the West," in *The Women's West*, ed. Susan Armitage and Elizabeth Jameson (Norman: University of Oklahoma Press, 1987), 9–18; and

Katherine Morrissey, "Engendering the West," in *Under an Open Sky: Rethinking America's Western Past*, ed. William Cronon, George Miles, and Jay Gitlin (New York: W. W. Norton, 1992), 132–44.

7. Sandra Myres, *Westering Women and the Frontier Experience, 1800–1915* (Albuquerque: University of New Mexico Press, 1982); Dorothy Gray, *Women of the West* (Millbrae CA: Les Femmes Press, 1976); and Lillian Schissel, *Women's Diaries of the Westward Journey* (New York: Schocken Books, 1982), 59–71.

8. John M. Faragher, *Women and Men on the Overland Trail* (New Haven: Yale University Press, 1979).

9. Patricia Limerick, *Legacy of Conquest: The Unbroken Past of the American West* (New York: W. W. Norton, 1987); White, *"It's Your Misfortune,"* and William Cronon, George Miles, and Jay Gitlin, "Becoming West: Toward a New Meaning for Western History," in Cronon, Miles, and Gitlin, *Under an Open Sky*, 3–27.

10. Sarah Deutsch, "Coming Together, Coming Apart: Women's History and the West," *Montana: The Magazine of Western History* 41 (spring 1991): 57–73, 61; Elizabeth Jameson, "Women as Workers, Women as Civilizers: True Womanhood in the American West," in Armitage and Jameson, *The Woman's West*, 145–64.

11. Gerda Lerner, "Reconceptualizing Differences among Women," *Journal of Women's History* 2, no. 3 (winter 1990): 106–22; and Elizabeth Fox-Genovese, "Between Individualism and Fragmentation: American Culture and the New Literary Studies of Race and Gender," *American Quarterly* 42 (March 1990): 7–34.

12. Sarah Deutsch, *No Separate Refuge: Culture, Class and Gender on an Anglo-Hispanic Frontier in the American Southwest, 1880–1940* (New York: Oxford University Press, 1987); Paula Petrik, *"No Step Backward": Women and Family on the Rocky Mountain Mining Frontier, Helena, Montana, 1865–1900* (Helena: Montana Historical Society Press, 1987).

13. John Mack Faragher, "Twenty Years of Western Women's History," *Montana: The Magazine of Western History* 41 (spring 1991): 71–73 (quote is on p. 73).

14. Ethnicity analysis of all town-dwelling men and women, 1880, 1900, 1910 census. To do a demographic analysis of Sweetwater County, I took a random sample of one hundred households for each census year—1880, 1900, and 1910. Throughout this study, the terms "men," "women," or "adult" refer to persons over age fifteen unless otherwise specified, and the term "census" refers to the Sweetwater County census manuscript. For complete discussion of quantitative methodology for this study, see the appendix.

15. Ethnicity analysis of adult men and women, Sweetwater County census, 1880, 1900, 1910.

16. Ethnicity analysis of foreign-born men and women; 1880 census. Other nationalities composed much smaller fractions of the foreign-born population at this time: Japa-

nese, 13.6 percent; Scandinavians, 11.1 percent; Canadians, 10.5 percent; and Germans, 5.5 percent.
17. Ethnicity analysis of foreign-born men and women, 1900 census.
18. Ethnicity analysis of foreign-born men and women; 1900, 1910 census.
19. Earl Stinneford, "Mines and Miners: The Eastern Europeans in Wyoming," in *Peopling the High Plains: Wyoming's European Heritage*, ed. Gordon Olaf Hendrickson (WSAHD, 1977), 121–48, 124.
20. Sweetwater County census, 1880, 1900, 1910. Unguren, interview; Gardner, interview.
21. Swanson, interview; George Osselton, "As I Remember Lionkol," unpublished memoir (WAS).
22. Elinore Pruitt Stewart, *Letters of a Woman Homesteader* (1914; reprint, Boston: Houghton Mifflin, 1982), 215; Culbertson and Howell, interview; and Mae E. Mickelson, *Bits and Pieces: Your Own Western History Magazine* (Newcastle WY: October 1969).
23. Robert Wiebe, *The Search for Order, 1877–1920* (New York: Hill & Wang, 1967); Kathy Peiss, *Cheap Amusements: Working Women and Leisure in Turn-of-the-Century New York* (Philadelphia: Temple University Press, 1986); Alice Kessler-Harris, *Out to Work: A History of Wage-Earning Women in the United States* (New York: Oxford University Press, 1982); and Neil Wynn, *From Progressivism to Prosperity: World War I and American Society* (New York: Holmes and Meier, 1986).
24. Carl Frederick Kraenzel, *The Great Plains in Transition* (Norman: University of Oklahoma Press, 1955), 138, table 4.
25. Sylvia Van Kirk, *Many Tender Ties: Women in Fur Trade Society, 1670–1870* (Norman: University of Oklahoma Press, 1980). Van Kirk underscored links between intimate partnership and community life. See also Jameson, "Women as Workers," 145–64: women in Colorado mining towns perceived little division between their family and community responsibilities.
26. Glenda Riley, "Western Women's History: A Look at Some of the Issues," MMWH 41 (spring 1991): 66–70, 69.
27. Faragher, "Twenty Years of Western Women's History," MMWH, 73; Faragher, "History from the Inside Out: Writing the History of Women in Rural America," *American Quarterly* 33 (winter 1981): 537–57; Virginia Scharff, "Gender and Western History: Is Anybody Home on the Range?" MMWH 41 (spring 1991): 62–65.
28. Robert V. Hine, *The American West: An Interpretive History* (Boston: Little Brown, 1973), vii.
29. Roderick Nash, *Wilderness and the American Mind* (New Haven: Yale University Press, 1978), 141–60; Henry Nash Smith, *Virgin Land: The American West as Symbol and Myth* (Cambridge: Harvard University Press, 1951), 92–111.

30. Paula Nelson, *After the West Was Won: Homesteaders and Town-Builders in Western South Dakota, 1900–1917* (Iowa City: University of Iowa Press, 1986).
31. Susan Johnson, "Sharing Bed and Board: Cohabitation and Cultural Differences in Central Arizona Mining Towns, 1863–1873," in Armitage and Jameson, *The Women's West*, 77–91. Johnson found that Anglo mining communities invoked Victorian gender ideology to deflect the liberalizing implications of new behaviors among women.
32. See the appendix for explanation of variables used in demographic analysis of Federal census manuscripts for Sweetwater County, 1880, 1900, and 1910.
33. Bruce Rosenberg, *The Code of the West* (Bloomington: Indiana University Press, 1982), 3–4; Clyde Milner, "The View from Wisdom: Four Layers of History and Regional Identity," in Cronon, Miles, and Gitlin, *Under an Open Sky*, 203–22.
34. Alan Lomax, Introduction to *The Folk Songs of North America* (New York: Doubleday, 1975), xv–xxx.
35. Barbara Allen, "Story in Oral History: Clues to Historical Consciousness," *Journal of American History* 79, no. 2 (September 1992): 606–11; Sherna Gluck, "What's So Special about Women? Women's Oral History," *Frontiers: A Journal of Women's Studies* 2 (summer 1977): 3–14.
36. Of these one hundred interviews, I drew illustrative stories from about thirty of them, based on their quality as the more vivid and detailed narratives. Those I did not cite echoed material more thoroughly covered in other narratives.
37. Ora Wright and Lenora Wright, *Our Valley, Eden Valley, Wyoming* (Portland OR: Gann, 1987); Sublette County Artists Guild, eds., *Tales of the Seeds-Ke-Dee*.
38. Theresa Jordan, ed., *Cowgirls: Women of the American West, An Oral History* (New York: Doubleday, 1984).
39. Clyde Milner, "The Shared Memory of Montana Pioneers," *Montana: The Magazine of Western History* 37, no. 1 (winter 1987): 2–13.

1. SWEETWATER COUNTY: DESERT HIGHWAY, COMPANY TOWN, COWBOY WEST

1. A. Howard Cutting, "Journal of an Overland Trip, 1863," Overland manuscript collections, Henry H. Huntington Library, San Marino CA; Isabella Bird, *A Lady's Life in the Rocky Mountains* (1883; reprint, New York: Ballantine Books, 1971), 22.
2. Wright and Wright, *Our Valley*, 8; Florence Kerr and Margaret Sowers, "Historical Sketch of Sweetwater County," WPA Historical Records Survey, WSAHD, 5–17; T. A. Larson, *History of Wyoming* (Lincoln: University of Nebraska Press, 1965), 1–2.
3. Tributaries of the Green River also include the Henry's Fork and State Creek.
4. Kerr and Sowers, "Historical Sketch," 5–17; T. A. Larson, *History of Wyoming*, 1–2.

Notes to Pages 16–21

5. Larson, *History of Wyoming*, 3–7, 137.
6. Ray Allen Billington, *Westward Expansion: A History of the American Frontier*, 4th ed. (New York: MacMillan, 1974), 379–88; Larson, *History of Wyoming*, 12–13.
7. Lola Homsher and Mary Lou Pence, *The Ghost Towns of Wyoming* (New York: Hastings House, 1956), 12–15; Larson, *History of Wyoming*, 13–16; Dee Brown, *Bury My Heart at Wounded Knee* (New York: Holt, Rinehart, & Winston, 1970), chapters 4–7, pp. 67–170.
8. Homsher and Pence, *Ghost Towns*, 15.
9. Larson, *History of Wyoming*, 33–34.
10. Billington, *Western Expansion*, 572; Larson, *History of Wyoming*, 20–35; White, *"It's Your Misfortune,"* 94–118.
11. Larson, *History of Wyoming*, 37–41.
12. Homsher and Pence, *Ghost Towns*, 197–98.
13. Kerr and Sowers, "Historical Sketch," 6–8.
14. Homsher and Pence, *Ghost Towns*, 197.
15. Homsher and Pence, *Ghost Towns*, 196–202.
16. Edward M. Lee, "The Woman Movement in Wyoming," *The Galaxy* 13 (June 1872): 755–60, in Huntington Library Collections. Quoted in Larson, *History of Wyoming*, 79–80.
17. Larson, *History of Wyoming*, 79–80.
18. Larson, *History of Wyoming*, 108.
19. Kerr and Sowers, "Historical Sketch," 9–10; *History of the Union Pacific Coal Mines, 1868–1940* (Omaha: The Colonial Press, 1940) [hereafter cited as *U.P. History*], 46–47.
20. Leskovec, interview.
21. *U.P. History*, 46–51; Dudley Gardner and Val Brinkerhoff, *Historical Images of Sweetwater County* (Virginia Beach VA: Donning Company Publishers, 1993), 49–50.
22. *U.P. History*, 47–48; Larson, *History of Wyoming*, 37–38, 114–15, 378; A. Dudley Gardner and Verla Flores, *Forgotten Frontier: A History of Coal Mining in Wyoming* (Boulder: Westview Press, 1989), 26.
23. Union Pacific Superintendent Dyer O. Clark, quoted in Gardner and Flores, *Forgotten Frontier*, 103–4.
24. Gardner and Flores, *Forgotten Frontier*, 28–29.
25. Kerr and Sowers, "Historical Sketch," 16–17; Paul Crane, "The Chinese Massacre," *Annals of Wyoming* 12 (January 1940): 47–55, and 12 (April 1940): 153–61; John Paige, "Country Squires and Laborers: British Immigrants in Wyoming," in Hendrickson, *Peopling the Plains*, 1–23; Larson, *History of Wyoming*, 113–14, 143; KLS radio transcripts, "Chinese in Evanston," WSAHD, OH-429.

26. Gardner and Flores, *Forgotten Frontier*, 83.
27. Analysis of ethnicity for adult men and women, Sweetwater County census, 1880, 1900.
28. *U.P. History*, 52.
29. *U.P. History*, 48–52; Larson, *History of Wyoming*, 147, 196; Gardner and Flores, *Forgotten Frontier*, 40–41, 72–73, 79.
30. Gardner and Flores, *Forgotten Frontier*, 52–71.
31. Analysis of residency for women, Sweetwater County census, 1900.
32. Huston, interview.
33. Kerr and Sowers, "Historical Sketch," 18; Larson, *History of Wyoming*, 164–65, 173; Dorothy E. Cook, "History of the Sheep Industry in Wyoming," Wyoming WPA, April 23, 1941, WSAHD MSS-WPA-327.
34. Kerr and Sowers, "Historical Sketch," 18.
35. Kerr and Sowers, "Historical Sketch," 18; Larson, *History of Wyoming*, 108–9.
36. Huston, interview.
37. Larson, *History of Wyoming*, 173–76.
38. Larson, *History of Wyoming*, 177–79.
39. "Abner Luman," *Progressive Men of the State of Wyoming* (Chicago: A. W. Brown, 1903), 194–96.
40. *Wyoming Agricultural Statistics* (Cheyenne: Wyoming State Department of Agriculture, 1923), 29; quoted in Cook, "History of the Sheep Industry," 8.
41. "Abner Luman," *Progressive Men*, 195; Phyllis Luman Metal and Doris Platts, *Cattle King on the Green River: The Family Life and Legends of Abner Luman, A Cowboy King of the Upper Green River Valley in the Twenties* (Wilson WY: Sunshine Ranch & Friends, 1983).
42. Paige, "Country Squires and Laborers," 14–15.
43. Residency analysis for men and women, 1880, 1900 census. Only 90 out of 699 adult residents lived in rural areas.
44. Cook, "History of the Sheep Industry," 6.
45. Secretary of the Territory, *Resources of Wyoming, 1889: The Vacant Public Lands and How to Obtain Them* (Cheyenne: The Daily Sun Electric Print, 1889), 64.
46. "Sweetwater County; One Vast Coal Bed Underlying a Fine Grazing Country," *Rock Springs Miner*, Special Illustrated Edition, May 17–June 17, 1897, 1, WSAHD MSS-WPA-1695.
47. Larson, *History of Wyoming*, 306.
48. Territorial Secretary, *Resources of Wyoming*, 64–65.
49. Larson, *History of Wyoming*, 303.
50. "Eden Irrigation Project Is Sold," *Rock Springs Miner*, August 13, 1926, 4.

51. Larson, *History of Wyoming*, 336; *U.P. History*, 138–41.
52. *U.P. History*, 150–53.
53. *U.P. History*, 141.
54. David Kathka, "The Italian Experience in Wyoming," in Hendrickson, *Peopling the Plains*, 68–94, 75–77.
55. Krmpotich, interview; Pivik, interview.
56. Earl Stinneford, "Mines and Miners," 124–25.
57. Gardner and Flores, *Forgotten Frontier*, 116–17.
58. "Basic Wage Rates and Hours of Service; . . . Taken from Payrolls and Wage Salaries, Union Pacific Railroad and Coal Company," in *U.P. History*, xli.
59. Larson, *History of Wyoming*, 336–41; Kathka, "The Italian Experience," 74.
60. Gardner and Flores, *Forgotten Frontier*, 117–26.
61. *Rock Springs Rocket*, January 27, 1911, February 3, 1911.
62. Gardner and Flores, *Forgotten Frontier*, 125–26.
63. Ethnicity analysis of adult men and women, Sweetwater County census, 1900, 1910.
64. Ethnicity analysis of adult men and women, Sweetwater County census, 1900, 1910. During this period, some Hungarians were listed on the census manuscripts as "Austrian."
65. Kathka, "The Italian Experience," 72; Dean Talagan, "Faith, Hard Work, and Family: The Story of the Wyoming Hellenes," in Hendrickson, *Peopling the Plains*, 149–68, 163; and Stinneford, "Mines and Miners," 124.
66. Gordon Olaf Hendrickson, "Immigration and Assimilation in Wyoming," in Hendrickson, *Peopling the Plains*, 175–79; quote, 179.
67. Stinneford, "Mines and Miners," 125.
68. Letter to Dee Garceau from Mary Lou Anselmi Unguren, June 5, 1994; Unguren, interview.
69. Kathka, "The Italian Experience," 73; Leskovec, interview; Taucher, interview.
70. Kovach, interview.
71. Ronald C. Brown, *Hard Rock Miners: The Intermountain West, 1860–1920* (College Station: Texas A & M University Press, 1979), 75–98.
72. Richard Lingenfelter, *The Hard Rock Miners: A History of the Mining Labor Movement in the American West, 1863–1893* (Berkeley: University of California Press, 1974), 23–27; quote, 23.
73. Gardner and Flores, *Forgotten Frontier*, 98; H. B. Humphrey, *Historical Summary of Coal Mine Explosions in the United States, 1810–1958* (Washington DC: Government Printing Office, 1960), 17, 22, 38–41.
74. Gardner and Flores, *Forgotten Frontier*, 151–56.
75. Larson, *History of Wyoming*, 346–47.

76. Larson, *History of Wyoming*, 362.
77. Larson, *History of Wyoming*, 366–72; Bret Wallach, "Sheep Ranching in the Dry Corner of Wyoming," *Geographical Review* 71 (1981): 51–63; see 53–54.
78. Josephine Jons, "The Ranches in Sublette County," Wyoming WPA, 1938, WSAHD MSS-WPA-1277, 4.
79. Larson, *History of Wyoming*, 385.
80. Gardner and Brinkerhoff, *Sweetwater County*, 64; Wire and Stewart, interview.
81. Robert Rhodes, *Booms and Busts on Bitter Creek: A History of Rock Springs, Wyoming* (Boulder: Pruett, 1987), 116–18; Gardner and Flores, *Forgotten Frontier*, 126–27; Larson, *History of Wyoming*, 396–98.
82. "Basic Wage Rates," *U.P. History*, xli; Larson, *History of Wyoming*, 398.
83. Maureen Greenwald, *Women, War, and Work: The Impact of World War I* (Westport CT: Greenwood Press, 1980); Rhodes, *Booms and Busts*, 117–19; Gardner and Brinkerhoff, *Sweetwater County*, 98.
84. Wright and Wright, "Club History, copied from Stella Engle's Year Books," *Our Valley*, 181–83, Women's Club of Rock Springs, Club Records, Rock Springs WY Public Library, Archival Collections; Gardner and Brinkerhoff, *Sweetwater County*, 101; Donald Hodgson and Vivien Hills, "Dream and Fulfillment: Germans in Wyoming," in Hendrickson, *Peopling the Plains*, 56; and Rhodes, *Booms and Busts*, 120.
85. *Wyoming State Business Directory* (Denver: Gazetteer, 1914), 418–30.
86. Kessler-Harris, *Out to Work*; changes in Sweetwater coal town women's work patterns are explored in chapter 7 of this volume.
87. Larson, *History of Wyoming*, 414–16.
88. Larson, *History of Wyoming*, 416; Wallach, "Sheep Ranching," *Geographical Review*, 53.
89. Single women homesteaders are investigated in chapter 6 of this volume.
90. Gardner and Flores, *Forgotten Frontier*, 161; Larson, *History of Wyoming*, 411–13.
91. Gardner and Flores, *Forgotten Frontier*, 158–61; Rhodes, *Booms and Busts*, 146–47.
92. The role of women's household work in the coal town economy is fully addressed in chapter 7 of this volume.
93. Larson, *History of Wyoming*, 412.
94. Gardner and Flores, *Forgotten Frontier*, 158–59.
95. Paige, "Country Squires and Laborers," 1–23; Hodgson and Hills, "Dream and Fulfillment," 35–65; Talagan, "Faith, Hard Work, and Family," 149–68; Kathka, "The Italian Experience," 68–94; and Stinneford, "Mines and Miners," 121–48.
96. Stinneford, "Mines and Miners," 130; Kathka, "The Italian Experience," 84; and Paige, "Country Squires and Laborers," 20–21.
97. Hodgson and Hills, "Dream and Fulfillment," 42–43; Kathka, "The Italian Experience," 82–84.

Notes to Pages 33-39

98. Frolic, interview; Metelko, interview; and Stinneford, "Mines and Miners," 141–42.
99. Women's Club of Rock Springs, Club Records, Rock Springs WY Public Library Archives.
100. Susan Strasser, *Never Done: A History of American Housework* (New York: Pantheon Books, 1982), 85, 96–100.
101. Ferdani and Constantino, interview.
102. *U.P. History*, 52, 152. Metelko, interview; Leskovec, interview; Krmpotich, interview.
103. Frolic, interview; Metelko, interview; Leskovec, interview; Strasser, *Never Done: A History of American Housework*, 78–85.
104. Wire, interview; Wright and Wright, *Our Valley*, 130–31.
105. Stinneford, "Mines and Miners," 124; David Cookson, "The Basques in Wyoming," in Hendrickson, *Peopling the Plains*, 107–8; Kathka, "The Italian Experience," 68, 88; Larson, *History of Wyoming*, 412; Leskovec, interview.
106. United States Bureau of the Census, *United States Census of Population: 1890 Population* (Washington DC: U.S. Department of Commerce, 1890), xxxi.
107. Turner, "The Significance of the Frontier," in Billington and Ridge, *America's Frontier Story*, 18; Nash, "The Wilderness Cult," *Wilderness and the American Mind*, 141–60.
108. Smith, *Virgin Land*, 92–111.
109. Chapter 7, this volume, explores how popular images of the cowboy West influenced ranchers themselves.
110. Jack Forbes, "Frontiers in American History and the Role of the Frontier Historian," *Ethnohistory* 15 (spring 1968): 203–35, 208; Deutsch, "Coming Together, Coming Apart," MMWH, 58–61.
111. Forbes, "Frontiers in American History," 221.
112. Carlos Schwantes, "The Concept of the Wage Worker's Frontier: A Framework for Future Research," *Western Historical Quarterly* 18 (January 1987): 39–55, 46.
113. Schwantes, "Wage Worker's Frontier," 41.
114. Kathka, "The Italian Experience," 73; Leskovec, interview.
115. Analysis of sex of town-dwellers, Sweetwater County census, 1880, 1900, 1910.
116. Schwantes, "Wage Worker's Frontier," 44.
117. Stinneford, "Mines and Miners," 213.

2. FAMILY NETWORKS: A WEB OF SUPPORT

1. Witka, interview.
2. Witka, interview.
3. John Bodnar, *The Transplanted: A History of Immigrants in Urban America* (Bloom-

ington: Indiana University Press, 1985); Ewa Morawski, *For Bread with Butter: Life Worlds of East Central Europeans in Johnstown, Pennsylvania, 1890–1940* (Cambridge: Cambridge University Press, 1985); Micaela DiLeonardo, "The Myth of the Urban Village: Women, Work, and Family among Italian-Americans in Twentieth-Century California," in Armitage and Jameson, *The Women's West*, 277–90; and David Emmons, *The Butte Irish: Class and Ethnicity in an American Mining Town, 1875–1925* (Urbana: University of Illinois Press, 1989), 13–34.

4. Emmons, *The Butte Irish*, 13–34; DiLeonardo, "Women, Work, and Family," 277–90; and John Bodnar, "Family and Community in Pennsylvania's Anthracite Region, 1900–1940," *Pennsylvania Heritage* 9, no. 3 (summer 1983): 13–17.

5. Metelko, interview; Semos, interview; Taucher, interview; Krmpotich, interview; Leskovec, interview; Powell, interview by Burns and Cranford. See also Gardner and Flores, *Forgotten Frontier*, 85.

6. For rural Italy, see Judy Smith, *Family Connections: A History of Italian and Jewish Immigrant Lives in Providence, R.I., 1900–1940* (Albany: State University of New York Press, 1985); for Finnish, Italian, and Polish family networks in the old country, see Jean Burnet, ed., *Looking into My Sister's Eyes: An Exploration in Women's History* (Toronto: Multicultural History Society of Ontario, 1986).

7. Semos, interview.

8. Semos, interview.

9. Taucher, interview. See also Metelko, interview; Leskovec, interview, Krmpotich, interview; and Yugovich, interview.

10. *U.P. History*, 46–47; T. A. Larson, *History of Wyoming*, 147, 196; and Gardner and Flores, *Forgotten Frontier*, 52–55, 116–17.

11. Occupational analysis of children age fourteen and younger; 1880, 1900, 1910 census.

12. Metelko, interview; Leskovec, interview; Frolic, interview.

13. United States Census Bureau, *Thirteenth Census of the United States*, vol. 4, *Population, 1910, Occupational Statistics [Wyoming]* (Washington DC: Government Printing Office, 1914).

14. Taucher, interview; Semos, interview.

15. Mean age for men and women, 1880, 1900, 1910 census.

16. In 1880, 6.7 percent of foreign-born adults were over fifty; in 1900, 10.9 percent; and in 1910, 4.9 percent. Age analysis for foreign-born men and women; 1880, 1900, 1910 census.

17. Gardner and Flores, *Forgotten Frontier*, 38–39.

18. Age analysis for foreign-born adults; 1880, 1900, 1910 census combined.

19. "We Nominate as Women of the Week, Mrs. Anna Magnagna," *Rock Springs Miner*, July 9, 1950.

20. The custom of close supervision of young, unmarried, immigrant women by parents, relatives, or other adults is explored in chapter 3 of this study.
21. Metelko, interview.
22. Metelko, interview.
23. Metelko, interview.
24. Household membership analysis for unmarried, foreign-born women over age fifteen; 1880, 1900, 1910 census samples combined.
25. Household membership analysis for unmarried foreign-born women over fifteen; 1910 census.
26. Bodnar, *The Transplanted*, xviii; DiLeonardo, "The Myth of the Urban Village," 277–90.
27. "Rock Springs, That Grew into a Great City," *U.P. History*, 46–47.
28. Census manuscripts showed the ethnic diversity of working-class neighborhoods. For example, "Great Flat," typical of Rock Springs neighborhoods in the 1900 census, showed the first house inhabited by Italians, the next by Austrians, the next by Norwegians, the next by Finns, the two beside that by Italians, and the three following that by Danes. The 1910 census showed the same pattern.
29. Ethnicity analysis of adult men and women; 1900, 1910 census. Out of 654 town dwellers sampled, 432, or 66 percent, were foreign born. By 1921, Rock Springs alone boasted forty-one nationalities. See *Wyoming State Business Directory* (Denver: Gazetteer, 1921), 358. Men outnumbered women 3 to 1. Analysis of ethnicity and gender for adult residents; 1900, 1910 census.
30. Leskovec, interview; Krmpotich, interview; Gardner and Flores, *Forgotten Frontier*, 88.
31. Zelenka, interview; Krmpotich, interview; Swanson, interview; Kovach, interview; and Zampedri, interview.
32. Leskovec, interview; Krmpotich, interview; and Taucher, interview; Stinneford, "Mines and Miners," 126–27; and Schwantes, "The Wage-Worker's Frontier," 39–55. Demographic analysis based on a random sample of one hundred households per census year did not always yield the same streets from one decade to the next. Hence, it was not possible to check for residential persistence. Evidence from personal narratives, however, consistently referred to the transience of neighborhoods.
33. Gardner and Flores, *Forgotten Frontier*, 107; Larson, *History of Wyoming*, 109–11, 378–80.
34. Gardner and Flores, *Forgotten Frontier*, 107.
35. Leskovec, interview; Bozovich, interview.
36. Bodnar, *The Transplanted*, 178.
37. Krmpotich, interview.

38. Krmpotich and Krmpotich, interview.
39. Krmpotich, interview.
40. Krmpotich, interview.
41. Krmpotich, interview.
42. Krmpotich, interview. Similarly, Swedish immigrant Anna Semos adopted two of her sister's children following her sister's death. Semos, interview.
43. Thompson, interview.
44. Thompson, interview.
45. Jameson, "Women as Workers," 145–64, 149.
46. Jameson, "Women as Workers," 149.
47. Ethnicity analysis, adult rural women; 1880, 1900, 1910 census. Analyses of the rural population were calculated from a subsample of twenty-one rural households from each census year; sixty-three rural households, total.
48. Mean age, rural adults; 1880, 1900, 1910 census. In 1880, the average age of rural men and women was 32; in 1900, 34.7; and in 1910, 31.6.
49. Wright and Wright, *Our Valley*.
50. Wright and Wright, *Our Valley*, 5.
51. Wright and Wright, *Our Valley*, 5–6.
52. Wright and Wright, *Our Valley*, 5–6.
53. Wright and Wright, *Our Valley*, 97.
54. Wright and Wright, *Our Valley*, 30; John Wright household, 1910 Sweetwater County census; and Frank Wright household, 1910 Sweetwater County census.
55. Wright and Wright, *Our Valley*, 98.
56. "Urban" refers both to coal towns like Rock Springs and Superior and to the railroad town of Green River.
57. Cora Beach, "Mrs. Caroline Eggs," in *Women of Wyoming* (Casper WY: S. E. Boyer, 1927), 2:298–300; Eggs-Gaensslen family history, unpublished manuscript written by Eleanor Eggs Gaensslen for the Sweetwater County Historical Society, October 11, 1981, Sweetwater County Historical Society Archives, Green River WY [hereafter Eggs-Gaensslen Family History].
58. Beach, "Mrs. Caroline Eggs," 2:298–300.
59. Beach, "Mrs. Caroline Eggs," 2:298.
60. Beach, "Mrs. Caroline Eggs," 2:299–300.
61. Eggs-Gaensslen Family History.
62. Beach, "Mrs. Caroline Eggs," 2:300; Eggs-Gaensslen Family History.
63. Schofield, interview.
64. Graf, interview; *Wyoming State Business Directory* (Denver: Gazetteer), 1914:280–81; 1918:280, 294; 1921:244–46; 1925:239, 241.

3. "I GOT A GIRL HERE": COURTSHIP, ETHNICITY, AND COMMUNITY

1. John Faragher, *Women and Men on the Overland Trail* (New Haven: Yale University Press, 1979); Lillian Schlissel, "Family on the Western Frontier," in *Western Women: Their Land, Their Lives*, ed. Lillian Schlissel, Vicki Ruiz, and Janice Monk (Albuquerque: University of New Mexico Press, 1988), 81–92; Elizabeth Hampsten, "Lena Olmsted and Oscar Phillips: Love and Marriage," in Armitage and Jameson, *The Women's West*, 127–42; and Grace Logan Schaedel, "The Story of Ernest and Lizzie Logan—A Frontier Courtship," *Annals of Wyoming* 54 (summer 1982): 48–61.
2. Elizabeth Lunbeck, "'A New Generation of Women': Progressive Psychiatrists and the 'Hypersexual' Female," *Feminist Studies* 13 (fall 1987): 513–44; Elizabeth Perry, "The General Motherhood of the Commonwealth: Dance Hall Reform in the Progressive Era," *American Quarterly* 37 (fall 1985): 719–33; and James R. McGovern, "The American Woman's Pre World War I Freedom in Manners and Morals," in *Our American Sisters: Women in American Life and Thought*, ed. Jean Friedman and William Shade (Lexington MA: D. C. Heath, 1982), 479–99.
3. Ellen Rothman, *Hands and Hearts: A History of Courtship in America* (Cambridge: Harvard University Press, 1987), 203–95.
4. Kathy Peiss, *Cheap Amusements: Working Women and Leisure in Turn-of-the-Century New York* (Philadelphia: Temple University Press, 1986), 88–114; Elizabeth Ewen, *Immigrant Women in the Land of Dollars: Life and Culture on the Lower East Side, 1890–1925* (New York: Monthly Review Press, 1985).
5. *Green River Star*, February 1, 1907, WSAHD. In an illustration accompanying this article, the "short skirt" was still fairly long, showing only lower calves, ankles, and feet.
6. Margaret Sangster, "Watch the Expenditures," *Green River Star*, January 4, 1907.
7. Lois Banner, "The Gibson Girl," in *American Beauty* (Chicago: University of Chicago Press, 1983), 154–74.
8. *Green River Star*, April 17, 1907, WSAHD.
9. *Green River Star*, April 17, 1907, WSAHD.
10. *Green River Star*, April 17, 1907, WSAHD.
11. "The Duping of Polly," *Green River Star*, July 17, 1908, WSAHD.
12. *Green River Star*, December 13, 1907, WSAHD.
13. *Green River Star*, December 13, 1907, WSAHD.
14. *Green River Star*, December 13, 1907, WSAHD.
15. "The School for Courtship," *Rock Springs Rocket*, February 23, 1911, 6; "All Women Today," *Rock Springs Rocket*, January 5, 1912, 5.
16. Mean age at marriage for women, 1900, 1910 census. The mean age at marriage cited for 1880 represents a rough estimate because the 1880 census did not include the

number of 0ears a person had been married. Thus the 1880 figure is based on narrative evidence: eleven life histories of women from Sweetwater County who married during the period 1870–1890. For these women, the average age at marriage was 20.63. See Beach, *Women of Wyoming*: "Mrs. John N. Greub," 2:193–95; "Mrs. Thomas Crofts," 1:329–31; "Mrs. Patrick John Quealy," 2:359–61; "Mrs. Caroline Eggs," 2:298–300; "Mrs. Albert Kierle," 2:85–87; "Mrs. Albert Facinelli," 1:343; "Mr. and Mrs. John Blair," 1:242–45; "Mrs. Frank D. Ball," 367; "Mrs. William B. Shedden," 112–15; and "Mrs. William K. Lee," 280–81. Denice Wheeler, "Caroline Adams Dugdale Wade," *The Feminine Frontier: Wyoming Women, 1850–1900* (Green River WY: Sweetwater County Historical Society, 1987), 242–44. The average age at first marriage for women nationwide in 1900 was 21.9 and followed "a slow and measured decline thereafter." Ben Wattenberg, *This U.S.A.: An Unexpected Family Portrait of 194,067,296 Americans Drawn from the Census* (Garden City NY: Doubleday, 1965), 472.

17. Age cohort analysis of women, ages 30–34; 1880, 1900, 1910 census. A sample of all women, aged 30–34, from each census year, yielded a case base of 54 women in this age bracket. Of these, 51, or 94.4 percent, were married.
18. Pivik, interview. See also Burns, interview.
19. Margaret Deland, "The Change in the Feminine Ideal," The *Atlantic*, March 1910, 289–302; and W. L. George, "Her New Job: Earning Her Own Living," *Good Housekeeping*, January 1923, 14–15.
20. Pivik, interview.
21. Pivik, interview.
22. Household membership analysis for all unmarried men over age 15; 1880, 1900, 1910 census. Between 1880 and 1910, 75.5 percent of unmarried men boarded out; 15.2 percent lived with their parents; and 6.2 percent lived with relatives.
23. Household membership analysis for unmarried women over age 15; 1880, 1900, 1910 census.
24. "Basic Wage Rates and Hours of Service; . . . Taken from Payrolls and Wage Scales, Union Pacific Railroad and Coal Company," in *History of the Union Pacific Coal Mines, 1868–1940* (Omaha: Colonial, 1940), xli. Taucher, interview.
25. Leskovec, interview; Metelko, interview; and Graf, interview; Wright and Wright, *Our Valley*, 168–70. Grandy household, at which Carrie Wright boarded, 1910 census.
26. Household membership analysis of unmarried women; 1880, 1900, 1910 census. Between 1880 and 1910, 54.5 percent of unmarried women over age 15 lived with their parents; 9.1 percent lived with relatives; 16.8 percent boarded with a family.
27. Household membership analysis for unmarried, foreign-born women; 1880, 1900, 1910 census.

28. Household membership analysis for unmarried native-born women; 1880, 1900, 1910 census.
29. Household membership analysis for unmarried women, 1880 census.
30. Gardner and Flores, *Forgotten Frontier*, 140.
31. Makka household, 1900 census manuscript, WSAHD.
32. Household membership analysis for unmarried, foreign-born women; 1900 census.
33. Household membership analysis for unmarried women, ages 16–25; 1910 census.
34. Analysis of marital status for men and women; 1880, 1900, 1910 census.
35. Stinneford, "Mines and Miners," 121–48; Sulentich, interview.
36. Analysis of sex and marital status for adult residents; 1910 census.
37. Ethnicity analysis of men and women; 1900, 1910 census.
38. Stinneford, "Mines and Miners," 124, table 1.
39. Stinneford, "Mines and Miners," 124, table 1.
40. In using the term "Southern Slav" as a shorthand for Slovenian, Croatian, Serbian, and other Balkan subgroups formerly encompassed by Yugoslavia, I do not assume that these subgroups consistently shared cultural solidarity. However, the evidence from Sweetwater County suggests that in these coal towns, Southern Slav subgroups such as Serbs, Slovenes, and Croats did share similar values regarding courtship.
41. Leskovec, interview; Frolic, interview; Stinneford, "Mines and Miners," 130–31.
42. Pivik, interview; Leskovec, interview.
43. Kovach, interview; Krmpotich, interview; Pivik, interview; Leskovec, interview; Frolic, interview; and Metelko, interview.
44. Pivik, interview.
45. Pivik, interview.
46. Taucher, interview.
47. Taucher, interview.
48. Taucher, interview.
49. Taucher, interview.
50. Taucher, interview.
51. Pivik, interview; Leskovec, interview. Louise Luzan Leskovec also remembered dating only those of the same nationality.
52. Pivik, interview.
53. Powell, interview by author.
54. Unguren, interview.
55. Leskovec, interview.
56. Pivik, interview; Leskovec, interview; and Frolic, interview; Peiss, *Cheap Amusements*, 90–92. Traditional working-class dances "took place in an environment controlled . . . by familial supervision and community ties" (p. 91).
57. Peiss, *Cheap Amusements*, 93–114.

58. Frolic, interview. See also *Wyoming Business Directory*: Green River, 244–47; Megeath, 315; Reliance, 350; South Superior, 400–401; Superior, 405–6; and Rock Springs, 358–68.
59. Buchan, interview.
60. Peiss, *Cheap Amusements*, 100–114.
61. Leskovec, interview.
62. Krmpotich, interview.
63. Analysis for endogamy, date of immigration, and date of marriage among foreign-born married couples; 1910 census. Women who had married the same year that they immigrated were not included in this sample since those marriages might have resulted from relationships begun in the old country. For the years 1910–1929, see Pivik, interview; Leskovec, interview; Krmpotich, interview; Frolic, interview; Sulentich, interview; and Melinkovich, interview.
64. Deanna Pagnini and S. Philip Morgan, "Intermarriage and Social Distance among U.S. Immigrants at the Turn of the Century," *American Journal of Sociology* 96 (September 1990): 405–32.
65. Analysis for date of immigration, date of marriage, and ethnicity of spouse among foreign-born adult men and women; 1910 census.
66. Leskovec, interview; Pivik, interview; Frolic, interview; and Metelko, interview.
67. Krmpotich, interview; Metelko, interview; Taucher, interview; Leskovec, interview; and LeFaivre, interview.
68. Krmpotich, interview. A husband's search for work often took place within an ethnic network; hence endogamous marriage was important to them too. John Bodnar, *Worker's World: Kinship, Community, and Protest in Industrial Society, 1900–1940* (Baltimore: Johns Hopkins University Press, 1982); Melinkovich, interview.
69. Tolar, interview; Melinkovich, interview. Tolar, a former Rock Springs resident, recalled how her Croatian grandfather refused to live with his brothers "because they had married English women."
70. Higginson, interview; Mae Mickelson, "The Twentieth-Century Club and Mr. And Mrs. Cyrus F. Fish," in Sublette County Artists Guild, *Tales of the Seeds-Ke-Dee*, 203–26, 209; Wilda Springman, "Early Day Pastimes," in Sublette County Artists Guild, *Tales of the Seeds-Ke-Dee*, 362–63.
71. Mae Mickelson, "The Life of a Southwestern Wyoming Cowboy and His Wife," *Bits and Pieces: Your Own Western History Magazine* (Newcastle WY: October 1969): 13–14.
72. Higginson, interview; Howell and Culbertson, interview; and Fern Dumbrill Spencer, "A Woman's Memoirs of Homesteading," appendix to Charles Floyd Spencer, *Wyoming Homestead Heritage* (Hicksville NY: Exposition, 1975), 175–99.
73. Ethnicity analysis of rural men and women; 1880, 1900, 1910 census. From a sample of 136 rural adults, 1880–1910, 72.8 percent were native born; and 27.2 percent were

foreign born. Among native-born, rural residents, 41.4 percent came from the Midwest; 15.2 percent came from the Northeast; 14.1 percent came from the South; and 29.3 percent came from the Far West.
74. Ethnicity analysis of rural adult men and women; 1880, 1900, 1910 census. Between 1880 and 1910, 91.9 percent of foreign-born rural residents came from Great Britain.
75. Howell and Culbertson, interview, 9–10.
76. Howell and Culbertson, interview, 10.
77. Howell and Culbertson, interview, 10.
78. Mrs. Nathan Hodson narrative, in Wright and Wright, *Our Valley*, 143.
79. "The Wild Rippling Water," author unknown; words and music in Austin Fife, *Cowboy and Western Songs* (Logan: Utah State University Press, 1967), 7.
80. "The Wild Rippling Water," author unknown; words and music in Austin Fife, *Cowboy and Western Songs* (Logan: Utah State University Press, 1967), 7.
81. "Bucking Broncho," author unknown; lyrics in Wyoming WPA Folksong Collection, WSAHD WPA-MSS-261.
82. "Bucking Broncho," author unknown; lyrics in Wyoming WPA Folksong Collection, WSAHD WPA-MSS-261.
83. "I'll Give You My Story," author unknown. Folksinger Rosalie Sorrels learned this song from Dick Person of Cascade, Idaho. See p. 3, album insert, *Folksongs of Idaho and Utah*, annotated by Kenneth Goldstein (New York: Folkways Records, 1961), side 1.
84. "I'll Give You My Story," author unknown. Folksinger Rosalie Sorrels learned this song from Dick Person of Cascade, Idaho. See p. 3, album insert, *Folksongs of Idaho and Utah*, annotated by Kenneth Goldstein (New York: Folkways Records, 1961), side 1.
85. Wire, interview.
86. Wire, interview.
87. Wire, interview.
88. Wire, interview.
89. Wire, interview.

4. "MY WIFE JUST DOESN'T LIKE IT HERE": MARRIAGE AND PATRIARCHAL AUTHORITY IN TRANSITION

1. Powell, interview by Burns.
2. Judith E. Smith, "Family History and Feminist History," *Feminist Studies* 17 (summer 1991): 349–64, 350. See also Stephanie Coontz, *The Way We Never Were: American Families and the Nostalgia Trap* (New York: Harper Collins, 1992).
3. John Mack Faragher, *Women and Men on the Overland Trail* (New Haven: Yale University Press, 1979).

4. Linda Peavy and Ursula Smith, *Women in Waiting in the Westward Movement: Life on the Home Frontier* (Norman: University of Oklahoma Press, 1994), 6–8.
5. Lillian Schlissel, "The Malick Family in the Oregon Territory, 1848–1867," in Susan Armitage and Elizabeth Jameson, *Far from Home: Families of the Westward Journey* (New York: Schocken Books, 1989), 3–106.
6. Paula Petrik, "If She Be Content: The Development of Montana Divorce Law, 1865–1907," *Western Historical Quarterly* 18 (July 1987): 261–91, 289; Petrik, *No Step Backward*, 56–96.
7. Melody Graulich, "Violence against Women: Power Dynamics in Literature of the Western Family," in Armitage and Jameson, *The Women's West*, 111–26.
8. Faragher, *Women and Men on the Overland Trail*, 2; Peavy and Smith, *Women in Waiting*, 17–28.
9. Witka, interview; Krmpotich, interview; Leskovec, interview.
10. For ninety-seven immigrant couples who married before migrating to the United States, then immigrated separately, the average length of separation caused by immigration was 3.55 years. Marital date and immigration date analysis; 1900, 1910 census.
11. Pivik, interview; Metelko, interview; Frolic, interview; Eggs-Gaensslen Family History, 1–4; Powell, interview by Burns; Leskovec, interview; Witka, interview; Krmpotich, interview.
12. See chapter 2 of this study.
13. Higginson, interview. Dorothy Higginson was Annie Caldwell Austin's daughter.
14. Higginson, 1.
15. Peavy and Smith, *Women in Waiting*, 41; Sherna Gluck, ed., *Rosie the Riveter Revisited: Women, the War, and Social Change* (New York: Meridian Books, 1987); Karen Anderson, *Wartime Women: Sex Roles, Family Relations, and the Status of Women during World War II* (Westport CT: Greenwood Press, 1981), 78–83; Mary Beth Norton, *Liberty's Daughters: The Revolutionary Experience of American Women, 1750–1800* (Boston: Little Brown, 1980).
16. Wheeler, "Caroline Wade," *The Feminine Frontier*, 243.
17. Wheeler, "Caroline Wade," 243–44.
18. Wheeler, "Caroline Wade," 243–44.
19. Wheeler, "Caroline Wade," 243.
20. Powell, interview by Burns.
21. Powell, interview by Burns.
22. Powell, interview by Burns.
23. Powell, interview by Burns.
24. Powell, interview by Burns.
25. Leskovec, interview.

Notes to Pages 78–82

26. Leskovec, interview.
27. Powell, interview by Burns.
28. Powell, interview by Burns.
29. Powell, interview by Burns.
30. Powell, interview by Burns.
31. Powell, interview by author; Burns, interview. Powell and Burns confirmed that it was common for daughters-in-law to move onto their husbands' parents' family farm, and that on extended family farms in Croatia, the mother-in-law held the powerful position of senior woman in charge of the household.
32. Beach, "Mrs. William K. Lee," 2:280.
33. Beach, "Mrs. William K. Lee," 2:280.
34. Pivik, interview; Powell, inteview by Burns; Krmpotich, interview; Tolar, interview; and Buchan, interview.
35. Metelko, interview.
36. Ruth Ellen Day Wright household, 1910 census; Wheeler, "Caroline Wade," 242–43; and "Dead: A Good Woman Gone to Her Reward" (obituary of Maggie Kinney), *Rock Springs Miner*, February 17, 1892.
37. Pivik, interview; Leskovec, interview; Witka, interview; Tolar, interview; Semos, interview; and Taucher, interview.
38. Graf, interview; Beach, "Mrs. Thomas Crofts," 1:330–31; Stevens and Shinazy were Anna Crofts's daughters, described in the text on Mrs. Crofts.
39. To gauge the average number of children born to each married woman (the 1880 census did not provide this information), I judged age forty and older a reasonable cutoff age for sampling women who had completed their childbearing years because the narrative evidence from Sweetwater County indicated that most women stopped childbearing by their late thirties: Beach, *Women of Wyoming*, 2:242–45, 280–82, 367, and 386–88.

    The 1880 census included twenty-three married women, age forty and older; among them, the average number of surviving children at home was 4.39.
40. Mean number of children for women at the end of their childbearing years, age forty and older; 1900, 1910 census.
41. Elinore Stewart, *Letters on an Elk Hunt, by a Woman Homesteader* (1915; reprint, Lincoln: University of Nebraska Press, 1979), 160.
42. Elizabeth Fuller Ferris, Introduction to *Letters on an Elk Hunt*, v–xiii, xi.
43. Elinore Stewart, *Letters of a Woman Homesteader* (1924; reprint, Boston: Houghton Mifflin, 1988), 191.
44. Stewart, "The Memory Bed," dated October 25, 1914, in Stewart, *Letters on an Elk Hunt*, 160–61.
45. Ferris, Introduction to Stewart, *Letters on an Elk Hunt*, xii.

46. Beach, *Women of Wyoming*: "Mrs. Eugene Amoretti," 1:166–68; "Mrs. Philip Harsch," 1:172–73; "Mrs. Archibald Blair," 1:196–98; "Mrs. Hannah Harrison," 1:199–200; "Mrs. Daniel B. Budd," 1:224–26; "Mrs. Robert H. Hall," 1:238–39; "Mr. and Mrs. John Blair," 1:242–45; "Mrs. William A. Johnson," 1:258; "Mrs. P. C. Bunning," 1:316–18; "Mrs. Thomas Crofts," 1:329–31; "Mrs. Albert Facinelli," 1:343; "Mrs. Frank D. Ball," 1:367; "Mrs. Julia E. Snyder," 1:501–2; "Mrs. Anna P. Davis," 1:521; "Mrs. Herman Gould Nickerson," 1:550–52; "Mrs. William B. Shedden," 2:112–15; "Mrs. John N. Greub," 2:193–95; "Mrs. William K. Lee," 2:280–81; "Mrs. David G. Thomas," 2:286–87; and "Mrs. Patrick John Quealy," 2:359–60; Wheeler, "Caroline Wade," 242–43. Marie Amorettu, Charlotte Blair, Anna Crofts, Effie Ball, Sarah Shedden, Minnie Greub, Susan Quealy, and Caroline Wade all lost at least one child to infant death.
47. The number of surviving children per mother was less than the number of births per mother among 82.8 percent of married women, age forty and older, 1900 census.
48. Margaret Riley household, Green River WY; 1900 census.
49. Mean number of births per mothers age forty and older; mean number of surviving children at home per mothers age forty and older; 1900 census.
50. Mean number of births per mothers age forty and older; mean number of surviving children at home per mothers age forty and older; 1910 census.
51. Beach, *Women of Wyoming*: "Mrs. George Brown Pryde," 2:115; "Mrs. Thomas Crofts," 1:329–31. (Annie Shinazy was one of Anna Crofts's daughters, as was Lavinia Karg.) Leskovec, interview.
52. Even allowing for discrepancies between the *total number of births per mother* and *estimated family size based on surviving children at home*, second-generation women had fewer children. Estimated family size fell from 4.4 children per mother in 1880, to 3.5 in 1900, to 2.7 in 1910. The total number of births per mother fell from 6.0 in 1900 to 4.7 in 1910.
53. Analysis of marital status for women; 1900, 1910 census. For description of 1880 average drawn from anecdotal evidence, see note 23 of this chapter.
54. Age cohort analysis of women, age 30–34, for marital status; 1800, 1910 census.
55. Beach, "Mrs. Thomas Crofts," 1:330–31.
56. Beach, "Mrs. John Greub," 2:193–95.
57. Beach, "Mrs. Thomas Crofts," 1:330–31.
58. Katz and Stern argued that while "contraceptive technology made the task [of birth control] easier . . . it was neither a cause nor a precondition of the fertility decline." Michael Katz and Mark Stern, "History and the Limits of Population Policy," *Politics and Society* 10 (1980): 225–45, 240.
59. Jolly Dry Farmers Club, *Calico Hill: Recalling the Early Years, Good Times, and*

Hardships of Homesteaders (Cheyenne: Pioneer, 1973), 11–12. See also Wilda Springman, "Grandma Sykes" and "Upper Middle Piney," in Sublette County Artists Guild, *Tales of the Seeds-Ke-Dee*, 197–202, 199; Ethel Van Dorsin Jewett, "Rosa Lieb Ball," in Sublette County Artists Guild, *Tales of the Seeds-Ke-Dee*, 284–91, 290; Margaret Bayer, "Pauline Kreuger Bayer," in Sublette County Artists Guild, *Tales of the Seeds-Ke-Dee*, 292–97, 297.

60. Jolly Dry Farmers Club, *Calico Hill*, 11–12.
61. Wire, interview.
62. Daniel Scott Smith, "Family Limitation, Sexual Control, and Domestic Feminism in Victorian America," in *A Heritage of Her Own: Toward a New Social History of American Women*, ed. Nancy Cott and Elizabeth Pleck (New York: Simon and Schuster, 1980), 222–45, 226; David Sanderson, "The Emergence of a Two-Child Norm among American Birth Controllers," *Population and Development Review* 13 (spring 1987): 1–41.
63. Mean number of surviving children per mother; 1880, 1900, 1910 census.
64. Scott-Smith, "Family Limitation," 222–45.
65. Powell, interview by author.
66. LeFaivre, interview.
67. Lena Anselmi Huntley's reasons for limiting family size are explored later in this chapter.
68. Paul Campisi, "Ethnic Family Patterns: The Italian Family in the United States," *American Journal of Sociology* 53 (fall 1984): 434–47. See also Ira Rosenwaike, "Two Generations of Italians in America: Their Fertility Experience," *International Migration Review* 7 (fall 1973): 271–80.
69. Virginia Yans-McLaughlin, *Family and Community: Italian Immigrants in Buffalo, 1880–1930* (Ithaca NY: Cornell University Press, 1977).
70. John W. Briggs, "Fertility and Cultural Change among Families in Italy and America," *American Historical Review* 91 (December 1986): 1129–45; 1130–31.
71. Metelko, interview; Witka, interview; Semos, interview; Leskovec, interview; Powell, interview by Burns; Pivik, interview; and Taucher, interview.
72. Metelko, interview; Leskovec, interview; Frolic, interview; Pivik, interview; and Sulentich, interview.
73. Frolic, interview; Leskovec, interview; Metelko, interview; and Pivik, interview.
74. To respect the confidentiality of this interview, I eliminated the woman's family name since this excerpt paints an unflattering picture of her husband. This oral history is part of the WSAHD Oral History Collection, Cheyenne, Wyoming.
75. LeFaivre, interview.
76. Leskovec, interview.

77. Powell, interview by Burns.
78. Leskovec, interview. For mention of home births, see Zampedri, interview; and Mattinson, interview.
79. Leskovec, interview. See also "As I Remember Lionkol Mining Camp," unpublished memoir by George Osselton, WAS.
80. Ketchum, interview.
81. Wire and Stewart, interview; Mickelson, *Bits and Pieces*, 14.
82. Wire, interview.

5. GROUP PARTNERSHIP AND COWBOY MYTH: THE GENDERING OF RANCH WORK

1. Mrs. B. B. Brooks, "Ranch Life on the Big Muddy," *The Daily Sun Leader*, December 22, 1899, transcribed by Mae Cody for the Wyoming WPA, WSAHD MSS-WPA-394, 1.
2. Anne Webb, "Minnesota Women Homesteaders: 1863–1889," *Journal of Social History* 23 (fall 1989): 115–36; Jan and Cornelia Flora, "Structures of Agriculture and Women's Culture on the Great Plains," *Great Plains Quarterly* 8 (spring 1988): 195–205; and Katherine Harris, "Homesteading in Northeastern Colorado, 1870–1920: Sex Roles and Women's Experience," in Armitage and Jameson, *The Women's West*, 165–78.
3. Among Nebraska farmers, Deborah Fink also found a conservative ideology of gender which negated the liberalizing implications of farm women's work. See *Agrarian Women: Wives and Mothers in Rural Nebraska, 1880–1940* (Chapel Hill: University of North Carolina Press, 1992).
4. Sylvia Eppler, *Calico Hill: Recalling the Early Years, Good Times and Hardships of Homesteaders* (Cheyenne WY: Pioneer, 1973), 27–28, WSAHD MSS-466.
5. Eppler, *Calico Hill*, 27–28.
6. Eppler, *Calico Hill*, 27–28.
7. Eppler, *Calico Hill*, 27–28.
8. Occupation analysis of household heads, sample of fifty rural households; 1880, 1900, and 1910 census. Of the fifty households sampled, forty-five were ranches.
9. Katherine Jellison, *Entitled to Power: Farm Women and Technology, 1913–1963* (Chapel Hill: University of North Carolina Press, 1993).
10. Wright and Wright, *Our Valley*, 131.
11. Wright and Wright, *Our Valley*, 131.
12. Wright and Wright, *Our Valley*, 132.
13. Faris, interview.
14. Wright and Wright, *Our Valley*, 132; Jack, interview; Wire and Stewart, interview.
15. Wire, interview; Faris, interview; Wright and Wright, *Our Valley*, 99–131; Wire

and Stewart, interview; Brooks, "Ranch Life on the Big Muddy," 1; Mrs. Olive Kafka, "Excerpt of a Ranch Woman's Diary," WSAHD WPA-MSS-401.
16. Susan Armitage, "Household Work and Childrearing on the Frontier," *Sociology and Social Research* 63 (April 1979): 467–74; Richard Rathge, "Women's Contribution to the Family Farm," *Great Plains Quarterly* 9 (winter 1989): 36–47.
17. Joan Jensen, *Loosening the Bonds: Mid-Atlantic Farm Women, 1750–1850* (New Haven: Yale University Press, 1986); Nancy Grey Osterud, "The Valuation of Women's Work: Gender and the Market in a Dairy Farming Community during the Late Nineteenth Century," *Frontiers* 10 (summer 1988): 18–24.
18. Harris, "Homesteading in Northeastern Colorado," 171; Katherine Harris, *Long Vistas: Women and Families on Colorado Homesteads* (Niwot: University Press of Colorado, 1992).
19. Webb, "Minnesota Women Homesteaders," 115–36; Flora and Flora, "Structures of Agriculture and Women's Culture," 195–205; Jameson, "Women as Workers, Women as Civilizers," 150–51; and Harris, "Homesteading in Northeastern Colorado," 167–71.
20. "If All We Did Was to Weep at Home," in Myres, *Westering Women*, 261; Arbenz, "Ranch Life from the Western Woman's Point of View," 1–2; Sheryll Patterson-Black, "Women Homesteaders on the Great Plains Frontier," *Frontiers: A Journal of Women's Studies* 1, no. 1 (spring 1976): 67–78.
21. Bruce A. Rosenberg, *The Code of the West* (Bloomington: University of Indiana Press, 1972), 57–77, 60.
22. Milner, "The Shared Memory of Montana Pioneers.
23. Paula Nelson, *After the West Was Won: Homesteaders and Town Builders in Western South Dakota, 1900–1917* (Iowa City: University of Iowa Press, 1986).
24. Stewart, *Letters of a Woman Homesteader*, 280–81. Wright and Wright, *Our Valley*, 130–33; Mrs. Nathan Hodson narrative, in Wright and Wright, *Our Valley*, 143–44; interview, Wire by Garceau; and Wilcox family narrative, in Jolly Dry Farmers Club, eds., *Calico Hill: Recalling the Early Years, Good Times, and Hardships of Homesteaders* (Cheyenne: Pioneer Printing, 1973), 40–45.
25. Stewart, *Letters*, 281–83.
26. Minnie Sitzman narrative, in Wright and Wright, *Our Valley*, 281.
27. Faris, interview, JF/5–8. See also Josephine Dearth narrative, in Wright and Wright, *Our Valley*, 234; and Metal and Platts, *Cattle King on the Green River*, 116–18.
28. Wright and Wright, *Our Valley*, 131.
29. Household membership analysis for rural households; 1880, 1900, 1910 census.
30. Luman, interview, DL/7–11.
31. Metal and Platts, *Cattle King*, 92. Wire, interview.

32. Alan Lomax, Introduction to *The Folk Songs of North America* (New York: Doubleday & Co., 1975), xv–xxx; xxi.
33. Author unknown, "The Washing Day," words and music in *Songs of the West*, ed. Paul Glass and Louise Singer (New York: Grosset and Dunlap, 1966), 44–46.
34. Lomax, *Folk Songs* 124; telephone conversation between author and folklorist-folksinger Linda Allen, Bellingham WA, December 14, 1987.
35. Mrs. Sarah A. Price, "The Housewife's Lament," words and music in *The Folk Songs of North America*, ed. Alan Lomax (New York: Doubleday, 1975), 133–34.
36. Household membership analysis; 1880, 1900 and 1910 census. Between 1880 and 1910, among the rural adult male population, 63.5 percent had neither wife nor adult female relatives. Of these, only 1 percent hired a housekeeper; 30.7 percent boarded with a family; and 68.2 percent lived in all-male households.
37. Katherine Harris documented the flexibility of gender roles on late-nineteenth- and early-twentieth-century Colorado homesteads. Harris, "Homesteading in Northeastern Colorado," 168.
38. George Squires Herrington, ed., "LeVancia Bent's Diary of a Sheep Drive, Evanston, Wyoming to Kearney, Nebraska, 1882," *Annals of Wyoming* 24 (January 1952): 24–51; 24–26.
39. Herrington, "LeVancia Bent's Diary," 32.
40. Luman, interview, DL/11.
41. Faris, interview, JF/6–9. Wire, interview; and Wire and Stewart, interview. For additional accounts of women doing "heavy, outdoor ranch work," see Jack, interview; and Mildred Homer, "Elizabeth and Andrew Homer, Pioneers," in Sublette County Artists Guild, *Tales of the Seeds-Ke-Dee*, 263–71, 267–68.
42. Sommers, interview.
43. Sommers, interview, VS/4–5.
44. Sommers, interview, VS/4–5.
45. Bell, interview, 26. Although Bell grew up on a ranch in southeast Wyoming, outside of Sweetwater County, conditions there required the same group effort as in southwest Wyoming.
46. Faris, interview, JF/9; see also Introduction to Rankin, *Spoken Words*, 6.
47. Wire, interview; Beth Farris, Foreword to Stewart, *Letters on an Elk Hunt*, xii.
48. Bruce Siberts's story is found in Walker D. Wyman, *Nothing but Prairie and Sky* (Norman: University of Oklahoma Press, 1954).
49. William Savage, ed., *Cowboy Life: Reconstructing an American Myth* (Niwot: University Press of Colorado, 1993); Robert Murray Davis, "*The Virginian*: Inventing the Westerner," in *Playing Cowboys: Low Culture and High Art in the Western* (Norman: University of Oklahoma Press, 1992), 3–29; Robert V. Hine, "The Cowboy and the

Cult of Masculinity," in *The American West: An Interpretive History* (Boston: Little, Brown, 1973), 125–38; and Neal Lambert, "Owen Wister's Virginian: The Genesis of a Cultural Hero," *Western American Literature* 6 (summer 1971): 99–107.
50. Helen C. Sargent, "Charlotta Hartley Albert," in Sublette County Artists Guild, *Tales of the Seeds-Ke-Dee*, 351–60, 354.
51. Elsie Cooksley Lloyd and Amy Cooksley Chubb narrative, in Jordan, *Cowgirls*, 2–12; 7.
52. Elsie Cooksley Lloyd and Amy Cooksley Chubb narrative, in Jordan, *Cowgirls*, 9.
53. Bell, interview, 24. See also Pearl Budd Spencer narrative, in Sublette County Artists Guild, *Tales of the Seeds-Ke-Dee*, 85–103. Explaining that her aunt, Sadie Budd Osterhout, had "helped her brothers with wrangling cows," Spencer hastened to add that Sadie was skilled in the domestic arts as well, as if to prevent the reader from assuming that Sadie was masculinized by her work with cattle: She "learned to be a good cook and to sew a fine seam and embroidery. Her father also bought her a piano" (p. 97).
54. Metal and Platts, *Cattle King*, 62–63.
55. Metal and Platts, *Cattle King*, 126.
56. Metal and Platts, *Cattle King*, 127–28.
57. Wire, interview; Wright and Wright, *Our Valley*, 100–130; Faris, interview, JF/7.
58. Sommers, interview, VS/5.
59. Wire, interview.
60. Sommers, interview, VS/7.
61. Luman, interview, DL/2.
62. Luman, interview, DL/3.
63. Luman, interview, DL/3.
64. Sommers, interview, VS/9.
65. Faris, interview, JF/6; Wire, interview. See also Miller, interview, MM/3.
66. Jack, interview. See also, Cooksley sisters' narrative, in Jordan, *Cowgirls*, 4.
67. Bell, interview, 25; Cooksley sisters' narrative, in Jordan, *Cowgirls*, 11.
68. Luman, interview, DL/3; Miller, interview, MM/3.
69. Bell, interview, 20–28, 24.
70. Bell, interview, 20–28, 24.
71. Bell, interview, 21.
72. Bell, interview, 20–28. See also Cooksley sisters' narrative, in Jordan, *Cowgirls*, 2–12; and Metal and Platts, *Cattle King*, 55–69, 126–28, 141.
73. Climate, topography, and ranching methods in northern Colorado were so similar to southwest Wyoming that I have chosen to include Davis in this discussion.
74. Barbara Fox Davis narrative, in Jordan, *Cowgirls*, 65–74, 66.

75. Barbara Fox Davis narrative, in Jordan, *Cowgirls*, 69; Sam Davis narrative, in Jordan, *Cowgirls*, 73–74, 73.
76. Barbara Fox Davis narrative, in Jordan, *Cowgirls*, 69–70.
77. Barbara Fox Davis narrative, in Jordan, *Cowgirls*, 72.
78. Barbara Fox Davis narrative, in Jordan, *Cowgirls*, 72.
79. Wire and Stewart, interview; Wire, interview.
80. Ranchers' narratives from the 1930s through 1960s indicate that women's work with beef cattle gradually became more commonplace, until by the 1960s, it, too came under the routine umbrella of "outside chores." Jerri Wattenberg narrative, in Jordan, *Cowgirls*, 30–37; Biddy Bonham narrative, in Jordan, *Cowgirls*, 38–46.

6. SINGLE WOMEN HOMESTEADERS AND INDEPENDENCE: PLACES ON THE MAP, PLACES IN THE MIND

1. Bell, interview, 25–26. See also Theresa Jordan, *Riding the White Horse Home: A Western Family Album* (New York: Pantheon, 1993).
2. The majority of narratives and land records used for this chapter came from Sweetwater County, but there are a few sources drawn from other Wyoming counties as well.
3. Hine, *The American West*, vii, 322–23. William Kittredge further explores the West as a mythic construct in his family memoir, *A Hole in the Sky* (New York: Alfred A. Knopf, 1992).
4. Kittredge, *A Hole in the Sky*, 12–29, 232–38.
5. Larson, *History of Wyoming*, 173–75, 362.
6. Wright and Wright, *Our Valley*; and Sublette County Artists Guild, *Tales of the Seeds-Ke-Dee*. See also chapter 5 in this volume.
7. For complete citation of Stewart's publications, see note 50 of this chapter. For modern reprints, see Stewart, *Letters of a Woman Homesteader*, and Stewart, *Letters on an Elk Hunt by a Woman Homesteader*.
8. Stewart, *Letters of a Woman Homesteader*, 214–15.
9. Stewart, *Letters of a Woman Homesteader*, 279.
10. Myres, *Westering Women*, 259, 270; Paula Mae Bauman, "Single Women Homesteaders in Wyoming, 1880–1930," *Annals of Wyoming* 58 (spring 1986): 39–53, 46; and Patterson-Black, "Women Homesteaders on the Great Plains Frontier," 74.
11. The *Atlantic Monthly* introduced Stewart's "Letters" with the following "Editor's Note": "These are the genuine letters, written without thought of publication, simply to tell a friendly story . . . to a former employer in Denver." The *Atlantic Monthly*, October 1913, 433.
12. Cover copy, Stewart, *Letters of a Woman Homesteader* (Boston: Houghton Mifflin,

Notes to Pages 115–119

1982); Gretel Erlich, "Foreword," in Stewart, *Letters of a Woman Homesteader* (Boston: Houghton Mifflin, 1988), xiii–xxi, xix.

13. Susan Hallgarth, "Women Settlers on the Frontier: Unwed, Unreluctant, Unrepentant," *Women's Studies Quarterly* 17, nos. 3–4 (1989): 23–34, 29.
14. Sherry Smith, "Single Woman Homesteaders: The Perplexing Case of Elinore Pruitt Stewart," *Western Historical Quarterly* 22 (May 1991): 163–84, 175.
15. Smith, "The Perplexing Case," 180–83; Suzanne George, *The Adventures of the Woman Homesteader: The Life and Letters of Elinore Pruitt Stewart* (Lincoln: University of Nebraska Press, 1992).
16. A "family head" was defined as a married couple or as a single adult, minimum age twenty-one, and a U.S. citizen (or one who has filed a declaration of intent to become a U.S. citizen). Homestead Act. *U.S. Statutes at Large* 12, p. 392; reprinted in Henry Steele Commager, ed., *Documents of American History*, 7th ed. (New York: Appleton-Century-Crofts, 1963), 1:410–11.
17. Larson, *History of Wyoming*, 173.
18. Larson, *History of Wyoming*, 173.
19. Formerly a part of Sweetwater County, the upper Green River Valley split off in 1922 to become Sublette County.
20. Josephine Jons, "The Ranches on the Green River Near Daniel, Wyoming," Wyoming WPA, 1938, WSAHD WPA-MSS-1277, 7 [hereafter cited as "Ranches"].
21. Jons, "Little Cottonwood," in "Ranches," 5.
22. Jons, "On the Green River," in "Ranches," 6.
23. Larson, *History of Wyoming*, 173–76; a married couple could not prove up on adjacent claims while sharing the same residence.
24. Fern Dumbrill Spencer, "A Woman's Memoirs of Homesteading," appendix to Charles Floyd Spencer, *Wyoming Homestead Heritage* (Hicksville NY: Exposition Press, 1975), 175–99.
25. Kirkbride, *From These Roots*, 121.
26. Larson, *History of Wyoming*, 173–75; Zay Philbrook, "My Wyoming Timber Claim," *Sunset Magazine* (December 1918): 22–23; and Wright and Wright, *Our Valley*, 7.
27. Eppler, *Calico Hill*, 27; Wright and Wright, *Our Valley*, 91.
28. Wire and Stewart, interview; regarding hired help needed for tasks such as fence building or cabin raising, see Wright and Wright, *Our Valley*, 98–100.
29. Philbrook, "My Wyoming Timber Claim," 23. Philbrook listed the following expenses: Surveyor, $32.00; Filing Fee, $10.00; 160 acres appraised at $430.00; Construction of one-room cabin, $100.00; and notary fees, maps, water rights, and title fees, $49.00. Together, these expenses totaled $621.00.
30. Occupation and household membership analysis, 1880, 1900, 1910 Sweetwater County census. For example, the 1900 census listed the Amelia Miller household as follows:

Miller, Amelia, Head, Age 39, Widowed, Stockgrower; Miller, Alfred A., Son, Age 19, Single, Sheepherder; Miller, James F., Son, Age 16, Single, Farm Laborer.

31. Barrett household, 1880 census; "Green River Pioneer Woman Succumbs to Long Illness," *Green River Star*, August 1930, 1, 2; "Mary Barrett," Enrollment Form, Wyoming Pioneers, WSAHD WPA-MSS-37. The younger Mary Barrett's birthdate appeared on the 1880 census as 1863; the 1900 census listed it as 1865.
32. Barrett household, 1880 census.
33. Barrett household, 1900 census.
34. Household membership analysis, 1880, 1900, 1910 census. For example, the Noble household appeared as follows in the 1880 census: Noble, William M., [Head], age 34, Farmer; Noble, Jennie R., Wife, age 33, Keeping house; McLaughlin, John, Bro-Law, age 31, Farmer; McLaughlin, Edith, Wife, age 27, Keeping house; Noble, Jane A., Widowed, age 55 [no occupation listed]. In the 1880 census, family heads were listed first in each household. In the 1900 and 1910 census, family heads were identified as "Head." In the above household, Jane Noble's adult son William was recognized as the household head.
35. *Rock Springs Miner*, July 15, 1916, WSAHD WPA-MSS-37.
36. *Rock Springs Miner*, July 15, 1916, WSAHD WPA-MSS-37.
37. "Green River Pioneer Woman Succumbs," *G.R. Star*, 1–2.
38. Jack, interview; Beach, "Mrs. Adam Cooper," in *Women of Wyoming*, 1:76–78; "Mrs. Anna Magnagna," *Rock Springs Miner*, July 9, 1950; and Margaret Duncan Brown, *Shepherdess of the Elk River Valley* (Denver: Golden Bell, 1967) further exemplify ranch women who took over a family outfit.
39. Jons, "South Piney," in "Ranches," 1.
40. Jons, "On the Green River," in "Ranches," 7.
41. Jons, "South Cottonwood," in "Ranches," 5.
42. Kirkbride, *From These Roots*, 121.
43. Culbertson and Howell, interview, 12. Myres found evidence of this pattern in her broad survey, *Westering Women*, 258.
44. Culbertson and Howell, interview.
45. Florence Blake Smith, *Cow Chips 'N Cactus: The Homestead in Wyoming* (New York: Pageant, 1962), 20–21; Bell narrative, in Jordan, *Cowgirls*, 25; [Which?] Spencer, "A Woman's Memories," in Spencer, *Wyoming Homestead*, 188–89; and Kirkbride, *From These Roots*, 121.
46. Charles Rankin, "Teaching: Opportunity and Limitation in Wyoming," *Western Historical Quarterly* 21 (May 1990): 147–70, 158.
47. Bell narrative, in Jordan, *Cowgirls*, 26; see property records of Eleanor Baxter, Latitia Kelsey, Susan J. McLauchlin, and Annie Nelson, all of whom proved up on claims and sold them to ranchers. Wyoming County Clerk Records, Book 95, 160,

344, 506, and 508, respectively. Records also listed in Appendix A, Bauman, "Single Women Homesteaders in Wyoming," 50–51.
48. Stewart's "Letters" drew favorable review, including notice in the *Dial*, July 1, 1914, 21; the *Nation*, July 16, 1914, 75; the *New York Times*, June 7, 1914, 259; and *Overland Monthly*, August 1, 1914, 820.
49. Elinore Stewart, "The Return of the Woman Homesteader," *The Atlantic Monthly*, May 1919, 590–96; and "Snow: An Adventure of the Woman Homesteader," *The Atlantic Monthly*, December 1923, 780–85.
50. The following articles appeared in popular magazines between 1913 and 1928:

   Elinore Stewart, "Letters of a Woman Homesteader," *The Atlantic Monthly*, October 1913; November 1913; December 1913; January 1914; February 1914; April 1914.

   Joanna Gleed Strange, "The Last Homesteads," *Collier's*, January 1913, 24.

   Mabel Lewis Stuart, "The Lady Honyocker," *The Independent*, July 1913, 133–37.

   Elinore Stewart, "Letters on an Elk Hunt, by a Woman Homesteader," *The Atlantic Monthly*, February 1915; March 1915; April 1915; May 1915; June 1915.

   Metta M. Loomis, "From a Schoolroom to a Montana Ranch," *Overland Monthly*, January 1916, 59–64.

   A. Fullerton, "Our Homesteaders," *Canadian Magazine*, January 1916, 249–68.

   A. Armstrong, "Homesteading without a Chaperone," *Sunset*, June 1916, 25–26.

   A. May Holaday, "The Lure of the West for Women," *Sunset*, March 1917, 61.

   Anna W. Case, "Experiences in Locating a Home on Public Lands in the West," *Overland Monthly*, February–April 1918, 159–64, 257–62, 346–52.

   F. I. Beebe, "Homesteading on the Windswept," *Sunset*, August 1918, 21–23.

   Mrs. J. C. Osborne, "Five Years on a Homestead," *Overland Monthly*, July–September 1918, 36–41, 172–79, 247–53.

   Zay Philbrook, "My Wyoming Timber Claim: A Woman Pioneer in the Bighorn Mountains," *Sunset*, December 1918, 22–23.

   Elinore Stewart, "Return of the Woman Homesteader," *The Atlantic Monthly*, May 1919, 590–96.

   F. I. Beebe, "Society on the Windswept," *Sunset*, June 1919, 17–20.

   Gladys Belvie Whitaker, "Girl Homesteader's Ordeal," *Overland Monthly*, July 1920, 67–70.

   Kate L. Heizer, "Via the Homesteading Route," *Sunset*, March 1921, 36–37.

   H. C. Davis, "A Home in the Wildwood," *Sunset*, March 1923, 68, 72.

   H. C. Davis, "On a Grazing Homestead," *Sunset*, November 1923, 17–18.

   Elinore Stewart, "Snow: An Adventure of the Woman Homesteader," *The Atlantic Monthly*, December 1923, 780–85.

A. May Holaday, "Pluck and a Thousand Acres," *St. Nicholas*, May–June 1926, 674–78, 687–92.

R. Rhodes, "Homemade Homestead Home," *Sunset*, June 1928, 26–27.

A. May Holaday, "Pat of Homestead Valley," *St. Nicholas*, July 1928, 717–21.

51. Stanford Layton, *To No Privileged Class: The Rationalization of Homesteading and Rural Life in the Early Twentieth-Century American West* (Provo UT: Brigham Young University Press, 1988).
52. Smith, "The Perplexing Case," 181.
53. Kessler-Harris, *Out to Work*, 108–79, 217–49; Robyn Muncy, *Creating a Female Dominion in American Reform, 1890–1935* (New York: Oxford University Press, 1991); Peiss, *Cheap Amusements*; Rothman, *Hands and Hearts*; Nancy Cott, *The Grounding of Modern Feminism* (New Haven: Yale University Press, 1987); Elaine Schowalter, ed., *These Modern Women: Autobiographical Essays from the Twenties* (New York: Feminist Press, 1989); and Lois Banner, *American Beauty* (Chicago: University of Chicago Press, 1985).
54. Stuart, "Lady Honyoker," 133.
55. Stuart, "Lady Honyoker," 133–37.
56. Stuart, "Lady Honyoker," 133–34.
57. Strange, "The Last Homesteads," 24.
58. Strange, "The Last Homesteads," 24.
59. Loomis, "From a Schoolroom to a Montana Ranch," 59.
60. Loomis, "From a Schoolroom to a Montana Ranch," 63–64. For additional articles by woman homesteaders who cited improved health and self-reliance as results of holding down a claim, see Beebe, "Society on the Windswept"; Davis, "A Home in the Wildwood"; and Rhodes, "Homemade Homestead Home."
61. Loomis, "From a Schoolroom to a Montana Ranch," 64. Armstrong echoed this theme in "Homesteading without a Chaperone."
62. Whitaker, "Girl Homesteader's Ordeal," 67.
63. Whitaker, "Girl Homesteader's Ordeal," 69–70.
64. Heizer, "Via the Homesteading Route," 52.
65. Heizer, "Via the Homesteading Route," 52. The following also highlighted the social equality of single woman homesteaders: Beebe, "Society on the Windswept"; Stuart, "The Lady Honyocker"; Strange, "The Last Homesteads"; and Loomis, "From a Schoolroom to a Montana Ranch."

7. FROM *KLENICKSO* TO MAIN STREET: TOWN WOMEN'S WORK

1. Lucy and Oliver Smith household, Rock Springs, 1880 census; Beach, "Mrs. Albert Kierle," 2:85–87. For descriptions of household work in Wyoming towns, see Thompson, interview; Metelko, interview; and Kovach, interview; see also Susan

Strasser, *Never Done: A History of American Housework* (New York: Pantheon Books, 1982): 32–49, 162–79.

2. Occupation analysis for unmarried, income-earning women, 1880 census. The total number of single women in the 1880 sample of one hundred households was twenty-two. Of those, sixteen worked as domestic servants.

3. Analysis of subregion (rural or mining-railroad town), marital status, occupation, and ethnicity for women, 1880 census. The 1880 census yielded thirteen single, town-dwelling women who worked as domestics, eight of whom served private families. The remainder worked in homes that kept boarders.

4. Beach, *Women of Wyoming*, 2:85; *Wyoming State Gazetteer and Business Directory* (R. L. Polk, 1908), 60, 176 [hereafter cited as *Wyoming Gazetteer*]. *Wyoming State Business Directory* (Denver: Gazetteer, 1914), 420 [hereafter cited as *Wyoming Directory*]. *Rock Springs Miner*, June 1907.

5. Beach, *Women of Wyoming*, 2:85.

6. Thompson, interview. Between 1908 and 1925, the city directories for Green River and Rock Springs combined listed an average of only four women per year who managed a large downtown hotel. *Wyoming Gazetteer* 1908: 135–36, 175–79; and *Wyoming Directory* 1914:279–83, 418–30; 1918:294–97, 438–49; 1925:238–42, 346–58.

7. Rhodes, *Booms and Busts*, 66–67.

8. Kessler-Harris, *Out to Work*, 128, 141; Strasser, *Never Done*, 167–76.

9. Kessler-Harris, *Out to Work*, 128–37; Strasser, *Never Done*, 169–72; David Katzman, *Seven Days a Week: Women and Domestic Service in Industrializing America* (Urbana: University of Illinois Press, 1981), 269–77.

10. Analysis of occupation and subregion for women; 1880, 1900, 1910 census.

11. Larson, *History of Wyoming*, 141–44, 336–37.

12. Analysis of ethnicity for all adult men and women; 1880, 1900, 1910 census. After 1910, Eastern European migration to Wyoming continued strong. Stinneford, "Mines and Miners," 124.

13. Analysis of class status of household head, for all town-dwelling households; 1880, 1900, 1910 census. Proportionally, the middle-class population fell from 60 percent of town-dwellers in 1880 to 46.2 percent in 1910.

14. In 1880, 61.5 percent of household servants worked for private families in middle-class homes. By 1900, 66.6 percent of household servants worked for families who kept boarders in working-class homes. Analysis of occupation, class of household head, and household membership, for town-dwelling women; 1880, 1900 census.

15. Frolic, interview.

16. Analysis of occupation, class of household head, and household membership, for town-dwelling adult women; 1910 census.

17. See Faye Dudden, *Serving Women: Household Services in Nineteenth Century America*

(Middletown CT: Wesleyan University Press, 1983) for discussion of regional economic and demographic influences on employer/servant relations in an earlier time.
18. Leskovec, interview.
19. Leskovec, interview.
20. Leskovec, interview.
21. Taucher, interview.
22. Taucher, interview.
23. Taucher, interview.
24. Taucher, interview.
25. Between 1880 and 1910, 76.2 percent of household servants were single; 19 percent were widowed. Analysis of marital status and occupation for women; 1880, 1900, 1910 census.
26. Homemaking tasks are described in Thompson, interview; Powell, interview; Leskovec, interview; and Taucher, interview.
27. For discussion of family structures and life-cycle stage as factors in women's work patterns, see Laura Anker, "Women, Work, and Family: Polish, Italian, and Eastern European Immigrants in Industrial Connecticut, 1890–1940," *Polish American Studies* 45 (summer 1988): 23–49. Schneider, "Patterns for Getting By," 517–41; and Kathleen Underwood, "The Pace of Their Own Lives: Teacher Training and the Life Course of Western Women," *Pacific Historical Review* 55 (November 1986): 513–30.
28. Analysis of marital status and occupation for town-dwelling adult women; 1800, 1900, 1910 census.
29. Miller and Miller, interview.
30. Analysis of class status of household head, household membership, and ethnicity for married women; 1880 census.
31. Analysis of class status of household head, household membership, and ethnicity for married women; 1910 census.
32. Analysis of class status of household head, household membership, and ethnicity for married women; 1910 census.
33. In 1900, 61 percent of the adult population was male. Among adult men, 64.8 percent were single. By 1910, 67.7 percent of the adult population was male; and 65.5 percent of these were unmarried. Analysis of gender and marital status, for all adults; 1900, 1910 census.
34. Analysis of household membership for married women keeping boarders; 1900, 1910 census.
35. Leskovec, interview.
36. Pivik, interview.

37. Kessler-Harris, *Out to Work*, 125. Kessler-Harris cited a study by early twentieth century social worker Margaret Byington, *Homestead: The Households of a Mill Town* (1910; reprint, Pittsburgh: University of Pittsburgh Press, 1974), chapter 10, which stated that working-class Slavic families typically kept from one to four lodgers in their four-room company houses. This bears a demographic resemblance to Eastern European households in Sweetwater coal towns. Byington observed that in 50 percent of these households, income from boarders contributed as much as 25 percent of the family income. (pp. 152–54). It seems reasonable to infer that the same was true of Eastern Europeans in Sweetwater coal towns.
38. Anker, "Women, Work and Family," 35; and Schneider, "Patterns for Getting By," 529–34.
39. Powell, interview by author.
40. Anker, "Women, Work and Family," 29.
41. Powell, interview by Burns.
42. Pivik, interview. See also Stinneford, "Mines and Miners," 123.
43. Stinneford, "Mines and Miners," 123.
44. Gardner and Flores, *Forgotten Frontier*, 136. Despite Prohibition, a brisk bootleg trade persisted during the 1920s. Rhodes, *Booms and Busts*, 125–46.
45. Leskovec, interview. See also Gardner and Flores, *Forgotten Frontier*, 126–27.
46. Miners whose hours were cut back sometimes could still earn enough to pay room and board for themselves, though not enough to support a family. Thus, women still had paying boarders during slack times at mines, and the income earned from boarders helped keep a family solvent.
47. Anker, "Women, Work and Family," 31; Schneider, "Patterns for Getting By," 529–34; Kessler-Harris, *Out to Work*, 241–42; Strasser, *Never Done*, 151; Mary Murphy, "Women's Work in a Man's World," *The Speculator* (winter 1984): 18–25; Jameson, "Women as Workers," 150.
48. Schneider, "Patterns for Getting By," 535.
49. Anker, "Women, Work and Family," 32. Similarly, Strasser noted that "women served often as surrogate mothers, wives, and sisters for their boarders." See *Never Done*, 155.
50. Leskovec, interview.
51. Leskovec, interview.
52. Leskovec, interview.
53. In contrast, married immigrant women in eastern industrial cities entered wage work outside the home as early as the turn of the century. Kessler-Harris, *Out to Work*, 138; Anker, "Women, Work and Family," 31–33; and Schneider, "Patterns for Getting By," 526–27.

54. These two towns became the hubs of Sweetwater County. Smaller coal towns such as Superior, Reliance, and Megeath did not develop commercial activity to the extent that these towns did.
55. For further discussion of regional economy, ethnicity, class, and education as factors in women's work patterns, see Mary Lou Locke, "Out of the Shadows and into the Western Sun: Working Women of the Late Nineteenth-Century Urban Far West," *Journal of Urban History* 16 (February 1990): 175–204; and Emmons, *The Butte Irish*, 71–76.
56. *U.P History*, 138–41; 150–53; Kathka, "The Italian Experience," 75–77; Krmpotich, interview; Pivik, interview.
57. Rhodes, *Booms and Busts*, 66–71, 74–75, 95, 104.
58. Rhodes, *Booms and Busts*, 99, 101, 104.
59. *Wyoming Directory* 1914:418–30.
60. Occupational analysis of income-earning adult women; 1880, 1910 census.
61. Analysis of class and residential location; 1900, 1910 census. See also, Rhodes, *Booms and Busts*, 67–70, 106–12.
62. *Wyoming Gazetteer* 1908:176–79.
63. *Wyoming Directory* 1914:419, 424, 428.
64. See John and Mary Taylor household, South Front St., Annie and Lizzie Brown household, First St.; Marie and Sarah Abraham household, West flat, First Addition; David and Annie Muir household, West flat, First Addition; Jennie Anderson household, South Front St.; Patrick and Margaret Rega household, East of No. One Mine; Maude McCoy, boarder in Robert and Melissa Read household, Front St.; and Wyoming General Hospital, W. B. Ray, Superintendent, one mile south of railroad; Rock Springs, 1900 census.
65. Mary and Ellen Murphy household, Green River, Wyoming; and Jean and Anthony Jeffers household, Green River, Wyoming; 1910 census. See also Teresini, Fisher, Dean, Davy, Bills, Sodergun, Paulson, Hasting, Bennett, Garth, and Whalen households, Green River and Rock Springs, 1910 census.
66. Unfortunately, none of the women holding downtown jobs who appeared in the 1900 and 1910 census samples were available for interviews; neither had any of them left behind taped interviews or written memoirs. Hence their motivations remain inarticulated.
67. Analysis of ethnicity for women; 1900 census. Analysis of occupation, marital status, and ethnicity for adult women; 1900 census.
68. Analysis of ethnicity for women; 1910 census. Analysis of occupation, marital status, and ethnicity for women; 1910 census.
69. Jean and Anthony Jeffers household, Green River, Wyoming, 1910 census. For Pearl Neuber, see *Wyoming Directory* 1914:418; 1921:359; 1925:437.

Notes to Pages 140–145

70. See Schneider, "Patterns for Getting By," 524–25; and Anker, "Women, Work and Family," 29. Anker found that 78 percent of the Eastern Europeans whom she studied in industrial Connecticut entered the job market through kin or ethnic ties.
71. Graf, interview; Eggs-Gaensslen Family History, 1–4; *Wyoming Gazetteer* 1908:135; *Wyoming Directory* 1914:280–81; 1918:280, 294; 1921:244–45; 1925:239, 241.
72. Graf, interview; Eggs-Gaensslen Family History, 1–4; *Wyoming Directory* 1925:241.
73. Metelko, interview.
74. Metelko, interview.
75. Metelko, interview.
76. Metelko, interview.
77. Metelko, interview.
78. Metelko, interview.
79. Metelko, interview.
80. Margaret quit full-time work when she married but continued to work as a Union Pacific cashier part-time. Metelko, interview.
81. Rhodes, *Booms and Busts*, 112.
82. Among the twenty-two life histories, ten include first-generation immigrant women who came over from Europe as adults. Nine out of ten of these women kept boarders or worked in domestic service upon arrival in Sweetwater County. All of those who kept boarders were married; and those in domestic service, single.

    Another ten of the twenty-two life histories were for single, foreign-born women who emigrated from Europe as children or youths. Among these women, the 50 percent who graduated from American high schools and earned income thereafter worked outside the home in non-domestic occupations. See Leskovec, interview; Frolic, interview; Pivik, interview; Taucher, interview; Metelko, interview; Semos, interview; Witka, interview; Powell, interview by Burns; Krmpotich, interview; and Sulentich, interview.
83. Leskovec, interview.
84. Leskovec, interview.
85. Taucher, interview.
86. Taucher, interview.
87. Taucher, interview.
88. Leskovec, interview.
89. Semos, interview.
90. "Basic Wage Rates," *U.P. History*, xli. See also, Larson, *History of Wyoming*, 398.
91. Rhodes, *Booms and Busts*, 116–19. Kessler-Harris, *Out to Work*, 219–24. Kessler-Harris noted that the wartime expansion of industrial production and temporary absence of male labor did not significantly alter women's work patterns beyond the war years.

92. *Wyoming Directory* 1918:438–49.
93. *Wyoming Directory* 1918; for Pearl Grumer, see 295; Mrs. Forshea, 294; Nellie Saleen, 449; and Rachel Van Deusen, 448.
94. Kessler-Harris, *Out to Work*, 224.
95. Gardner and Flores, *Forgotten Frontier*, 158–59. Rhodes, *Booms and Busts*, 146–47.
96. *Wyoming Directory* 1925:238–41, 347–58.
97. Gardner and Flores, *Forgotten Frontier*, 62.
98. Gardner and Flores, *Forgotten Frontier*, 60–63. For commercial expansion, ca. 1920s, see *Wyoming Directory* 1925:238–41, 347–58.
99. *Wyoming Directory* 1918:294–97, 438–49; 1929:238–42, 246–359, 347–58. I omitted women who ran boarding houses, since commercialized domesticity did not represent a new occupational category.
100. *Wyoming Directory* 1925:238, 240, 244.
101. *Wyoming Directory* 1925:238, 240, 244.
102. Business listings for the State Bank of Green River, the First National Bank of Green River, the North Side State Bank of Rock Springs, the Rock Springs National Bank and the First National Bank of Rock Springs, in 1908, 1914, and 1918 showed only male employees in the position of Assistant Cashier. *Wyoming Gazetteer* 1908:135, 176, 178; 1914:281, 417, 421, 424, 427; and 1918:294, 296, 441, 445, 446.
103. *Green River Star*, January 26, 1923, 5, Sweetwater County Library, Rock Springs WY.
104. *Wyoming Directory* 1925:239.
105. Kessler-Harris, *Out to Work*, 249.
106. *Wyoming Directory* 1925:239, 348.
107. The *Wyoming Directory* in 1914 listed six women who ran small businesses outside the realm of commercialized domesticity. By 1925, thirteen women entrepreneurs listed retail businesses. *Wyoming Directory* 1914:280–81, 418–30; 1925:238–41, 347–58.
108. LeFaivre, interview.
109. Leskovec, interview; Metelko, interview; Graf, interview; and Semos, interview.
110. Leskovec, interview; Metelko, interview; and Semos, interview.

8. "GRASPING AT THE SHADOW": THE PARADOX OF CHANGE

1. Deutsch, "Coming Together, Coming Apart," 59.
2. *Big Piney Examiner*, October 20, 1915; reprinted in Sublette County Artists Guild, *Tales of the Seeds-Ke-Dee*, 222. The upper Green River Valley served by this newspaper was part of Sweetwater County until 1922, when it split off to become part of the newly formed Sublette County.
3. *Big Piney Examiner*, October 20, 1915; reprinted in Sublette County Artists Guild, *Tales of the Seeds-Ke-Dee*, 222.

4. Metal and Platts, *Cattle King on the Green River*.
5. Jordan, *Cowgirls*; see especially chapter 9, "Cowgirls and the Crowd: The Early Years; Wild West and Rodeo, 1885–1941," 187–236, 195.
6. By the 1970s, when Theresa Jordan interviewed ranch women throughout the West, work with beef cattle was no longer assumed to be a masculine occupation. Jordan, *Cowgirls*, 29–65, 93–173.
7. William Cronon, Katherine Morrissey, Howard Lamar, and Jay Gitlin, "Women and the West: Rethinking the Western History Course," *Western Historical Quarterly* 17 (July 1986): 269–90, 272.

APPENDIX

1. Although abstracts of the 1890 Federal census are available, the actual street-by-street, household-by-household manuscripts were destroyed in a fire. Hence I could not include the 1890 census in this analysis.
2. The case base for upper-class women proved too small to allow generalization. Only 2.3 percent of the female population were upper class, 1880–1910; while 97.7 percent were middle or working class. Hence I abandoned "upper class" as a category of analysis.
3. Emmons, *The Butte Irish*.

Selected Bibliography

The Important Things of Life draws extensively from the oral histories of Sweetwater County residents. The most vivid and detailed of these include interviews with Helen Korich Krmpotich, Elsie Oblock Frolic, Margaret Plemel Metelko, Louise Luzan Leskovec, Dorothy Pivik, Mary Jesersek Taucher, Bertha Witka, Ann LeVar Powell, Anna Semos, Louise Spinner Graf, Beatrice Jack, and Dorothy Austin Higginson (Cheyenne: Wyoming State Archives and Historical Department [hereafter cited as WSAHD, 1976–77). Early-twentieth-century ranch women are featured in Carol Rankin, ed., *Spoken Words of Four Ranch Women* (Cheyenne: WSAHD, 1979), which includes interviews with Jesse McMaster Faris, Verla Richie Sommers, Doris Bailey Luman, and Mildred Mickelson Miller. Additionally, the State Archives yielded interviews with Jean Hodge Thompson and Mrs. B. B. Brooks, transcribed by WPA workers during the late 1930s.

Another source of valuable oral histories is the collection compiled by A. Dudley Gardner and housed at the Wyoming State Archaeological Services in Rock Springs. Most useful among these were interviews with Henry Kovach, Mary Yugovich, Jack and Pat Krmpotich, Joe Bozovich, Joe Melinkovich, James Zelenka, Edwin Swanson, Henry Zampedri, Helen Mattinson, and Elinore Bastalich Tolar. Lastly, in the author's possession are her interviews with Jerrine Stewart Wire, Ann Begovich Burns, Ann LeVar Powell, Pat Huntley LeFaivre, Mary Lou Anselmi Unguren, and Elinore Gaensslen Schofield.

Equally rich in nuance and detail were four published memoirs: Theresa Jordan's annotated collection of oral histories with ranch women, *Cowgirls: Women of the American West* (New York: Doubleday, 1984); Ora and Lenora Wright's memoir of rural life in the Green River drainage, *Our Valley, Eden Valley, Wyoming* (Portland OR: Gann Publishing Co., 1987); Sublette County Artists' Guild narratives, *Tales of the Seeds-Ke-Dee* (Denver: Big Mountain Press, 1963); and Phyllis Luman Metal's family memoir, *Cattle King on the Green River: The Family Life and Legends of Abner Luman, A Cowboy King of the Upper Green River Valley in the Twenties* (Wilson WY: Sunshine Ranch & Friends, 1983).

This study also relied upon data gleaned from the Sweetwater County census manuscripts of the *Tenth, Twelfth,* and *Thirteenth Federal Census of the United States* (Washington DC: Government Printing Office, 1880, 1900, 1910), on microfilm at the Wyoming State Archives and Historical Department in Cheyenne.

Secondary literature spanned the fields of the history of the U.S. West, Wyoming regional history, the history of women in the American West, family history, women's labor history, and ethnic history. For a broad synthesis of revisionist scholarship in western history, see Richard White, *"It's Your Misfortune and None of My Own": A New History of the American West* (Norman: University of Oklahoma Press, 1991); and Patricia Nelson Limerick, *Legacy of Conquest: The Unbroken Past of the American West* (New York: W. W. Norton, 1987). Recent debate over the nature of frontier history is reviewed in John Faragher, "The Frontier Trail: Rethinking Turner and Reimagining the American West," AHR 98 (February 1993): 106–17; and Allen Bogue, "The Significance of the History of the American West: Postscripts and Prospects," WHQ 24 (February 1993): 45–68. A narrative history organized around traditional definitions of frontier can be found in Ray Allen Billington, *Westward Expansion,* 5th ed. (New York: MacMillan, 1982).

Essays on the mythology of the American West include Henry Nash Smith's classic study, *Virgin Land: The American West as Symbol and Myth* (1950; reprint, Cambridge: Harvard University Press, 1970); Robert V. Hine, *The American West: An Interpretive History* (New York: Little, Brown, 1973); and more recently, William Kittredge's poignant but unsparing memoir, *A Hole in the Sky* (New York: Alfred A. Knopf, 1992).

Meditations on storytelling, cultural identity, and the construction of memory appear in Clyde Milner, "The View from Wisdom: Four Layers of History and Regional Identity," *Under an Open Sky: Rethinking America's Western Past,* ed. William Cronon, George Miles, and Jay Gitlin (New York: W. W. Norton, 1992), and Barbara Allen, "Story in Oral History: Clues to Historical Consciousness," JAH 79 (September 1992): 606–11. For reflections on cowboy myth, consult William Savage, ed., *Cowboy Life: Reconstructing an American Myth* (Niwot: University Press of Colorado, 1993), and Robert M. Davis, *Playing Cowboys: Low Culture and High Art in the Western* (Norman: University of Oklahoma Press, 1992).

Regional history is illuminated by A. Dudley Gardner and Verla Flores, *Forgotten Frontier: A History of Coal Mining in Wyoming* (Boulder CO: Westview, 1989); Gordon Olaf Hendrickson, ed., *Peopling the High Plains: Wyoming's European Heritage* (Cheyenne: WSAHD, 1977); T. A. Larson, *A History of Wyoming* (Lincoln: University of Nebraska Press, 1965); and Robert Rhodes, *Booms and Busts on Bitter Creek: A History of Rock Springs, Wyoming* (Boulder CO: Pruett, 1987). A photographic archive of the region is presented in A. Dudley Gardner and Val Brinkerhoff, *Historical Images of Sweetwater County* (Virginia Beach VA: Donning, 1993).

Regarding the impact of westward migration on gender systems, John Faragher's study,

Selected Bibliography

Women and Men on the Overland Trail (New Haven: Yale University Press, 1979) focuses on mid-nineteenth-century middle-class emigrants from the rural Midwest. Similarly, Robert Griswold reviews the fate of Victorian gender ideology in the West, in "Anglo Women and Domestic Ideology in the American West in the Nineteenth and Early Twentieth Century," in *Western Women: Their Land, Their Lives*, ed. Lillian Schlissel, Vicki Ruiz, and Janice Monk (Albuquerque: University of New Mexico Press, 1988), 15–34.

Discussions of recent historiographical trends in western women's history highlight multicultural scholarship that now enriches the field. See, for example, Sarah Deutsch, Virginia Scharf, Glenda Riley, and John Faragher's contributions to "The History of Women in the West: A Search for Understanding amid Diversity," *MMWH* 41 (spring 1991): 57–73. See also Katherine Morrissey, "Engendering the West," in Cronon, Miles, and Gitlin, *Under an Open Sky*, 132–44; and essays by Susan Armitage and Elizabeth Jameson in *The Women's West* (Norman: University of Oklahoma Press, 1987).

Breaking new ground are monographs which suggest an ecology of gender, demonstrating ways that women's roles have evolved through the regional adaptations of distinctive ethnic groups, classes, and cultures. Exemplars include Paula Petrik, *"No Step Backward": Women and Family on the Rocky Mountain Mining Frontier, Helena, Montana, 1865–1900* (Helena: Montana Historical Society, 1987); Sarah Deutsch, *No Separate Refuge: Culture, Class and Gender on an Anglo-Hispanic Frontier in the American Southwest, 1880–1940* (New York: Oxford University Press, 1987); and Peggy Pascoe, *Relations of Rescue: The Search for Female Moral Authority in the American West* (New York: Oxford University Press, 1990).

In the field of family history, recent studies have raised the issue of conflict between women's and men's interests within the family, exploring how political reaction to and social expression of such conflict changes over time. See Linda Gordon, *Heroes of Their Own Lives: The Politics and History of Family Violence* (New York: Viking, 1988), and Stephanie Coontz, *The Way We Never Were: American Families and the Nostalgia Trap* (New York: Harper Collins, 1992). For discussion of familial conflict related to westward migration, see Lillian Schlissel, "The Malick Family in the Oregon Territory, 1848–1867," *Far from Home: Families of the Westward Journey* (New York: Schocken Books, 1989), 3–106; and Linda Peavy and Ursula Smith, *Women in Waiting in the Westward Movement: Life on the Home Frontier* (Norman: University of Oklahoma Press, 1994).

Documenting changes in courtship which accompanied the emergence of a separate youth culture during the early twentieth century are Kathy Peiss, *Cheap Amusements: Working Women and Leisure in Turn-of-the-Century New York* (Philadelphia: Temple University Press, 1986); and Ellen Rothman, *Hands and Hearts: A History of Courtship in America* (Cambridge: Harvard University Press, 1987).

Historians of women's work address a range of topics relevant to this study. Useful con-

Selected Bibliography

ceptual approaches to the construction of women's place within family economies are found in Tamara Hareven, *Family Time and Industrial Time: The Relationship between Family and Work in a New England Industrial Community* (Cambridge: Cambridge University Press, 1982); and Louise Lamphere, *From Working Daughters to Working Mothers: Immigrant Women in a New England Industrial Community* (Ithaca NY: Cornell University Press, 1987). Faye Dudden links changes in work relations among domestic servants to regional economic and demographic change in *Serving Women: Household Service in Nineteenth-Century America* (Middletown CT: Wesleyan University, 1983). Susan Strasser offers a comprehensive history of women's household work in *Never Done: A History of American Housework* (New York: Pantheon, 1982). Wartime changes in early-twentieth-century women's work patterns are explored in Maureen Greenwald, *Women, War, and Work: The Impact of World War I* (Westport CT: Greenview, 1980). Finally, a useful overview of women's wage labor appears in Alice Kessler-Harris, *Out to Work: A History of Wage-Earning Women in the United States* (New York: Oxford University Press, 1982).

Finally, regional studies of homesteading further illuminate rural women's work, family, and community roles. See Katherine Harris, *Long Vistas: Women and Families on Colorado Homesteads* (Niwot: University Press of Colorado, 1992); and Paula Nelson, *After the West Was Won: Homesteaders and Town-Builders in Western South Dakota, 1900–1917* (Iowa City: University of Iowa Press, 1986). Reexamining gender ideology and rural women's work are Deborah Fink, *Agrarian Women: Wives and Mothers in Rural Nebraska, 1880–1940* (Chapel Hill: University of North Carolina Press, 1992), and Katherine Jellison, *Entitled to Power: Farm Women and Technology, 1913–1963* (Chapel Hill: University of North Carolina Press, 1993).

INTERVIEWS CITED

Bell, Marie Jordan. Interviewed by Theresa Jordan. In *Cowgirls: Women of the American West: An Oral History*, ed. Theresa Jordan. New York: Doubleday, 1984.

Bozovich, Joe. Interview by Dudley Gardner. Transcript of tape recording, December 1987. WAS.

Burns, Ann Begovich. Interview by author. Rock Springs WY, May 24, 1994.

Buchan, Marion, and Mary Buchan. Interview by Ann Burns and Nancy Cranford. Tape recording, OH-551, January 15, 1977. WSAHD.

Coburn, Helen. *See* Culbertson, Mary, and Helen Coburn Howell.

Culbertson, Mary, and Helen Coburn Howell. Interview by L. L. H. Transcription, WPA-798, June 26, 1936. WSAHD.

Faris, Jesse McMaster. Interview by Carol Rankin. In *Spoken Words of Four Ranchwomen*, ed. Carol Rankin. Unpublished transcription, MSS-987, WSAHD.

Ferdani, Tony, and Quinto Constantino. "The Italian Experience in Wyoming," interview by David Katha. In *Peopling the Plains*, ed. Gordon Olaf Hendrickson. WSAHD.

Selected Bibliography

Frolic, Elsie Oblock. Interview by Ann Burns and Nancy Cranford. Tape recording, OH-553, January 8, 1977. WSAHD.

Gardner, A. Dudley. Interview by author. Transcription. Rock Springs WY, May 25, 1994.

Graf, Louise Spinner. Interview by W. H. Barton. Tape recording, July 15, 1977. WSAHD.

Higginson, Dorothy Austin. Interview by Dennis Roe. Tape recording, OH-543, February 12, 1977. WSAHD.

Howell, Helen Coburn. *See* Culbertson, Mary, and Helen Coburn Howell.

Huston, J. M. Interview by Josephine Jons. Unpublished manuscripts of interviews, MSS-1277, 1938. WPA.

Jack, Beatrice. Interview by Randie Wallner. Tape recording, OH-255, July 26, 1974. WSAHD.

Ketchum, Beatrice. Interview by A. Dudley Gardner. Transcript of tape recording, 1992. WAS.

Krmpotich, Helen Korich. Interview by Ann Burns and Nancy Cranford. Tape recording, OH-555, January 16, 1977. WSAHD.

Krmpotich, Jack, and Pat Krmpotich. Interview by Peggy Vawter. Transcript of tape recording, Rock Springs WY, 1992. WAS.

Kovach, Henry. Interview by Todd Horn. Transcript of tape recording, May 16, 1987. WAS.

LeFaivre, Pat Huntley. Interview by author. Green River WY, May 26, 1994.

Leskovec, Louise Luzan. Interview by Ann Burns and Nancy Cranford. Tape recording, OH-557, November 15, 1976. WSAHD.

Luman, Doris Bailey. Interview by Carol Rankin. In Rankin, *Spoken Words*. Unpublished transcription, MSS-987, WSAHD.

Mattinson, Helen Knezovich. Interview by Donna Acker Mattinson. Transcript of tape recording, October 23, 1991. WAS.

Melinkovich, Joe. Interview by Percilla Martin. Transcript of tape recording, October 28, 1991. WAS.

Metelko, Margaret Plemel. Interview by Ann Burns and Nancy Cranford. Tape recording, OH-559, February 16, 1977. WSAHD.

Miller, Mildred Mickelson. Interview by Carol Rankin. In Rankin, *Spoken Words*. Unpublished transcription of interviews, MSS-987, WSAHD.

Miller, Catherine, and Joseph Miller. Interview by Shirley Black. Transcript of tape recording, February 1987. WAS.

Peternell, Phyllis. Interview by Andy Peternell. Transcript of tape recording, October 12, 1991. WAS.

Pivik, Dorothy. Interview by Nancy Cranford. Tape recording, OH-564, January 11, 1977. WSAHD.

Selected Bibliography

Powell, Ann LeVar. Interview by Ann Burns. Tape recording, OH-566, 1977. WSAHD [hereafter cited as Powell, interview by Burns].

Powell, Ann LeVar. Interview by author. Rock Springs WY, May 27, 1994 [hereafter cited as Powell, interview by author].

Schofield, Elinore Gaensslen. Interview by author. Green River WY, May 26, 1994.

Semos, Anna Waananen Berg. Interview by Amy Peterson. Tape recording, OH-254, April 28, 1974. WSAHD.

Sommers, Verla Richie. Interview by Carol Rankin. In Rankin, *Spoken Words*. Unpublished transcription of interviews, MSS-987, WSAHD.

Sulentich, Anna. Interview by Amy Peterson. Tape recording, OH-569, 1976. WSAHD.

Swanson, Edward. Interview by Kathy Brailey. Transcript of tape recording, September 9, 1990. WAS.

Taucher, Mary Jersersek. Interview by Ann Burns and Nancy Cranford. Tape recording, OH-570, December 4, 1976. WSAHD.

Thompson, Jean Hodge. Interview by unidentified WPA field worker. Transcript of tape recording, WPA-1101, November 14, 1936. WSAHD.

Tolar, Elinore Bastalich. Interview by Glen Biggs. Transcript of tape recording, summer 1988. WAS.

Unguren, Mary Lou Anselmi. Interview by author. Rock Springs WY, May 27, 1994.

Wire, Jerrine Stewart, and Robert Stewart. Interview by Annick Smith and Beth Ferris. Transcript of tape recording, 1979. Wilderness Women Project, Missoula MT.

Wire, Jerrine Stewart. Interview by author. Tape recording, Croyden PA, March 23, 1986.

Witka, Bertha Savo Husa. Interview by Amy Peterson. Tape recording, OH-251, April 18, 1974. WSAHD.

Yugovich, Mary. Interview by Lori Harper. Transcript of tape recording, November 11, 1988. WAS.

Zampedri, Henry. Interview by A. Dudley Gardner. Transcript of tape recording, February 4, 1985. WAS.

Zelenka, James. Interview by Shirley Green. Transcript of tape recording, March 3, 1987. WAS.

Index

Abraham, Sarah, 139
Adams, Caroline. *See* Wade, Caroline Adams Dougdale
agricultural prices, 30–31
Albert, Charlotta Hartley, 103
Anderson, Jennie, 139
Anker, Laura, 136
Anselmi, Joseph, 138
Anselmi, Lena, 84–87, 148, 150
Anselmi, Mary Lou. *See* Unguren, Mary Lou Anselmi
Anselmi, Rudy, 63
Armitage, Susan, 92
Asian population, 20–21
Austin, Annie Birzilla Caldwell, 76
Austin, Norris, 76

bachelors, 57, 59, 135
Bailey, Doris, 96, 100, 106–7
Ball, Jigg, 121
Barrett, Edward, 119–20
Barrett, Hattie, 119–20
Barrett, James, 120
Barrett, Mary Armsbury, 119–21, 127, 154
Barrett, Patrick, 119
Barrett Sheep Company, 119–21
Bell, John, 108
Bell, Marie Jordan, 101–2, 104, 108, 110, 112–13
Bennett, Mary, 139

Bent, LeVancia, 99–100
Berg, Anna Waananen. *See* Semos, Anna Waananen Berg
Berg, Gust, 144
Bertagnolli, Alexander, 138
Bertagnolli, Henry, 26, 138
Bertagnolli, Joe, 138
Big Piney, 30, 152
Bills, Anna, 139
birth control, 83–84
Birzilla, Annie, 76
Bitter Creek, 18
Blair, Archibald, 19–20
Blair, Duncan, 19–20
Blairtown, 20
boarders, 134–36, 149
Bodnar, John, 44–45
Bogeti, Mary, 136
Bolin, Auntie, 84
Bonderant, Claire, 67
Briggs, John, 85
British population, 5–6, 21, 28
Brooks, Mrs. B. B., 89
Brooks, Mae, 146
Brown, Lizzie, 139
Bryan Station, 18
Buchan, Marion, 64
Buchan, Mary, 81
Budd, Charles, 121
Budd, Jennie, 121–22
Burns, Ann, 64

Index

Burnt Fork, 12–13, 70, 76, 94, 114–15, 119

Campisi, Paul, 85
Carey Act of 1894, 25
cattle prices, 30
cattle ranching development, 23–24
Chase, Elsie Ann Johnson, 66–67
Chase, Jesse, 66–67
child labor, 21, 40–42
Chug Creek, 108, 112
Clark, Mary A., 139
climate, 16
coal: discoveries, 19–20; mine safety, 21, 27, 29–30, 32, 46; prices, 32
Coburn, Helen, 67–68, 121
commercial roles for women, 137–41, 145–47
Connor, Margaret, 147
Converse, Martha, 139
Cooksley, Amy, 103–4, 106
Cooksley, Elsie, 103–4, 106
courtship rituals, 54–56. *See also* marriage
cowboy ethic, 102–6, 152
cowcamp, 102–6, 110–11, 152–53
Cranford, Nancy, 64
Crofts, Anna, 83
Cronon, William, 156
Crosby, LaPrele, 147
crossover work by women, 99–102
Crouch, Ida, 27
Culbertson, Mary, 67, 121
Cunnington, Margaret, 117, 119
Cutting, A. Howard, 15–16, 24

Daniel, 121
Davis, Anna, 146
Davis, Barbara Fox, 108–9, 111
Davis, Sam, 108–9
Davy, Mary, 139
Dean, Tessa, 139

Deutsch, Sarah, 5, 151
Dines, 31, 44–45
Dodge, Ira, 67
domestic service, 130–34, 144
Dugdale, Caroline Adams. *See* Wade, Caroline Adams Dugdale
Dugdale, William, 76
Dumbrill, Fern. *See* Spencer, Fern Dumbrill
Dumbrill, Olive, 118, 119

Eastern European population, 5–6, 21, 28, 60; marriage and, 60–61
Eden Land and Irrigation, 25
Eden Valley, 48–50, 68, 91–92, 95
Eden Valley Irrigation Project, 25
education, 141–42
Eggs, Carl, 50
Eggs, Caroline Spinner, 50–51
Eggs, Charles, 51, 141
Eggs, Eleanor. *See* Gaensslen, Eleanor Eggs
Eggs, George, 50
endogamy, 64–66, 72. *See also* marriage
Eppler, Sylvia, 90, 118
Erlich, Gretel, 115
ethnic groups, 21; Asian, 20–21; British, 5–6, 21, 28; Eastern European, 5–6, 21, 28, 60; German, 5, 28; Scandinavian, 21, 28; Southern Slavs, 60–64, 133–34
ethnic neighborhoods, 28–29, 44–45
exogamy, 64–66, 72. *See also* marriage

family size, 80–82, 85–86
Faragher, John, 5, 8
Faris, Jesse McMaster, 92, 95, 100–102, 107
Faris, Wilma, 100, 107
Fisher, Celia, 139
folksongs, 11, 96–99

Index

Forbes, Jack, 36–38
Forshea, Mrs. W. H., 145
Fort Bridger, 17
Fort Laramie Treaty of 1868, 17
Fox, Barbara. *See* Davis, Barbara Fox
Fox, Bessie, 121
fraternal organizations, 32–33
Frolic, Elsie Oblock, 75, 132
frontier: definition of, 4, 35; myth of, 36

Gaensslen, Eleanor Eggs, 50–51, 75, 141
Gaensslen, Emil, 50–51
Gaensslen, Hugo, 51, 141
Gardner, Dudley, 21
Garth, Evie, 139
Gaunt, Anna V., 139
gender and work. *See* work relationships
geography, 16
George, Suzanne, 116
German population, 28
Gitlin, Jay, 156
Graf, Louise Spinner, 51, 81, 140–41, 148
Green River: business in, 26–27, 50–51, 119, 137; newspaper in, 54–56; professional women in, 139–41, 145, 146–47; and the railroad, 17–18, 22
Greub, Minnie Hepp, 83
Grumer, Pearl, 145

Haley, Lot, 66, 117
Hallgarth, Susan, 115–16
Hanna, 27
Harris, Alice Kessler, 147
Hasting, Nellie, 139
Hazlett, Ida Crouch, 27
Heizer, Kate, 125–26
Hendrickson, Gordon, 28
Heppener, Ursala Metelko, 43–44

Hidy, Minnie, 121
Hillsdale, 84, 91, 121
Hine, Robert, 9, 113
Hodge, Jean, 47–48
Hodson, Mrs. Nathan, 68
Holladay, Ben, 17
home ownership, 28–29, 45
homestead claims, numbers of, 31
homesteaders, single women, 9, 112–13, 154–55; alternative occupations of, 121; cooperation and, 118–19; literary presentation of, 10, 122–27, 154–55; motivation of, 114–17
Homsher, Lola, 18
household technology, 91–92
Huntley, Lena Anselmi, 84–87, 148, 150
Husa, Eino, 39
Huston, J. M., 22–23

infant mortality, 82–83
irrigation, 25

Jack, Beatrice, 107
Jameson, Elizabeth, 48
Jeffers, Jean, 139–40
Jellison, Katherine, 91
Jesersek, Mary. *See* Taucher, Mary Jesersek
Johnson, Elsie Ann, 66–67
Jons, Josephine, 22
Jordan, Marie. *See* Bell, Marie Jordan

Karg, Lavinia, 83
Kemmerer, 57
Kershisnik, Frank, 138
Ketchum, Beatrice, 87
Kierle, Alice Paterson, 47, 129–31
Kinney, Maggie, 81
kinship networks, 38–39; aged and, 42; children and, 40–41, 46–47; immigration patterns and, 40, 43, 48;

Index

kinship networks (*cont.*)
   native-born immigrants and, 48–49;
   siblings and, 42–43, 46–48, 52. *See also* marriage
Kirkbride, Alex D., 118
Kirkbride, Mabel, 118
Kirkbride, Mary, 118
Kirkbride, Peggy, 118, 121
Kirkbride, Sarah, 118
Kovach, Henry, 29
Krmpotich, Helen Korich, 26, 46–47, 64, 75, 81
Kujala, Annie, 58–59

labor unions, 21, 27, 32
Lamar, Howard, 156
Larsen, Bertha, 147
Larson, T. A., 19, 31
Layton, Stanford, 122
Lee, Ann Ramsay, 80–81
Lee, Edward M., 19
Lee, Margaret, 81
Lee, Mary, 81
Lee, William, 80–81
LeFaivre, Pat Huntley, 84
Leskovec, Louise Luzan: boarders and, 135, 136; and childbirth and children, 81, 83, 86–87; courtship and, 63–64; immigration of family of, 75, 78; and work, 132–33, 142–43, 144, 148
Leskovec, Matt, 64, 143
LeVar, Ann. *See* Powell, Ann LeVar
Lewis, John L., 32
Lionkol, 7, 31
Lomax, Alan, 96
Loomis, Metta, 124–26
Luman, Abner, 23–24
Luman, Bob, 100
Luman, Doris Bailey, 96, 100, 106–7
Luman, Phyllis. *See* Metal, Phyllis Luman

Luzan, Louise. *See* Leskovec, Louise Luzan
Lyons, Blanche, 121

MacLaughlin, Catherine, 147
Magnagna, Anna Rizzi, 42–43
Magnagna, Louis, 43
Makka, Emil, 59
Makka, Mary, 59
Mann, Frank, 121
marriage, 53; age at, 56–57; bachelors and, 57, 59; birth control and, 83–84; courtship rituals and, 54–56; Eastern European populations and, 60–61; endogamy, 64–66, 72; ethnic ties and, 64–66; exogamy, 64–66, 72; and family size, 80–86; matchmaking and, 61–63; and premarital sex, 68–70, 71; recreation and, 63–64; religion and, 63; rural *vs.* urban, 66–68; separation during, 74–78; single women and, 58–60; social order within, 78–80. *See also* homesteaders, single women; work relationships
matchmaking, 61–63
McAlister, J. E., 117
McAlister, May. *See* Sommers, May McAlister
McCoy, Maude, 139
McKay, Stella, 121–22
McMaster, Jesse. *See* Faris, Jesse McMaster
Megeath, 7, 44–46, 64, 135
Metal, Phyllis Luman, 96, 104–6, 153
Metelko, Frank, 43
Metelko, Louis, 142
Metelko, Margaret Plemel, 75, 81, 141–42, 148
Metelko, Ursala, 43–44
Mickelson, Jim, 30
Mickelson, Mae, 66–68

Index

Milner, Clyde, 12
Morgan, S. Philip, 65
Morrissey, Katherine, 156
Mrak, John, 60–61, 63
Muir, Mary, 139
Murphy, Mary, 139
mutual aid societies, 32–33

National Origins Act of 1924, 34
Native Americans, 16–17
Neuber, A. F., 140
Neuber, Pearl, 139–40
Nickolson, Frank, 117
North Piney, 117

Oblock, Elsie. *See* Frolic, Elsie Oblock

Pagnini, Deanna, 65
Paterson, Alice. *See* Kierle, Alice Paterson
Paulson, Dora, 139
Peiss, Kathy, 63
Pivik, Dorothy, 57, 61–64, 75, 81, 135
Plemel, Frank, 141–42
Plemel, Margaret. *See* Metelko, Margaret Plemel
Point of Rocks, 18, 33
population growth, 23, 30–31
Powell, Ann LeVar, 63, 74, 77–81, 84, 86–88
Powell, John Wesley, 23
premarital sex, 68–70
Price, Sarah, 96
prices: agricultural, 30–31; cattle, 30; coal, 32; sheep, 30, 32
Pruitt, Elinore. *See* Stewart, Elinore Pruitt
Pryde, Anne, 83

ranch consolidation, 30
recreation, 63–64
Regan, Marmis, 139

Reliance, 26, 28, 41, 44–45, 138
Richie, Verla, 100–101, 106–7
Riley, Glenda, 8
Riley, Margaret, 82
Rizzi, Anna. *See* Magnagna, Anna Rizzi
Rizzi, Dorothy, 43
Rizzi, Eugene, 42
Rizzi, John, 43
Rizzi, Marguerite, 43
Rock Springs: coal mining and, 19, 21–22, 41, 45; education in, 142; foreign settlers in, 39–45; growth of, 138, 145; mutual aid socities in, 32–33; politics in, 27; professional women in, 146–47
Rock Springs Massacre, 21
Rosenberg, Bruce, 11
Rowley, Sarah, 139

Saleen, Nellie, 145
Sargent, Helen, 67
Savo, Bertha. *See* Witka, Bertha Savo Husa
Scandinavian population, 6, 21, 28
Schneider, JoAnne, 136
Schofield, Elinore Gaensslen, 51
Schuster, Louise, 63
Schwantes, Carlos, 36–38
Sellon, Alice, 121–22
Sellon, Hattie, 121–22
Semos, Anna Waananen Berg, 40–42, 81, 144, 148
service industries, 31
sex, premarital, 68–70
sex ratio, 37, 44
sheep prices, 30, 32
sheep ranching, 24
Shinazy, Annie, 81, 83
Siberts, Bruce, 103
Siegert, Grace, 146

singles. *See* bachelors; homesteaders, single women; women, unmarried
Sitzman, Adolph, 95
Sitzman, Minnie Webster, 95
Skedd, Jennie A., 139
Slovenski Dom, 60
Smith, Daniel Scott, 84
Smith, Judith, 74
Smith, Laura E., 139
Smith, Oliver, 129
Smith, Sherry, 115–16, 122
Sodergrun, Mabel, 139
Sommers, A. P., 117, 121
Sommers, May McAlister, 117, 119
Sommers, Pearl V., 117
Sorrels, Rosalie, 69
Southern Slavic population, 60–64, 133–34
South Superior, 7, 45
Spencer, Fern Dumbrill, 117–18
Spinner, Caroline. *See* Eggs, Caroline Spinner
Spinner, George, 51
Squires, Emmeline, 99–100
Squires, George, 99–100
Stevens, Bertha, 81, 83
Stewart, Clyde, 87, 102, 115–16, 119
Stewart, Elinore Pruitt: as midwife, 70–71, 84; and childbirth and children, 82, 87; and homesteading, 94–95, 114–17; and writing, 114–17, 122
Stewart, Jerrine. *See* Wire, Jerrine Stewart
Stewart, Ruth C., 116
Stinneford, Earl, 26, 28
Strange, Joanna Gleed, 123
Stuart, Mabel Lewis, 123–26
suffrage, 1, 19, 152–53
Superior, mining in, 25–26, 138
Superior Coal Company, 25

Taucher, Mary Jesersek, 41, 42, 61–62, 81, 133–34, 137, 143–44
Taylor, Bessie, 139
Teresini, Mary, 139
Thompson, Jean Hodge, 47–48
Thompson, William, 48
Thornton, 117
Tolar, Elinor Bastalich, 81
Turner, Frederick Jackson, 4–5, 35

Unguren, Mary Lou Anselmi, 28–29, 63
Union Pacific Coal Company, 20; employment practices, 20–22; housing practices, 28, 33, 45; production, 22, 25–26; scrip payment methods, 21–22, 26
Union Pacific Railroad: arrival of, 17; development of settlements and, 18–19; employment practices of, 28; purchases coal mining land, 20
United Mine Workers of America (UMWA), 27, 32
Urie, 76–77

Van Deusen, Rachel, 145

Waananen, Anna. *See* Semos, Anna Waananen Berg
Wade, Caroline Adams Dugdale, 76–78, 81, 88
Wade, John, 76–77
wages, 31, 145
wage work: taking boarders, 134–36; domestic service, 129, 130–34, 144; education and, 141–42; and expanding commercial roles for women, 137–41, 145–47; and working-class population, 131
Westholder, Louis, 145
Whalen, Nellie, 139
Whitaker, Gladys Belvie, 125–26

Index

Winton, 7, 31, 44–45
Wire, Frank, 110
Wire, Jerrine Stewart, 70–71, 84, 87, 102, 106–7, 109–10, 151
Witka, Bertha Savo Husa, 39, 75, 81
women, unmarried, 58–59, 60. *See also* homesteaders, single women
women's associations, 33
women's work, 90–92
working-class population, 131
work relationships: children and, 106–11; cowcamp and, 102–6, 110–11, 152–53; crossover work by women, 99–102; division of labor, 92; economic contribution of women, 92–95, 99, 110; expanding commercial roles for women, 137–41, 145–47; expressed in folksongs, 96–99; household technology, 91–92; women's work, 90–92. *See also* homesteaders, single women; wage work

Worland, 67, 118, 121
Wright, Carrie, 48–49
Wright, Frank, 48–49
Wright, John, 48–49
Wright, Lenora, 12, 91–92, 96
Wright, Lizzie Mae, 49
Wright, Ora, 12, 49
Wright, Ruth Ellen Day, 48–49, 81
Wright, Walter, 49
Wright, William, 49

Yans-McLaughlin, Virginia, 85
Yates, Nellie, 121–22

In the Women in the West series

Martha Maxwell, Rocky Mountain Naturalist
By Maxine Benson

The Art of the Woman: The Life and Work of Elisabet Ney
By Emily Fourmy Cutrer

Emily: The Diary of a Hard-Worked Woman
By Emily French
Edited by Janet Lecompte

The Important Things of Life
Women, Work, and Family in Sweetwater County, Wyoming, 1880–1929
By Dee Garceau

The Adventures of the Woman Homesteader: The Life and Letters of Elinore Pruitt Stewart
By Susanne K. George

The Colonel's Lady on the Western Frontier: The Correspondence of Alice Kirk Grierson
Edited by Shirley A. Leckie

A Stranger in Her Native Land: Alice Fletcher and the American Indians
By Joan Mark

So Much to Be Done: Women Settlers on the Mining and Ranching Frontier
Edited by Ruth B. Moynihan, Susan Armitage, and Christiane Fischer Dichamp

www.ingramcontent.com/pod-product-compliance
Lightning Source LLC
Chambersburg PA
CBHW021147160426
43194CB00007B/721